economía

Volume **8** Number **1**

Journal of the Latin American and Caribbean Economic Association

Fall 2007

EDITORS
Eduardo Engel
Francisco Ferreira
Roberto Rigobon

LATIN AMERICAN AND CARIBBEAN
ECONOMIC ASSOCIATION

BROOKINGS INSTITUTION PRESS
Washington, D.C.

Articles in this publication were developed by the authors for the biannual *Economía* meetings. In all cases the papers are the product of the authors' thinking alone and do not imply endorsement by the staff members, officers, or trustees of the Brookings Institution or of LACEA, or of those institutions with which the authors are affiliated.

Published by
BROOKINGS INSTITUTION PRESS
1775 Massachusetts Avenue, N.W., Washington, D.C. 20036
www.brookings.edu

ISSN 1529-7470
ISBN-13: 978-0-8157-2087-4

For information on subscriptions, standing orders, and individual copies, contact Brookings Institution Press, P.O. Box 465, Hanover, PA 17331-0465. Or call 866-698-0010. E-mail brookings@tsp.sheridan.com. Visit Brookings online at www.brookings.edu/press.

Brookings periodicals are available online through Online Computer Library Center (contact the OCLC subscriptions department at 800-848-5878, ext. 6251) and Project Muse (http://muse.jhu.edu).

Volume 8 Number 1 economía

Journal of the Latin American and Caribbean Economic Association

Fall 2007

Nora Lustig, *Poverty Group of the United Nations Development Program (UNDP)*
José A. Ocampo, *United Nations*
Carmen Reinhart, *University of Maryland*
Roberto Rigobon, *Massachusetts Institute of Technology*
Andrés Rodríguez-Clare, *Pennsylvania State University*
Jaime Saavedra, *World Bank*
Pablo Sanguinetti, *Universidad Torcuato Di Tella, Buenos Aires*
Ernesto Schargrodsky, *Universidad Torcuato Di Tella, Buenos Aires*

ECONOMIA

Editors
Eduardo Engel, *Yale University*
Francisco Ferreira, *World Bank*
Roberto Rigobon, *Massachusetts Institute of Technology*

Editorial Associate
Jennifer Hoover

Managing Editor
Catherine Mathieu-Canuto

Webmaster
Miguel Rodriguez Lopez

Editorial Board
Rafael di Tella, *Harvard University*
Eduardo Engel, *Yale University*
Francisco Ferreira, *Pontifícia Universidade Católica do
    Rio de Janeiro and World Bank*
Carmen Pagés-Serra, *Inter-American Development Bank*
Roberto Rigobon, *Massachusetts Institute of Technology*
Andrés Rodríguez-Clare, *Pennsylvania State University*
Federico Sturzenegger, *Harvard University and Universidad Torcuato
    Di Tella, Buenos Aires*
Miguel Urquiola, *Columbia University*
Andrés Velasco, *Ministerio de Hacienda, Chile, Harvard University,
    and Universidad de Chile*

EDUARDO ENGEL
FRANCISCO H. G. FERREIRA
ROBERTO RIGOBON

Editors' Summary

Chile's economic performance over the last two decades is one of the few success stories in Latin America during this period. The country's per capita gross domestic product (GDP) grew at an average rate of 4.3 percent a year, and the fraction of the population living under the poverty line decreased from 45.1 to 13.7 percent. The contrast with other countries in the region is stark. For example, Brazil's per capita income, corrected for purchasing power parity (PPP), was 45 percent higher than Chile's in 1985, but it lagged by 30 percent two decades later. These trends have motivated the search for the determinants of the Chilean success story. Early and deep reforms following the prescriptions that eventually became known as the Washington Consensus are one line of explanation. The way in which Chile deviated from this blueprint is another factor.

In "Taxes and Growth in a Financially Underdeveloped Country: Evidence from the Chilean Investment Boom," Chang-Tai Hsieh and Jonathan Parker put forward a provocative thesis that goes beyond the standard explanations for Chile's performance. They argue that a reduction of the tax rate on retained profits from 50 to 10 percent in 1984 explains the investment boom underlying the so-called Chilean growth miracle. A central argument of their thesis is that taxation of retained profits is particularly distortionary in an economy with good growth prospects and poorly developed financial markets—as Chile arguably was after liberalizing the economy in the late 1970s and suffering the banking crisis of 1982—because it primarily reduces the investment of financially constrained firms. Consistent with this theory, they find a large increase in aggregate investment after the reform, which was entirely funded by an increase in retained profits.

Hsieh and Parker's thesis has its caveats, and both discussants do a good job of pointing them out. Yet sometime in the future, when the dust has settled and a synthesis emerges, their thesis is likely to represent a significant part of the explanation for Chile's success story.

Inequality is often cited as a possible explanation for Latin America's lackluster economic performance. Some of the mechanisms through which inequality may hinder growth relate to unequal opportunities and lack of economic mobility. In "Social Mobility and Preferences for Redistribution in Latin America," Alejandro Gaviria uses Latinobarómetro data to explore the relationship between intergenerational mobility and political attitudes in seventeen countries in Latin America. While it has long been known that inequality (say, in educational attainment) is higher in Latin America than in the United States, this paper presents the first multi-country study of differences in educational mobility. The news is not good: in addition to being considerably more unequal, Latin American countries tend to display lower levels of mobility across generations than do developed countries.

Does this matter for the outcome of the political process in Latin America? Using Latinobarómetro data on political attitudes, Gaviria finds that demands for redistribution are relatively high in Latin America. Preferences for redistribution are (negatively) correlated with socioeconomic status, more strongly than in other regions, suggesting that the Meltzer-Richards paradigm (that the poorer the median voter, the more redistribution he or she will demand) seems to apply to the region. But one's present position in the distribution is not all that matters: those who are most optimistic about mobility seem to demand less redistribution, as predicted by the hypothesis on prospects for upward mobility. Finally, people's own views of the causes of inequality also matter. Those who feel that poverty is caused by external circumstances, rather than lack of effort, or that hard work does not guarantee success, are more likely to favor an active redistribution policy than those who hold the opposite views. Sadly, a majority of Latin Americans believe that opportunities are not equal for all, that poverty is due to external circumstances, and that hard work is no guarantee of success. This probably reflects their own experiences of limited mobility, and it probably also helps shape their political demands for the role of the state. If the recent literature on the role of beliefs in shaping different politico-economic equilibria is right, then Gaviria's analysis of these correlations would suggest that Latin America might end up trapped in an equilibrium characterized by high redistribution, low effort, and a low belief in effort.

Taxes on retained profits and limited mobility are two nonstandard explanations for economic performance. Country size is another. In "Regional Integration: What Is in It for CARICOM?" Mauricio Mesquita Moreira and Eduardo Mendoza address an old concern in the Caribbean region—namely, whether the small size of the countries has implications for their development prospects. Regional integration has often been proposed as a solution for the problems of small countries, and it has been part of the Caribbean policy agenda for many decades. The authors explore this issue from many perspectives, beginning with whether size is truly a liability. Given the possibility of trade, a small country can achieve relevant economies of scale by specializing in a few sectors while importing other goods. In this way, being small may not be so costly in a globalized world where transportation costs and other trade barriers have fallen substantially. The authors review and extend some recent empirical research to show that the small Caribbean countries do not seem to be paying a significant price for their size. These considerations may explain why the Caribbean Community and Common Market (CARICOM) appears to have generated few benefits and significant costs. Additional factors include the slow implementation of the agreement in the early decades, the undeniable fact that the CARICOM members have very similar factor endowments, and the small size of the whole region.

The limitations of regional integration pose a particular challenge in light of the erosion of unilateral preferences for CARICOM exports to world markets and the growing global competition for aid and foreign direct investment. What, then, can be gained from regional integration? The authors convincingly argue that trade can alleviate the possible disadvantages associated with size for certain nontradable sectors, such as infrastructure, health, education, and other areas for which the minimum efficient scale surpasses most Caribbean countries. Although some efforts are under way in this direction, the paper concludes with a call for the region to take this much more seriously.

Weak governance is yet another possible explanation for poor economic performance in some Latin American countries. A prominent factor in this regard is capture of the political agenda by interest groups. Electoral campaign finance legislation is often discussed as a deterrent for this problem. Limiting contributions by interest groups or individuals, making political funding more transparent, and introducing state financing for political campaigns are among the central elements considered in such legislation.

In "Electoral Campaign Financing: The Role of Public Contributions and Party Ideology" Adriana Cuoco Portugal and Maurício Bugarin begin by reviewing the plethora of electoral campaign finance legislation and reform, both in Latin America and elsewhere. They also provide detailed evidence on how illicit political financing has ignited many crises in the region. The core of the paper develops a model to analyze the effects of public financing of electoral campaigns on policies announced by ideologically oriented parties, subject to pre-electoral lobbying. Parties' ideologies lead politicians to announce divergent platforms, even though this means losing some votes. Divergent platforms, in turn, make lobbies actually contribute to parties' electoral campaigns. The announced platforms are biased in favor of the parties' ideology and the interest groups' preferred policies. Finally, increasing public financing of electoral campaigns may generate unequal electoral competition and may significantly raise the chances of one party's becoming hegemonic, wiping out party competition in the long run.

The last paper in this issue examines the effects of Mexican interstate (internal) migration and international return migration (Mexican workers who return to Mexico after working abroad) on wages and employment in the *maquiladora* industry in Mexico. One motivation behind Scott Atkinson and Marilyn Ibarra's article, entitled "The Effect of Mexican Workforce Migration on the Mexican *Maquiladora* Labor Market," is the relocation of a number of firms in recent years from Mexico to China in search of lower labor costs.

Interstate or return migration in pursuit of employment in Mexican manufacturing assembly plants can either reduce or increase the market wage for unskilled and skilled workers, depending on whether it expands or contracts the supply of available labor. Migration can also shift labor demand to the right. This could reflect an increase in productivity if migrants are more skilled than local workers or an increase in the demand for goods produced by the migrants. The share of migrant workers is quite significant. Approximately 7.5 percent of the total number of workers are interstate migrants, while 5 percent are return immigrants.

The paper estimates cost and demand functions for Mexican skilled and unskilled labor in the textile *maquiladora* industry in twenty Mexican states for 1998–2001. The study concludes that the demand for labor is sensitive to costs, but more so for skilled than unskilled labor. Separately, the authors use the 2000 Mexican census to estimate the effect of return and interstate migration on the equilibrium wage in the manufacturing industry labor market. They find that interstate migration has a negative effect on wages, while international return migration has a modest positive effect. They then use a combination of these two models to compute the effects of both types of migration on the wages and employment of skilled and unskilled workers in the textile *maquiladora* industry, concluding that interstate migration has led to a reduction in wages and increased employment in this sector in a number of Mexican states.

Some final acknowledgments are in order. The fifteenth issue of *Economía* contains papers presented at the panel meeting held on May 11–12, 2007, in New Haven, Connecticut. Yale University's MacMillan Center, through its Edward J. and Dorothy Clarke Kempf Fund, cosponsored and graciously hosted the meeting. We are grateful to Jean Silk at the MacMillan Center's Council for Latin American and Iberian Studies for much help and support. Thanks are also due close to home: to the Associate Editors of *Economía*, the members of the panel, and Managing Editor Catherine Mathieu-Canuto. This issue benefited tremendously from their hard work.

CHANG-TAI HSIEH
JONATHAN A. PARKER

Taxes and Growth in a Financially Underdeveloped Country: Evidence from the Chilean Investment Boom

The performance of the Chilean economy since the mid-1980s has been extraordinary: Chile's per capita gross domestic product (GDP) grew at an average rate of 4.5 percent per year in the decade following 1983. While not as impressive as the growth miracles of the Asian developing economies in the postwar period, Chile's strong economic performance is unique among the developing economies in the Western Hemisphere. An important component of Chile's impressive growth was a saving and investment boom on the order of 10 percent of GDP. In this paper, we present evidence that a main cause of this investment and growth boom was a corporate tax reform that cut the tax rate on retained profits from nearly 50 percent to 10 percent over the period 1984–86.

This reform could have large effects. When firms face credit constraints, taxation of retained profits is more distortionary than taxation of dividends or household capital gains. By definition, the return to the marginal investment of a constrained firm is (weakly) greater than the after-tax real interest rate. Taxation of retained profits reduces precisely this potentially highly productive investment, since it draws down internal funds and therefore lowers the invest-

Hsieh is with the University of California at Berkeley; Parker is with Northwestern University.

We thank Daron Acemoglu, Robert Barro, Ben Bernanke, Ricardo Caballero, Angus Deaton, J. Bradford DeLong, Eduardo Engel, Erica Field, Christian Julliard, Peter Klenow, Nina Pavcnik, Thomas Philippon, Bruce Preston, Claudio Raddatz, Jose Scheinkman, Fabio Schiantarelli, Christopher Sims, James Tybout, and Rodrigo Valdes for helpful comments. For funding, we thank Dani Rodrik's project on analytical country studies on economic growth, the Sloan Foundation (Parker), the National Science Foundation grant SES-0096076 (Parker), and the research committee of the World Bank (Hsieh). Erica Field provided excellent research assistance. This paper formerly circulated as "Taxes and Growth in a Financially Underdeveloped Country: Explaining the Chilean Investment Boom."

1

ment of constrained firms by the amount of the tax. Unconstrained firms can largely avoid retaining profits and are able to fund investment through other means. Taxing retained earnings is thus potentially quite harmful in an economy with poorly developed financial markets, but otherwise favorable macroeconomic policies and conditions, such as Chile in the mid-1980s.[1] The 1984 tax reform, by reducing the tax rate on retained earnings, increased the internal funds of many credit-constrained firms and so may have been responsible for the increase in aggregate investment.

We present three types of evidence to assess our theory. First, we show that the timing and composition of the aggregate saving and investment boom are both consistent with the idea that the reduction in the taxation of retained profits was a major cause of the investment boom. Investment increased by 4.5 percent of GDP in the first year of the reform and had grown by over 10 percent of GDP five years after the reform, reaching 25 percent of GDP. The tax reform occurred at the beginning of the investment boom, whereas other reforms such as trade liberalization and the privatization of the public pension system significantly predate the boom. More importantly, the increase in investment was entirely funded by business saving, that is, by retained profits. Private saving and public saving remained largely unchanged.

Second, the cross-industry pattern of investment is also consistent with our theory. Using an annual survey that covers all Chilean manufacturing plants with more than ten employees, we show that investment rates rose after the reform primarily in industries that are heavily dependent on external finance. Industries classified by Rajan and Zingales as dependent on external finance had larger increases in investment in 1985, 1986, and 1987, although not in the first year of the reform, 1984.[2]

Finally, since we do not have clean measures of financial constraints at the firm level, we compare the investment rates of plants that are plausibly constrained to those that are plausibly unconstrained using the measures we do have. That is, we divide plants into those that are owned by firms that are more and less likely to face financing constraints and compare the investment behavior of plants owned by these different types of firms after the tax reform. Here, the evidence on our theory is weaker and more mixed. We find that the plants owned by firms that exhibited a high correlation of cash flow and investment before the reform increased their investment significantly more

---

1. These favorable macroeconomic policies represent other important causes of growth, which we discuss subsequently.
2. Rajan and Zingales (1998).

during the reform and to some extent following the reform compared with similar plants that had low prior correlations of cash flow and investment. We also find some evidence that plants owned by firms that previously had low short-term reserves increased their investment more during and to some extent following the reforms. However, we find no evidence that plants owned either by firms that pay rent or by smaller firms benefited disproportionately from the reform, although the distinction between small and large firms is less likely to measure the degree of financial constraints facing a firm in Chile than in the United States.

This paper is primarily related to two literatures. First, our analysis adds to the literature on the impact of tax policies on investment and the importance of financial constraints for investment.[3] Two papers are closely related to our current study. Calomiris and Hubbard use a firm's reaction to the retained profits tax of 1936–37 in the United States to identify liquidity-constrained firms and study their subsequent investment behavior.[4] We reverse this process. Rajan and Zingales examine the growth pattern of industries with differing needs for external financing in countries with different levels of financial development.[5] We compare the response of investment to Chile's 1984 tax reform across industries with differing needs for external financing.

Second, we contribute to the literature on the causes of economic development, particularly work focusing on the so-called Chilean miracle. Chilean observers frequently mention the 1984 tax reform as being potentially important in explaining the subsequent investment boom.[6] Previous research, however, focuses on other reforms undertaken by Chile, including the liberalization of the trade regime, the liberalization and deepening of financial markets, bankruptcy reform, and the privatization of the public pension system, rather than exploring the corporate tax reform as the underlying cause of Chile's growth performance.[7] To be clear, our argument is not that these other reforms are irrelevant for growth in general. Some of these reforms probably did raise

---

3. See Hubbard (1998); Bernanke and Gertler (1995); Bernanke, Gertler, and Gilchrist (1999); Hassett and Hubbard (2002), for reviews. Cummins, Hassett, and Hubbard (1996) discuss the difficulties inherent in cross-country estimation of the impact of taxes on investment; they present evidence that investment responds to tax incentives in general.

4. Calomiris and Hubbard (1995).

5. Rajan and Zingales (1998).

6. See Agosín (2001); Agosín, Crespi, and Letelier (1997); Budnevich and Jara (1997); Bustos, Engel, and Galetovic (1998); Larroulet (1987); Marfan and Bosworth (1994), for brief discussions of the 1984 tax reform.

7. See Bergoeing and others (2002); Edwards (1996); Gallego and Loayza (2000); Morandé (1998); Pavcnik (2002).

Chile's steady-state level of output per person, although we do not evaluate this claim. We provide evidence that the reduction in the tax on retained profits increased the accumulation of capital, and our preferred interpretation of this finding is that the tax reform led to rapid, rather than slow, convergence toward the steady state. In applying this lesson to financially underdeveloped economies more broadly, it is important to note that taxing retained earnings is highly distortionary only when there are productive investment opportunities.

The outline of the paper is as follows. The next section models the effect of taxes on retained profits when some firms are constrained from borrowing as much as they would like to invest at market interest rates. The paper then describes the 1984 tax reform in Chile and presents aggregate evidence that the corporate tax reform was a significant cause of Chile's rapid growth. A subsequent section details our use of the annual plant-level data from the Chilean manufacturing census, which we later use to test the industry- and plant-level predictions of our theory. We also discuss alternative explanations for Chile's investment boom, to provide a broad description of the Chilean experience. A final section concludes.

Investment and Taxes on Retained Earnings

This section explores how a tax on retained profits alters investment and productivity. To this end, we consider the investment decision of a household that owns a profitable firm and is unable to borrow to finance investment.[8] Firms and households face credit constraints and firms with highly productive investment opportunities are constrained from borrowing to invest at the optimal rate. We consider an economy like Chile's, in which there are three taxes levied on capital income: profits tax (τ_p), retained profits tax (τ_r), and dividend income tax (τ_d). The retained profits and dividend income tax rates are defined as the tax rate net of the profits tax. We assume that the economy is small and open so that the after-tax real interest rate is fixed at r^f.

Consider two firms that have the same initial capital stock (K_0) and profits (π), but differ in the productivity of the investment opportunities available to them. Firm H has a highly productive investment opportunity, while firm L does not. Figure 1 shows the marginal product of capital in the future for each

---

8. See appendix A of the working paper (Hsieh and Parker 2006) for additional formal exposition of the arguments in this section.

FIGURE 1. Investment and Credit Constraints

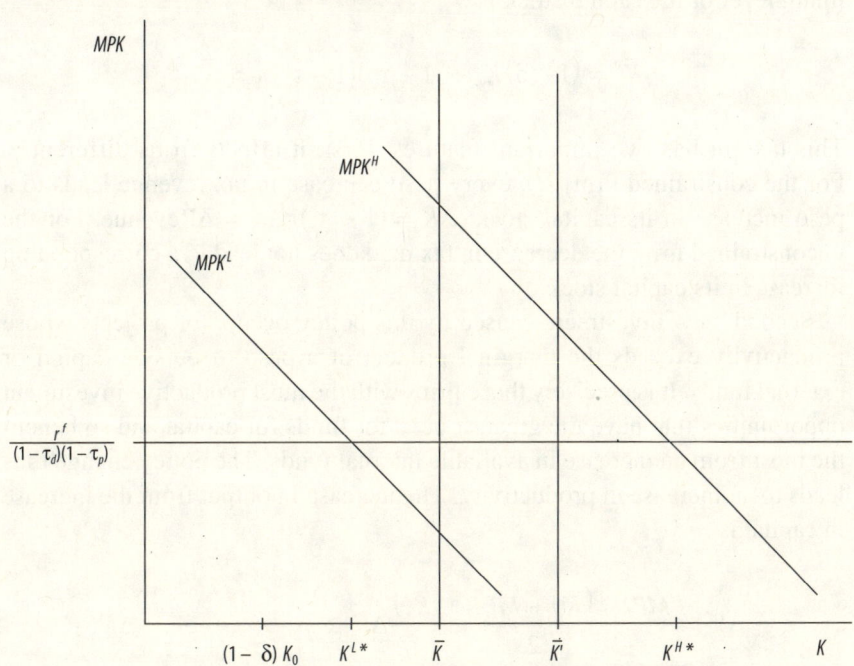

firm, with MPK^H lying above MPK^L. In a world with perfect capital markets, each firm would set the pretax marginal product of capital equal to the required pretax rate of return to investment, which is equal to the after-tax rate of return adjusted for the tax rates. The first-best levels of capital chosen would thus be K^{H*} and K^{L*}, and gross investment would equal $K^{H*} + K^{L*} - 2(1 - \delta)K_0$, where δ is the depreciation rate of old capital.

However, if we assume that these firms, and their owners, do not have access to external funds (debt or equity) to finance further investment, then their new investment is limited by their after-tax retained profits or $(1 - \tau_p)(1 - \tau_r)\pi$. Both the profits tax and the tax on retained profits decrease the funds available for investment. This bound on investment limits the future capital stock to

$$\bar{K} = (1 - \delta)K_0 + (1 - \tau_p)(1 - \tau_r)\pi.$$

Thus, firm H, with a highly productive investment opportunity, is unable to take full advantage of this opportunity ($\bar{K} < K^{H*}$).

Consider now a cut in the tax rate on retained profits to τ_r'. The new maximum level of the capital stock is

$$\bar{K}' = (1 - \delta)K_o + (1 - \tau_p)(1 - \tau_r')\pi > \bar{K}.$$

This tax cut has two important features. First, it affects firms differently. For the constrained firm (H), every peso decrease in tax revenue leads to a peso increase in its capital stock: $\Delta K = (1 - \tau_p)\pi\Delta\tau_r = \Delta\text{Revenue}$. For the unconstrained firm, the decrease in tax paid does not lead to a corresponding increase in its capital stock.

Second, new investment caused by this policy occurs for projects whose productivity exceeds the marginal product of a peso of outside capital or external funds. It is precisely those firms with the most productive investment opportunities that have the greatest need for funds for capital and so benefit the most from an increase in available internal funds. The policy change thus leads to an increase in productivity. The increase in output from the increase in capital is

$$\Delta Y = \frac{MPK^H(\bar{K}) + MPK^H(\bar{K}')}{2}\Delta K \geq \frac{r^f}{(1 - \tau_p)(1 - \tau_d)}\Delta K.$$

Comparatively, a cut in the dividend tax rate increases the incentive to invest by all firms, but highly profitable firms that are not paying dividends and are cash constrained are unable to raise their investment rates in response to such a tax cut. The marginal product of new investment generated from such a tax cut has the social marginal value of capital since it changes the investment rates of firms that are setting their capital stocks so as to equalize marginal products and interest rates. Alternatively, a cut in the profits tax rate increases the incentive to invest by all firms and allows further investment by cash-constrained firms, but it does not target the tax cut at highly productive investment opportunities. Similarly, a cut in the household tax on capital gains increases the frictionless demand for capital, but it does not increase the capital demand of constrained firms at the margin.

This graphical exposition is stylized in three ways. First, it is unlikely that any firms are truly constrained. Most, if not all, firms probably have access to funds at some price. For many firms, however, the costs of monitoring and enforcement may be extremely high, so that these firms face interest rates far above official rates. Such transaction costs associated with making loans act similarly to credit constraints.[9] Second, we have not been explicit about product markets. The size of unconstrained firms needs to be limited either by economies of scope, to generate diminishing returns in $F(.)$, or by demand, such as through monopolistic competition. Thus, the profit opportunities available to one firm are not available to all firms. If they were, the distribution of internal funds and credit constraints would be irrelevant for aggregate investment. Finally, in a multi-period world, a tax on retained profits reduces optimal investment for an unconstrained firm. Only for a firm without new investment (in excess of depreciation allowances) is there no tax benefit or government revenue lost and no change in incentives or value. However, the impact on the unconstrained firm remains significantly less than on the investment behavior of a constrained firm because the retained profits tax affects the marginal return to investment from the optimal level rather than from the tightening of a binding constraint.[10]

Given these arguments, how large an increase in capital stock do we expect from a cut in the tax on retained profits? These aggregate effects depend on whether a significant number of firms are credit constrained, so as a rough benchmark, we suppose that half of the firms (weighted by their capital stock) in Chile are credit constrained and are investing all their internal funds. The share of profits (before taxes) to value added can be approximated by the capital share of national income net of debt payments and depreciation, which we conservatively estimate to be 20 percent for Chile.[11] If the tax on retained profits falls from 50 percent to 10 percent, as happened in Chile, then the cash flow available to a firm increases from 10 percent to 18 percent of value added. If only credit-constrained firms invest the additional cash flow, then a lower bound on the effect of this tax policy change is a 4 percentage point increase in the investment share of GDP (8×0.5), which is slightly less than half of the increase in the investment share of GDP in Chile since the mid-1980s.

In sum, taxes on retained earnings remove cash from inside credit-constrained firms, where it is most valuable.

9. In 1984 the Chilean banking sector was still suffering from the aftereffects of the debt crisis. A number of banks had gone bankrupt, and a number had been taken over by the government. Thus, at this time, the sector that monitors loans and enforces legal debt contracts was small and probably had low technology, leading to high costs of external finance.

10. Although we do not study firm creation, the retained profits tax significantly changes the value of a new firm, and firm creation did increase following the reform.

11. From 1985 to 1998, the average capital share was 51 percent, and the average capital income net of depreciation was 41.2 percent of GDP (Central Bank of Chile 1999, table 1.57). Given that this number is larger than the capital share for a typical country and that interest payments typically account for a third of the capital share, 20 percent is a conservative estimate of the quantity of interest.

The 1984–86 Tax Reform

The Chilean tax system before 1984 was based on the principle that households and firms should be treated similarly in the tax code. This principle was implemented by setting the tax rate applied to firms' retained profits equal to that applied to dividends or distributed earnings. That is, the personal and corporate tax codes were structured so that whether profits were paid to the owner or to the firm was irrelevant for tax revenue collected.

More specifically, the tax treatment of capital income in Chile in the period before 1984 can be summarized in four points: profits were taxed at a 10 percent rate; retained profits (net of the corporate profits tax) were taxed at either the personal income tax rate of the owners (from 0 to 58 percent) for limited-liability corporations or a 40 percent rate for publicly traded companies; dividends (net of the corporate profits tax) were taxed at the personal income tax rate (ranging up to 58 percent); and realized capital gains were taxed as dividends if owned by an individual or as corporate profits if owned by a firm.[12] These taxes cumulate to a high effective tax rate on retained profits. Retained profits of publicly traded companies were first taxed at 10 percent (the corporate profits tax) and the residual net of the 10 percent tax was then taxed at 40 percent, for an effective tax rate of 46 percent on retained profits. The tax treatment of retained profits of limited liability corporations was similar, except that the residual net of the 10 percent corporate profits tax was taxed at the marginal income rate of the owner of the firm. This yields an effective tax rate on retained profits of $0.1 + 0.9\tau$ (where τ is the marginal income tax rate of the owner of the firm) for limited liability corporations. In 1980, the average marginal income tax rate of individuals who paid taxes on dividends and retained profits was 43 percent, which translates into a typical effective tax rate of almost 50 percent on retained profits.[13]

The Chilean government enacted a significant tax reform in January 1984. While the reform altered both the personal and corporate tax codes, the largest

---

12. Capital gains on assets held for less than a year were not taxed before 1984. The dividend tax rate indicated (up to 58 percent) was the rate on dividends of limited liability firms. The dividends tax for shareholders of publicly traded companies was slightly more complicated, involving two taxes: first, dividends were taxed at 40 percent; second, dividends net of the 40 percent tax were taxed at the personal income tax rate minus 0.4. The tax rate on dividends (net of the corporate profits tax) was therefore $0.6*\tau + 0.16$, where τ is the personal income tax rate. If the personal income tax rate was 40 percent, the dividends tax rate was equal to the personal income tax rate (and equal to the dividend tax rate for limited liability corporations).

13. Calculated from Servicio de Impuestos Internos (1980, p. 44).

TABLE 1. **Personal Income Tax Rates in Chile before and after the Reform**[a]

Tax bracket (1983–85)	Marginal tax rate			Tax bracket (1986)	Marginal tax rate (1986)
	1983	1984	1985		
0–32,140	0.00	0.00	0.00	0–32,140	0.00
32,140–80,350	0.08	0.07	0.06	32,140–96,420	0.05
80,350–128,560	0.13	0.12	0.11	96,420–160,700	0.10
128,560–176,770	0.18	0.17	0.16	160,700–224,980	0.15
176,770–224,980	0.28	0.27	0.26	224,980–289,260	0.25
224,980–273,190	0.38	0.37	0.36	289,260–385,680	0.35
273,190–321,400	0.48	0.47	0.46	385,680–482,100	0.45
Over 321,400	0.58	0.57	0.56	Over 482,100	0.50

a. The tax brackets are in pesos per month and are indexed for inflation. The 1986 tax bracket is quoted in January 1984 pesos per month.

change was the near-elimination of the tax on retained profits that had paralleled the tax on dividends. The effective tax on retained profits was lowered to 10 percent, effective immediately for limited liability corporations but phased in over three years for publicly traded companies.[14] The tax reform did not alter the tax on corporate profits (10 percent), and it left the tax treatment of capital gains largely unchanged.[15] With respect to dividend taxation, the tax reform widened personal income tax brackets and lowered marginal income tax rates slightly. Table 1 describes the personal income tax rates before and after the tax reform. In addition to the cut in income tax rates, the tax reform also provided a credit for corporate taxes paid that reduced the basis for the payment of the dividend tax. Table 2 summarizes the effective tax rate on dividends and retained profits before and after the tax reform.

Two additional features of the tax system had important effects on firms' finances. First, firms paid (and still pay) estimated taxes on retained earnings monthly. The change in the tax rate on retained profits thus had an immediate impact on cash flows. Second, the corporate tax code was stable from 1986 to 1988, but the tax on retained profits was eliminated entirely for the tax year 1989. The retained profits tax was then increased to 15 percent in 1990, and it remained at that level throughout the 1990s. We focus our analysis of firms on the period 1980–90.

Cuts in personal tax rates have two main effects on incentives. First, to the extent that the cuts in marginal tax rates on labor income are perceived as

14. The retained profits tax rate for publicly traded companies was lowered to 30 percent in 1984, 15 percent in 1985, and zero thereafter.

15. The 1984 tax reform removed the tax exemption on capital gains held for less than a year, but otherwise did not change the tax treatment of capital gains.

TABLE 2. Tax Rates on Corporate Profits and Dividends in Chile before and after the Reform[a]

	Publicly traded companies		Limited-liability companies	
Period	Retained profits	Distributed profits	Retained profits	Distributed profits
Pre-1984	0.460	$0.244 + 0.540\tau$	$0.100 + 0.900\tau$	$0.100 + 0.900\tau$
1984	0.370	$0.118 + 0.630\tau$	0.100	τ
1985	0.235	$0.04375 + 0.765\tau$	0.100	τ
Post-1985	0.100	τ	0.100	τ

a. τ is the marginal personal income tax rate.

highly persistent (as they turned out to be in Chile), then changes in tax rates provide no incentive to substitute labor intertemporally. Nevertheless, persistent tax cuts cause wealth effects that reduce labor supply and substitution effects from leisure to consumption that increase labor supply. The evidence on wage levels and hours of work across countries and over time suggests that these effects are of similar magnitude, but that the wealth effect dominates, so the Chilean reforms would have reduced labor supply. Given the small size of the rate changes, the labor income tax changes seem unlikely to have had a major role in causing the Chilean investment boom.[16]

Second, a reduction in the taxation of dividend income increases the incentive to save and accumulate capital. This aspect of the Chilean reform is unlikely to have played a large role in the observed economic boom, however, since Chile experienced an investment boom at the time of the reform, while saving rose only slowly. Chile borrowed significantly from abroad until 1988, when saving roughly equaled investment. Given the weak observed link between capital income taxation and economic growth across countries and the small changes that Chile actually implemented at this time, the changes in personal tax rates are unlikely to have significantly contributed to the Chilean economic boom.

Aggregate Evidence

The behavior of national saving and investment suggests that the reduction in the taxation of retained profits caused at least part of the rapid growth in Chile. Both saving and investment rose following the reform, from an average rate

---

16. The one caveat to this argument is that lower tax rates on labor income also increase the incentive to accumulate human capital. It is at least possible that the investment boom occurred to take advantage of the higher expected future human capital levels.

FIGURE 2.   **Sources of Saving in Chile**

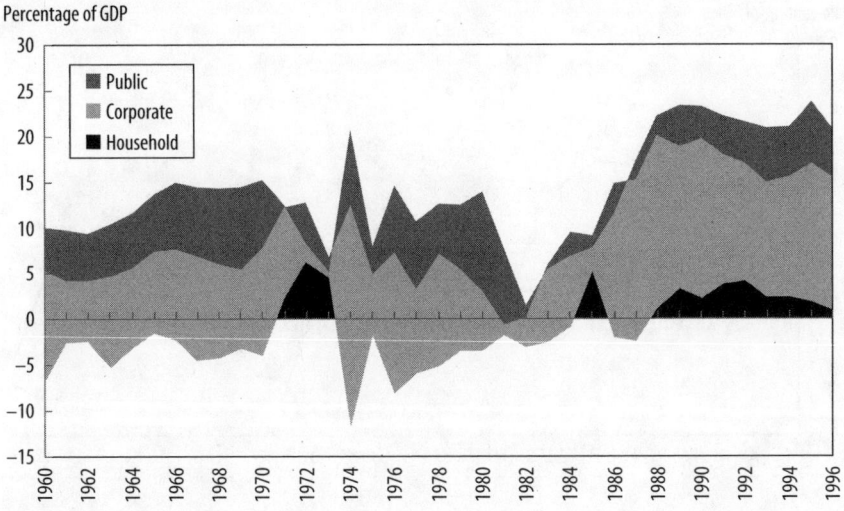

Percentage of GDP

Source: Bennett, Schmidt-Hebbel, and Soto (1999).

of 15 percent from 1960 to 1983 to an average rate of 25 percent in the first half of the 1990s.

Figure 2 shows that both the level and composition of saving underwent a striking change at the time of the tax reform. Business saving increased after the reform period of 1984–86, while household saving and public saving rose much less and with a longer lag. Our theory predicts that saving should rise as firms respond to the reduction in the tax on retained profits by retaining more profits, and that households should not decrease active saving to offset this change.[17] With respect to investment, the timing of the investment boom also supports our theory. Investment increased by 4.5 percent of GDP in the first year of the reform and by over 10 percent of GDP over five years, reaching 25 percent of GDP in 1989. The tax reform occurred at the beginning of the investment boom, while other reforms such as trade liberalization and the privatization of the public pension system significantly predate the boom.

17. This is consistent with cash-constrained firms' being owned by liquidity-constrained households. If liquidity constraints and cash constraints were not important, a reduction in the retained profits tax rate might merely result in a shift in the composition of savings from household to corporate savings, with no effect on aggregate savings.

F I G U R E 3 .   **Investment to GDP in Latin America**[a]

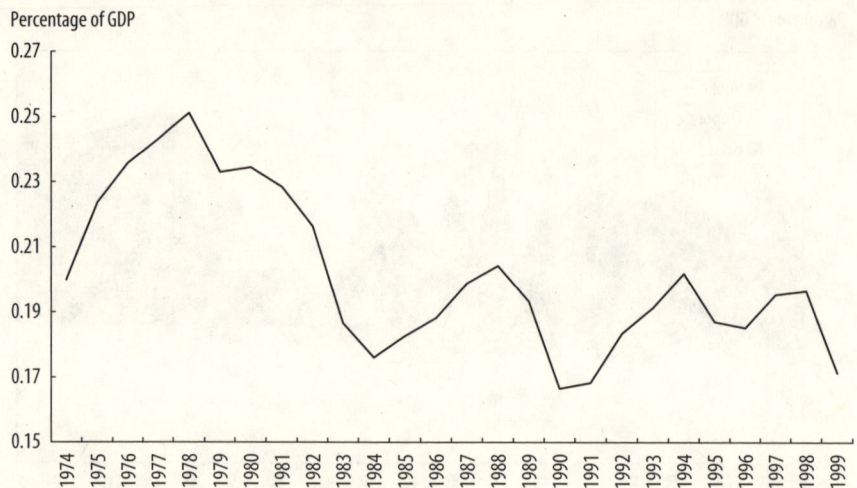

Percentage of GDP

Source: International Monetary Fund, *International Financial Statistics*.
a. Includes Argentina, Brazil, Colombia, Mexico, and Venezuela.

Chile also experienced an investment boom from 1976 to 1981, financed by large current account deficits, but this lending boom and subsequent collapse were common to many countries in Latin America.[18] As shown in Figure 3, only the later investment boom is particular to Chile, since the rest of Latin America stagnated in the 1980s following the debt crisis.[19]

Other aggregate evidence includes the change in the debt-to-asset ratio for firms during this period. In terms of theory, an unconstrained firm should increase its profit retention relative to dividend payments in response to the change in incentives associated with the reduction in the tax on retained earnings.[20] A constrained firm should increase its after-tax retained earnings and increase its investment. The national data cover only publicly traded companies, which by definition have some access to capital. The national data on debt ratios thus reflect the behavior of more unconstrained firms than the

18. The consensus view of these booms is that they were unsustainable lending booms driven by some combination of poorly regulated financial liberalization and a surge in capital inflows driven by external factors. See, for example, Díaz-Alejandro (1985).

19. The countries in our Latin American sample are Argentina, Brazil, Colombia, Mexico, and Venezuela.

20. The tax rate on dividends also fell slightly. In a frictionless world, the investment decision of an extant firm that pays dividends is undistorted by dividend taxation (Bradford 1981).

FIGURE 4.   **Debt to Total Assets of Publicly Traded Companies**

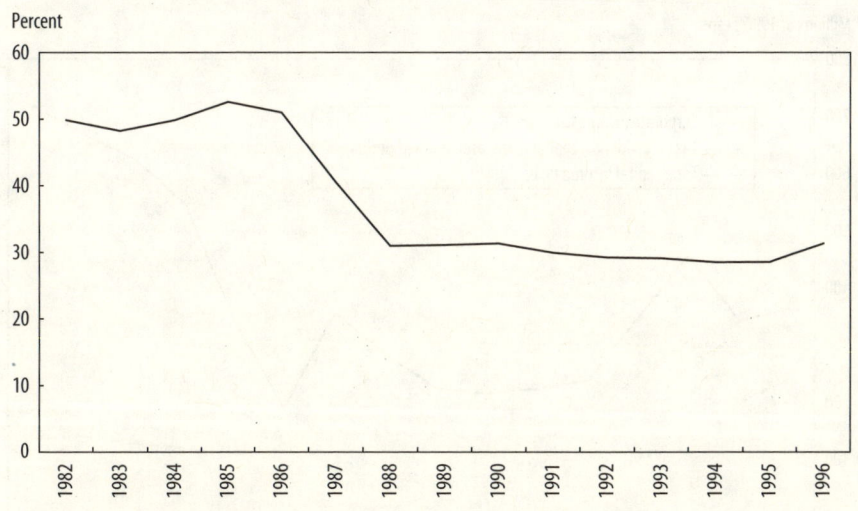

Source: Eyzaguirre and Lefort (1999).

national average. As figure 4 illustrates, publicly traded firms reduced their debt after the reforms, but only after a significant lag.[21]

Figure 5 shows the impact of the tax reform and investment boom on real tax revenues collected on capital income, from both the personal income tax and the corporate profits tax. The tax revenues from the category that includes retained profits declined from 250 million 1996 pesos in 1984 to less than 100 million 1996 pesos in 1987. At the same time, the revenues collected from the corporate income tax (the 10 percent tax on all firm profits) rose starting in 1984 as firms invested and grew. From 1989 on, with the exception of 1990, when the retained profits tax was set to zero for a year, the increase in taxes collected through the general profits tax more than replaced the lost revenues on retained profits. Figure 5 suggests that Chile was able to reduce the tax on retained earnings and increase tax revenues.

Having presented the basic aggregate facts, we next describe the data on firms and plants that we use to construct industry-level data, categorize plants

21. As in the United States, firms maintain fairly high levels of debt despite the favorable tax treatment of retained versus distributed profits. Bustos, Engel, and Galetovic (1998) report that from 1985 to 1995, publicly traded firms in Chile still carried so much debt that their profits net of interest payments (and depreciation allowances) were, on average, effectively zero (or slightly negative).

FIGURE 5. Tax Revenues from Capital Income[a]

Millions of 1996 pesos

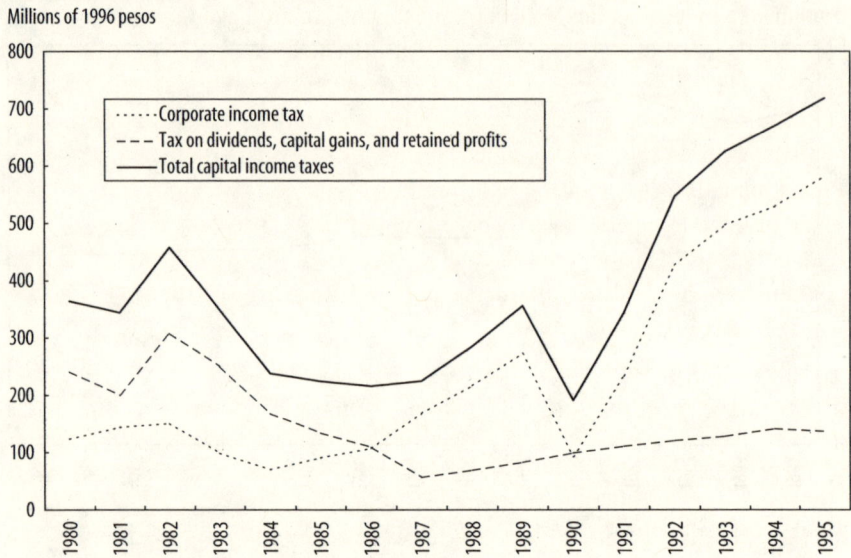

Source: *Ley de Presupuestos del Sector Público* (Budget Office, various years).
a. The figure displays taxes collected during a year, rather than taxes collected on activity during a year.

by constrained status, and test whether constrained plants indeed invested more following the reform.

The Chilean Manufacturing Census

The data for our analysis of industry and firm investment behavior are drawn from the Chilean manufacturing census (Encuesta Nacional Industrial Anual) conducted annually by the Chilean government's statistical office (Instituto Nacional de Estadística). The survey covers all manufacturing plants in Chile with more than ten employees and has been run annually since 1979. In addition to working with the raw data files, we also use data from an extract from this survey, compiled by the World Bank under the direction of James Tybout. Finally, the Chilean statistical agency also provided us with information on which plants were owned by the same firm. Thus, while we analyze plants, we are able to use the financial situation and behavior of firms to categorize plants as likely or unlikely to be credit constrained.

The advantages of the Chilean manufacturing census for our purposes are its near universal coverage, annual frequency, and the wealth of information contained about each plant. We combine the information available in the annual surveys from 1979 to 1990 with the World Bank extract, which covers only 1979 to 1986. The survey contains information on a wide variety of plant characteristics such as industry (four-digit International Standard Industrial Classification, or ISIC), factor inputs, energy use, days of production, and sales. Plants annually report investment, employment, and production. The book value of fixed assets is collected in 1980 and 1981. The census data for year t are collected in surveys conducted at the beginning of year $t + 1$. The data contain the value of flow variables over the entire year t and the value of stock variables as of the end of year t.

The census contains information on five types of investment: purchases of new capital, purchases of used capital, production of capital for own use, improvements in own capital by third parties, and sales of capital. Our measure of investment, to which our capital measure corresponds, is the sum of all five types of investment in machinery, equipment, and vehicles. That is, we exclude investment in land and buildings. Investment can be negative owing to sales of capital, and we treat negative reported investment as legitimate. A large number of plants report zero investment from purchases, production, improvements, and sales for all varieties of capital goods. Our primary database sets investment to missing only when the World Bank extract considers it missing. This treats the vast majority of zero investment reports as legitimate zeros and treats all such reports after 1986 (the last year of the World Bank extract) as legitimate. To check that this assumption is not driving our results, we create an alternative database that sets investment (and thus subsequent capital stocks) to missing if there is zero reported investment in all categories and types for two consecutive years. Our baseline results thus use data consistent with those used in previous research, while our alternative data set checks the robustness of our main results along this dimension. Our baseline results are generally robust, and we note any places where our results differ.

Our definition of capital corresponds to our definition of investment; it includes machinery, equipment, and vehicles and excludes buildings. We take our main measures of capital stock from the World Bank extract, which constructs the book value of capital stock in 1980 and 1981 using an inflation adjustment and a depreciation adjustment. To check that our results do not depend on these adjustments, we also construct a separate data extract based on the reported book value of capital as reported in the raw survey data. As with the alternative treatment of investment, our findings are generally robust to this alternative, and we note results for which inference depends on our baseline assumption.

A plant's capital stock in years other than 1980 and 1981 is calculated by iterating forward using investment and the capital accumulation equation,

$$(1) \qquad K_{j,t} = \left(1 - \delta_j\right) K_{j,t-1} + I_{j,t},$$

where j indexes either machinery and equipment or vehicles and the timing follows from the fact that investment in year t adds the capital reported at the end of year $t - 1$ to capital stock at the end of year t. We use the following depreciation rates: 10 percent for machinery and equipment and 20 percent for vehicles. These are the same rates used in the World Bank extract. In this procedure, we keep capital stocks positive, and we omit depreciation for plants that are missing from the survey for a year and drop plants missing for more than one year.

We use the machinery price index to deflate both investment and capital stock. We discard plants that die before the experiment that we seek to study (that is, any plant that does not exist after 1983). We drop all plants owned or run by the government. We consider investment to capital ratios greater than three or less than minus one to be miscoded or misreported and so treat them as missing observations. Finally, there is significant attrition of plants: one-quarter of plants attrit between 1984 and 1990 in our baseline sample.[22]

Evidence from Chilean Industries

This section presents our main results. We test whether, at the time of the tax reform, investment increases were concentrated in industries for which external finance is important. Rajan and Zingales construct measures of an industry's reliance on external finance by examining the use of external finance by U.S. companies.[23] They show that in countries with poorly developed financial markets, industries that are more reliant on external finance grow more slowly relative to the typical growth for that industry and for that country in aggregate. We take a similar tack to identify the impact of the tax cut on retained profits. If capital markets in Chile were poorly developed in the 1980s and if the 1984 tax cut disproportionately benefited credit-constrained plants, then investment rates

---

22. See the appendixes in the working paper (Hsieh and Parker 2006) for additional details, including a further description of the data construction.
23. Rajan and Zingales (1998).

should rise disproportionately in industries that are particularly reliant on external finance, relative to the typical rate for that industry and for Chile in that year.

We thus measure the extent to which industries that are more dependent on external finance have larger increases in investment rates after the reform, relative to their typical investment rates and to the average investment rate in that year. At the same time, we control for the fact that if the industry is capital intensive, it may increase its investment more in response to the tax reform. That is, we estimate the following equation:

$$(2) \qquad \frac{I_{n,t}}{K_{n,t}} = \alpha_n + \gamma_t + E_n \mathbf{D}_t \boldsymbol{\beta}_E + F_n \mathbf{D}_t \boldsymbol{\beta}_D + \xi_{i,t},$$

where $I_{n,t}$ and $K_{n,t}$ are the total investment and capital stock, respectively, for industry n in year t; α_n measures the average investment to capital ratio for industry n; γ_t measures the average investment to capital ratio in year t; E_n denotes dependence on external finance for industry n, as measured by Rajan and Zingales; $\mathbf{D}_t$ is a row vector of indicator variables for years after the tax reform begins; $\boldsymbol{\beta}_E$ is the coefficient vector of interest, measuring the amount by which $I_{n,t} / K_{n,t}$ is higher for industries that are highly dependent on external finance in each year after the reform; F_n are control variables; and $\xi_{i,t}$ denotes the error term. The control variables address the concern that the heterogeneity in post-1984 growth and investment is at least partly driven by factors other than external financial dependence and that these factors might be correlated with external financial dependence. If this were the case and we omitted the year interactions with F_n from our regressions, the estimated $\boldsymbol{\beta}_E$ would confound these factors with the importance of increased access to external funds. We consider two control variables, described subsequently.

Since we estimate this equation on industry-level data from 1982 to 1990, the typical growth rate of an industry is measured by its performance in 1982 and 1983. We also measure typical performance by 1982, 1983, 1989, and 1990, by dropping the last two years of interactions between external dependence and the time indicators and between capital intensity and the time indicators. The first two years have the advantage of being before the reform, but the disadvantage of including the 1982 recession, such that the pattern of growth across industries may be affected by the severity of the recession, even after we control for year effects. The last two years have the advantage of being years of healthy growth in Chile, but the disadvantage of being after the reform and after a significant growth boom, when capital markets are beginning to develop more generally.

We first run equation 2 including capital intensity as F_n. Since the economy boomed after 1984 and since capital-intensive industries tend to be cyclical, we would expect industries that are more capital intensive to grow more rapidly after 1984. Moreover, if capital intensity is correlated with dependence on external finance, as seems likely, then omitting this term would bias us in favor of finding that industries that are highly dependent on external finance grew more—as our theory predicts, but for a spurious reason. We measure capital intensity before the boom as the average of the 1981 and 1982 log of the ratio of the capital stock in industry n to the total wages in industry n. Thus, in this first set of regressions, the vector β_D measures the extent to which investment-to-capital ratios are larger for industries that are more capital intensive in each year after the reform, and the vector β_E captures the effect of dependence on external finance, controlling for capital intensity.

Table 3 shows the results of estimating equation 2 using weighted least squares, with the number of plants in an industry as weights, and making inference allowing for arbitrary cross-industry correlations.[24] Industries are defined according to the three-digit ISIC.[25] The first set of results examines the impact of the reform through 1990; the second set treats 1989 and 1990 as additional control years. The coefficients of interest, β_{E_t}, are negative and insignificant in 1984, positive in 1985, and positive and significant in both sets of results in 1986 and 1987. The last column of the table quantifies the relative impact of the reform across industries that differ in their degree of financial dependence. An industry one standard deviation above the average level of dependence on external finance is predicted to have increased its capital 6 percent according to the first set of results and 12 percent according to the second by the end of 1987 relative to a comparable industry one standard deviation below the average. Industries that are more dependent on external finance grew more rapidly than usual at the time of the reform.[26]

24. Here we use the degree of external dependence as a continuous variable, rather than using it to split the sample as we do subsequently with indicators of possibly constrained status in the plant-level analysis. We chose this functional form to better control for capital intensity. That said, the results are substantively similar if we instead split plants into thirds by the Rajan and Zingales (1998) measures and also include indicator variables for high, medium, or low capital intensity.

25. The exceptions are food processing and manufacture of fabricated metal, where large numbers of plants allow finer detail, and six industries with few plants that are grouped into three categories. See Hsieh and Parker (2006).

26. Results are similar across samples, similar if we omit the control for capital intensity, and similar if we compare the three groups: high, medium, and low dependence on external finance. Capital-intensive industries tend to have no consistent pattern of investment rates in 1984 or 1985, statistically insignificant higher investment rates in 1986, and lower investment rates in 1987 and 1988.

T A B L E   3 .   Industry Investment Rates as a Function of Dependence on External Finance[a]

Interaction of dependence on external finance and year	Coefficient	Standard error	Effect of 1 standard deviation increase in external finance dependency
Control years: 1982 and 1983			
1984	−0.003	0.004	−0.001
1985	0.039	0.004	0.016
1986	0.055	0.004	0.022
1987	0.067	0.004	0.027
1988	−0.011	0.004	−0.004
1989	0.056	0.004	0.023
1990	0.037	0.004	0.015
Cumulative	0.240		0.098
Control years: 1982, 1983, 1989, and 1990			
1984	−0.024	0.015	−0.010
1985	0.019	0.015	0.008
1986	0.035	0.014	0.014
1987	0.046	0.015	0.019
1988	−0.032	0.015	−0.013
Cumulative	0.045		0.018
No. of observations	306		

a. Regressions include industry and year effects and capital-labor ratio interacted with year effects. Standard errors are calculated allowing for arbitrary heteroskedasticity and cross-industry correlations within each year. Regressions are run on data from 1982 to 1990 and include only plants that survive until at least 1984. See text for further details.

Table 4 shows the results of adding a control for whether the industry exports, imports, or has little trade exposure.[27] That is, F_n includes both a measure of capital intensity and a measure of trade exposure. The real exchange rate declined over the 1980s, representing a boom for exporting industries. If exporting industries were more likely also to be reliant on external finance, then this correlation could be biasing the results in table 3. The results in table 4 are slightly weaker than those in table 3, suggesting some correlation, but the net impact, measured with some level of uncertainty, is still that industries that rely more on external finance saw larger increases in their investment rates after the tax reform than those that rely less on external finance.

These results provide some support for our thesis that many plants were having difficulty raising external funds in 1983, that plants in industries strongly dependent on external finance were the most hurt by these constraints, and that these plants made the largest increases in their investment in 1985–87. We now turn directly to plant-level evidence, comparing the investment behavior

27. We thank Nina Pavcnik for providing these data. Construction of the variable is described in Hsieh and Parker (2006).

TABLE 4. Industry Investment Rates and Dependence on External Finance, Controlling for Exporting Status of Industry[a]

Interaction of dependence on external finance and year	Coefficient	Standard error	Effect of 1 standard deviation increase in external finance dependency
Control years: 1982 and 1983			
1984	−0.009	0.002	−0.004
1985	0.033	0.003	0.013
1986	0.046	0.002	0.019
1987	0.059	0.002	0.024
1988	−0.033	0.002	−0.013
1989	0.039	0.002	0.016
1990	0.031	0.002	0.012
Cumulative	0.166		0.068
Control years: 1982, 1983, 1989, and 1990			
1984	−0.024	0.010	−0.010
1985	0.018	0.010	0.007
1986	0.031	0.010	0.013
1987	0.044	0.010	0.018
1988	−0.048	0.011	−0.020
Cumulative	0.021		0.009
No. of observations	270		

a. Regressions include industry and year effects and average net exports status interacted with year effects. Standard errors are calculated allowing for arbitrary heteroskedasticity and cross-industry correlations within each year. Regressions are run on data from 1982 to 1990 and include only plants that survive until at least 1984. See text for further details.

of plants that are likely and unlikely to be cash constrained and controlling for the typical industry investment levels to see if this dimension of the data also supports our theory.

Evidence from Chilean Plants

This section presents comparisons of the investment behavior of plants that are likely and unlikely to be having trouble raising external funds for productive investment. We measure the likelihood of being constrained based on the correlation of profits and investment before the reform, the amount of short-term capital held by the firm before the reform, whether a firm pays rent, and the size of the firm. When firms are split by investment-profit correlation, we find a significant effect of the reform, as predicted by our theory. We also find some evidence from the sample split by short-term assets. However, there is no detectable postreform investment boom of plants owned by small firms relative to those owned by large firms or of plants owned by firms that pay rent relative to those owned by firms that do not.

Our key dependent variable is investment in year t divided by capital at the start of the year (the end of the previous year):

$$\left(\frac{I}{K}\right)_{i,t} \equiv \frac{\sum_j I_{j,t}}{\sum_j K_{j,t-1}},$$

where j indexes types of capital. Table 5 provides a set of statistics on the number of plants and the mean, standard deviation, and median of investment-to-capital ratios by year. To characterize plants as likely or unlikely to have restricted access to capital, we merge plants owned by the same firm together into observations on firms. All firms and their associated plants are categorized into more and less likely to be liquidity constrained on the basis of observed firm characteristics before 1984. Most plants are themselves firms; approximately 350 plants are associated with multi-plant firms in the years of the reform.

We first measure the likelihood of a plant's being credit constrained by the correlation of cash flow and investment for the entire firm during the period before the reforms.[28] The argument for this measure is standard. Credit-constrained plants rely more heavily on internal funds to finance operations and so are unable to maintain investment when cash flow drops significantly. The size of the correlation of cash flow and investment therefore provides a good measure of the degree to which a plant relies on internal funds to finance investment. While standard, this measure of constrained status is, at best, error ridden. Several recent papers show that standard theoretical models of firm behavior can imply a significant correlation between cash flow and profits for unconstrained firms, possibly even greater than for constrained firms (depending on the stochastic processes of the price of output and the constraint).[29] Hence, the other approaches of this paper.

28. Our identification strategy is the reverse of that used by Calomiris and Hubbard (1995), who identify firms as credit constrained or not based on their response to a 1937 surtax imposed on retained earnings. Firms that retain profits despite paying between 7 and 27 percent additional taxes on such retained profits are called *credit constrained*. Constrained plants are found to display a higher correlation between investment and cash flow than firms that do not retain profits in the face of this tax. In contrast, we identify credit constraints by sensitivity to cash flow before the tax change, and we then examine whether constrained plants display a greater response to the tax change.

29. Gomes (2001); Cooper and Ejarque (2003).

TABLE 5. Number of Plants and Investment Capital Ratios, by Year and Sample[a]

Sample and year	No. of observations	Mean I/K	Standard deviation I/K	Median I/K
Baseline sample				
1981	3,283	0.115	0.303	0.000
1982	3,321	0.058	0.209	0.000
1983	3,209	0.059	0.213	0.000
1984	3,209	0.071	0.219	0.000
1985	3,013	0.068	0.212	0.000
1986	2,767	0.079	0.233	0.000
1987	2,635	0.103	0.251	0.009
1988	2,517	0.113	0.266	0.019
1989	2,433	0.139	0.289	0.029
1990	2,375	0.112	0.258	0.017
Alternative initial capital stock				
1981	3,286	0.111	0.266	0.000
1982	3,354	0.056	0.197	0.000
1983	3,235	0.057	0.199	0.000
1984	3,233	0.065	0.194	0.000
1985	3,028	0.065	0.204	0.000
1986	2,784	0.075	0.223	0.000
1987	2,653	0.102	0.252	0.009
1988	2,533	0.116	0.278	0.020
1989	2,434	0.134	0.275	0.027
1990	2,378	0.112	0.255	0.017
Alternative investment series				
1981	1,907	0.2005734	0.3781525	0.0788183
1982	1,757	0.1066308	0.2803740	0.0306863
1983	1,449	0.1037540	0.2584918	0.0302968
1984	1,309	0.1307663	0.2723599	0.0499551
1985	1,184	0.1205192	0.2390222	0.0457503
1986	982	0.1422860	0.2620428	0.0643813
1987	831	0.1469315	0.2320091	0.0764872
1988	791	0.1503537	0.2451368	0.0902295
1989	762	0.1831413	0.2607033	0.1085611
1990	727	0.1631771	0.2540562	0.0911481
Alternative capital stock and investment series				
1981	1,907	0.2041381	0.3452066	0.0847551
1982	1,783	0.1036753	0.2554344	0.0305476
1983	1,464	0.0945425	0.2267038	0.0277332
1984	1,321	0.1177184	0.2378064	0.0465582
1985	1,186	0.1001863	0.1807689	0.0409718
1986	986	0.1254738	0.2290787	0.0575351
1987	834	0.1308618	0.2008967	0.0660726
1988	794	0.1383945	0.2204166	0.0792377
1989	763	0.1688204	0.2344262	0.0992237
1990	730	0.1535068	0.2518668	0.0807679

a. The samples are defined as follows. In the baseline sample, the capital stock is initialized from the World Bank extract, and investment is set to missing following the World Bank extract. In the sample using the alternative capital stock, the capital stock is initialized as the reported book value, and investment is set to missing following the World Bank extract. In the sample using the alternative investment series, the capital stock is initialized from the World Bank extract, and investment is set to missing if it is zero in two consecutive years. In the sample using the alternative capital stock and the alternative investment series, the capital stock is initialized as the reported book value, and investment is set to missing if it is zero in two consecutive years.

Our exact measure is the correlation between the ratio of net profits to capital and the ratio of gross investment to capital over the period 1980–82, where we use the 1980 capital stock in place of the unavailable 1979 stock. While we choose this period because of our limited sample, we suspect that this is a good time period for observing which plants are credit constrained, since 1982 was a large, temporary downturn. Plants able to maintain some investment or avoid selling off capital in this deep recession are the most likely to have had owners with deep pockets, access to borrowing, or significant internal funds.

We divide our sample of plants into thirds based on our measure of the correlation of profits and investment. We expect the group with the highest correlations to be the most likely to be credit constrained and to benefit the most from the reduction in the tax on retained profits. We call these plants constrained, the middle third possibly constrained, and the lowest third unconstrained, although these terms do not imply that we believe this split to be perfect. Given this crude measure, some constrained plants have surely been classified in the unconstrained sample and vice versa. This should lead any estimates of the impact of the tax reform to be biased toward zero. Following these results, we present evidence from several alternative or complementary divisions of plants.

We begin by running the following regression:

$$(3) \qquad \ln\left(\frac{I}{K}\right)_{i,t} = \alpha_i + \gamma_t + C_i \mathbf{D}_t \boldsymbol{\beta}_C + PC_i \mathbf{D}_t \boldsymbol{\beta}_{PC} + \varepsilon_{i,t},$$

where α_i is a plant-specific fixed effect, γ_t is a year-specific fixed effect, C_i is an indicator of whether a plant is deemed constrained, PC_i is an indicator variable for whether a plant is possibly constrained, $\mathbf{D}_t$ is a row vector of indicator variables for years after the tax reform begins, and $\varepsilon_{i,t}$ captures other factors that affect a plant's investment choices, as well as measurement error in K and I. The elements of the column vectors $\boldsymbol{\beta}_C$ and $\boldsymbol{\beta}_{PC}$ measure the differential investment activity of plants during and after the tax reform relative to their previous investment rates and relative to the contemporaneous investment choices of plants deemed unlikely to be constrained. We use all available data on plants from 1982 to 1990 and, as before, vary whether 1989 and 1990 are used as control years by varying whether indicator variables for 1989 and 1990 are included in the vector $\mathbf{D}_t$.

Table 6 presents the estimates from equation 3 in the first and second columns of results. Plants with a high correlation of investment and profits

TABLE 6. Investment to Capital as a Function of Profit-Investment Correlations and Year[a]

Type of plant and year	Plant and year effects		Industry x year effects	
	(1)	(2)	(3)	(4)
High-correlation indicator			−0.021	−0.039
			(0.006)	(0.008)
High-correlation plants				
1984	0.049	0.063	0.044	0.063
	(0.012)	(0.013)	(0.013)	(0.014)
1985	0.032	0.046	0.031	0.049
	(0.012)	(0.013)	(0.013)	(0.014)
1986	0.024	0.038	0.024	0.042
	(0.013)	(0.014)	(0.013)	(0.014)
1987	0.008	0.023	0.008	0.026
	(0.013)	(0.014)	(0.014)	(0.015)
1988	0.031	0.046	0.033	0.051
	(0.013)	(0.014)	(0.014)	(0.015)
1989		0.039		0.045
		(0.014)		(0.015)
1990		0.024		0.036
		(0.014)		(0.015)
Medium-correlation indicator			−0.039	−0.058
			(0.006)	(0.008)
Medium-correlation plants				
1984	0.024	0.041	0.023	0.042
	(0.012)	(0.013)	(0.012)	(0.013)
1985	0.016	0.034	0.017	0.036
	(0.012)	(0.013)	(0.013)	(0.013)
1986	0.011	0.029	0.013	0.033
	(0.012)	(0.013)	(0.013)	(0.014)
1987	0.023	0.042	0.023	0.042
	(0.013)	(0.014)	(0.013)	(0.014)
1988	0.031	0.051	0.034	0.053
	(0.013)	(0.014)	(0.013)	(0.014)
1989		0.038		0.038
		(0.014)		(0.014)
1990		0.046		0.051
		(0.014)		(0.015)
No. of observations	24,590	24,590	24,590	24,590

a. Correlation categorizations are based on the three observations of investment-to-capital ratios and net-profit-to-capital ratios in 1980, 1981, and 1982. Regressions are run on data from 1982 to 1990 and include only plants that survive until at least 1984. See text for details. Standard errors are in parentheses.

through the boom-bust period of 1980–82 show rapid and large increases in investment rates following the tax cuts. Constrained plants, on average, raised their investment rates by 3 to 4 percentage points during the three years of the reform. These estimates control for the average investment rate of a given plant and for the average investment rate in each year. We find similar results if we use our alternative series for capital and investment. The effect of the reform seems to be persistent. The exercise provides little evidence that investment rates slowed even several years after the reform, although we find slightly more evidence for our alternative capital and investment series. The plants with medium correlations of profits and investment, which we consider possibly constrained, present a significant though smaller investment boom, again after we control for both time and plant effects.

Our plant-level results so far rely on the assumption that the differences in the correlation of profits and investment across plants are driven by differences in access to capital rather than differences in technologies and product-specific demands. This assumption might fail if our results are largely comparing plants in different industries. That is, one might be concerned that some industries use technologies that happen to produce a high correlation between profits and investment and also happened to boom after 1983. We address this alternative by controlling for the investment rate of each plant's industry in each year that we study and then turning to alternative identification strategies.

We first compare the investment behavior of differentially constrained firms relative to the average investment in that industry in that year. That is, we drop the firm and time effects in equation 3 and instead include a set of thirty-three three-digit industry-level dummies interacted with a complete set of time dummy variables. Denoting an industry-time dummy as α_{jt}, we write the estimating equation as

$$(4) \quad \ln\left(\frac{I}{K}\right)_{i,t} = \alpha_{j,t} + \gamma_C C_i + \gamma_{PC} PC_i + C_i \mathbf{D}_t \boldsymbol{\beta}_C + PC_i \mathbf{D}_t \boldsymbol{\beta}_{PC} + \xi_{i,t}.$$

The coefficients γ_C and γ_{LC} capture the average investment rates of constrained and possibly constrained plants, and the coefficient vectors $\boldsymbol{\beta}_C$ and $\boldsymbol{\beta}_{LC}$ measure the higher investment-to-capital rates for constrained and possibly constrained plants in each year relative to the average in that industry in that year. The last two columns of results in table 6 show that our conclusions are robust to this alternative specification. The relative investment rates of constrained and possibly constrained plants rose significantly during the reform. The coefficients on the indicator variables for constrained and possibly constrained firms are both negative, indicating that constrained firms invested at lower rates than unconstrained firms, as one might expect.

Nevertheless, we still treat a firm as constrained if its correlation is in the top third for all firms rather than relative to the typical correlation in its own industry. Thus we next divide plants by their investment-profits correlations relative to the average rate in their industry. We consider a plant to be constrained if it is among the top third of the plants in its four-digit industry in terms of the correlation between net profits and investment before the reform. The results of this exercise are substantively identical to the results in table 6, so we do not report them here. Plants we deem likely to be constrained experienced larger investment booms. The remainder of the results all classify the constrained status of plants relative to the average values in their industry.

Having established that plants with higher correlations of profits and investment benefited more from the reform, we now investigate alternative assumptions for identifying constrained and unconstrained plants. We consider three other measures of the degree to which a plant is short on internal funds: the ratio of short-term reserves to capital, the ratio of rental payments to capital, and the size of the firm. All of the splits are based on numbers in 1980 and 1981, when book values are reported and well before the tax experiment we are considering. On balance, the results of these alternative splits do not clearly support or refute our main hypothesis.

Table 7 shows the relative investment-to-capital ratios of plants deemed constrained by their holdings of short-term reserves in 1980 and 1981. Results are quite similar across the construction of the capital stock series. They are robust to whether the 1989 and 1990 years are treated as control years, but they differ with respect to the construction of the investment series. Table 7 thus presents results from the two different constructions of the investment series. The first two sets of results are derived from the baseline series and show no significant differential effect of the reform on plants with low short-term asset ratios in 1980 and 1981. The second two sets of results show some increase in investment following the reform, particularly when we control for the typical growth in each industry in each year, although the evidence is statistically weak.

One possible explanation for the lack of relative investment boom in this split of the data is that financially constrained firms may hold more liquid assets to avoid bankruptcy than plants that can borrow freely. Thus, plants with credit lines maintain low levels of short-term assets without bankruptcy risk and contaminate this variable as an indicator of constrained status. Another possibility is that the high inflation rate leads to a pattern of reserves that is

TABLE 7. Investment to Capital as a Function of the Ratio of Short-Term Assets to Capital[a]

Type of plant and year	Baseline series		Alternative investment series	
	Plant and year effects	Industry x year effects	Plant and year effects	Industry x year effects
	(1)	(2)	(3)	(4)
Low-asset indicator		−0.019		−0.016
		(0.006)		(0.010)
Low-asset plants				
1984	−0.005	−0.002	−0.001	0.031
	(0.011)	(0.012)	(0.020)	(0.022)
1985	0.012	0.013	0.020	0.035
	(0.011)	(0.012)	(0.021)	(0.023)
1986	0.008	0.010	0.020	0.035
	(0.012)	(0.013)	(0.023)	(0.025)
1987	−0.001	0.010	0.003	0.010
	(0.012)	(0.013)	(0.025)	(0.027)
1988	0.007	0.017	0.005	0.011
	(0.012)	(0.013)	(0.026)	(0.028)
Medium-asset indicator		−0.041		−0.049
		(0.006)		(0.009)
Medium-asset plants				
1984	−0.006	−0.004	−0.016	−0.003
	(0.011)	(0.012)	(0.019)	(0.020)
1985	0.013	0.016	0.006	0.019
	(0.012)	(0.012)	(0.020)	(0.021)
1986	0.007	0.006	0.003	−0.002
	(0.012)	(0.013)	(0.021)	(0.022)
1987	0.021	0.022	0.027	0.020
	(0.012)	(0.013)	(0.022)	(0.024)
1988	0.003	0.003	−0.008	−0.022
	(0.012)	(0.013)	(0.023)	(0.025)
No. of observations	24,666	24,666	9,404	9,404

a. All regressions include year and plant indicator variables. Categorizations are based on the ratio of short-term assets to capital in 1980 and 1981 relative to the industry average. Regressions are run on data from 1982 to 1990 and include only plants that survive until at least 1984. See text for details. Standard errors are in parentheses.

more dependent on monetary factors than real factors. In sum, we conclude that we find some weak support for our hypothesis and no evidence to reject it when we identify plants as constrained by comparing their level of short-term reserves to their industry's average level.

Our second alternative identification strategy is to assume that plants that are financially constrained and have highly productive investment opportunities may be able to rent physical capital to partially loosen the financial constraint.

TABLE 8.   Investment to Capital as a Function of Whether a Firm Pays Rent[a]

Type of plant and year	Baseline series		Alternative capital and investment series	
	Plant and year effects	Industry x year effects	Plant and year effects	Industry x year effects
	(1)	(2)	(3)	(4)
Rent-paying-plant indicator		0.024		0.027
		(0.005)		(0.008)
Rent-paying plants				
1984	−0.007	−0.009	0.010	−0.003
	(0.010)	(0.010)	(0.014)	(0.018)
1985	−0.018	−0.020	0.016	0.006
	(0.010)	(0.011)	(0.015)	(0.019)
1986	−0.003	−0.005	0.014	0.008
	(0.010)	(0.011)	(0.016)	(0.020)
1987	−0.015	−0.023	−0.003	−0.019
	(0.011)	(0.011)	(0.018)	(0.022)
1988	−0.017	−0.026	0.011	0.009
	(0.011)	(0.012)	(0.018)	(0.023)
No. of observations	24,666	24,666	9,618	9,618

a. Plants are categorized as rent payers based on 1980 and 1981 data. Regressions are run on data from 1982 to 1990 and include only plants that survive until at least 1984. See text for details. Standard errors are in parentheses.

That is, a financially constrained firm is more likely to rent than own the building in which it operates. In table 8 we investigate whether plants that report paying rental payments benefited more during the years of the reforms. Since most plants report paying no rent, we simply study those that do relative to those that do not. We find no evidence that plants that pay rent invested more following the reform. Our findings are similar whether or not we include 1989 and 1990 as control years, but they differ by capital and investment series, with the results with only one alternative series lying between the reported pairs of results.

Our final alternative identification strategy is to assume that small plants are more likely to be constrained. This is standard practice in the literature on credit-constrained plants in the United States, in which small plants are seen as having significantly lower access to credit markets. In Chile, however, four issues arise. First, previous studies typically measure the size of a plant by its capital stock, so we could use capital stocks in 1980 and 1981 to create a split. Only book capital is available, however, and the initial capital stock is subject to significant mismeasurement. This would create a bias toward small plants having high investment-to-capital ratios early in the sample. This bias, in turn, would create the incorrect illusion that small plants grew faster than large plants before the tax reform and potentially that their growth slowed relative to large plants as the tax reform was instituted. We provide a partial solution to this problem by splitting plants by the average number of employees in 1980 and 1981 rather than by the initial capital stock.

The second problem with using size as a proxy for financial constraints is that many of the smallest firms in Chile do not pay taxes at all or pay minimal taxes because the owners have low incomes. As table 2 shows, a firm owned by an individual with a low enough income to have a zero personal tax rate had the same 10 percent tax rate on profits before and after the reform.[30] Third, many small manufacturing plants in Chile are family-run businesses that are perhaps limited in size by economies of scope. The most notable example of this is that 14 percent of our sample comprises plants in ISIC 3117—namely, bakeries. In the United States, "small" firms in investment studies are usually small public firms, whereas in Chile less than one percent of plants were even public in 1980 and 1981. Thus, we are really comparing small plants with small plants. Finally, Chile's financial markets are currently significantly less developed than those in the United States, and the difference was even more marked in the early 1980s. Many relatively large plants in Chile do not have access to capital in the same way that relatively large companies in the United States do. In short, size is much less an indicator of access to capital in Chile and more an indicator of industry, for example. We provide a partial solution to these problems by splitting firms relative to the average size in their industry, as discussed previously.

Table 9 presents the results from dividing plants by size. To reemphasize how different this exercise is from previous studies of U.S. data, we note that in the typical industry in Chile, small plants are defined as averaging nineteen employees or fewer, while large plants are defined as averaging forty-four employees or more. Table 9 reports no evidence that the investment rates of small plants rose (or fell) disproportionately at the time of the tax reform.[31]

In sum, plants that had a high correlation between cash flow (net profits) and investment before the reform had the largest increases in investment rates after the reform. This finding is quite robust, although alternative measures of which firms are likely to be constrained do not support our main thesis.

---

30. All of our reported results are similar whether or not we exclude firms that paid no profits tax in the years before and including 1982.

31. Results are similar for the alternative definition of capital and for regressions that include 1989 and 1990 as postreform years.

TABLE 9.   Investment to Capital as a Function of Plant Size and Year[a]

Type of plant and year	Baseline series		Alternative investment series	
	Plant and year effects	Industry x year effects	Plant and year effects	Industry x year effects
	(1)	(2)	(3)	(4)
Small-plant indicator		−0.021		0.026
		(0.006)		(0.010)
Small plants				
1984	0.008	−0.005	0.038	0.019
	(0.011)	(0.013)	(0.020)	(0.021)
1985	−0.004	−0.019	0.016	0.008
	(0.011)	(0.013)	(0.020)	(0.022)
1986	−0.004	−0.015	−0.042	−0.031
	(0.012)	(0.013)	(0.022)	(0.024)
1987	0.038	0.031	−0.019	−0.003
	(0.012)	(0.014)	(0.024)	(0.026)
1988	0.020	0.008	−0.006	0.024
	(0.012)	(0.014)	(0.024)	(0.026)
Medium-sized-plant indicator		−0.009		−0.007
		(0.005)		(0.009)
Medium-sized plants				
1984	0.008	0.005	0.024	0.024
	(0.011)	(0.012)	(0.019)	(0.020)
1985	0.006	0.006	−0.001	0.008
	(0.011)	(0.012)	(0.020)	(0.020)
1986	−0.002	−0.003	0.032	0.031
	(0.012)	(0.012)	(0.021)	(0.022)
1987	0.008	0.004	0.016	0.014
	(0.012)	(0.012)	(0.023)	(0.024)
1988	0.023	0.022	0.033	0.042
	(0.012)	(0.013)	(0.023)	(0.024)
No. of observations	25,479	25,479	9,792	9,792

a. Size categorizations are based on the percent difference in firm employment from the industry average in 1980 and 1981. Regressions are run on data from 1982 to 1990 and include only plants that survive until at least 1984. See text for details. Results using the alternative capital series and including 1989 and 1990 interactions yield similar results. Standard errors are in parentheses.

Other Policy Reforms

This paper argues that in a country with undeveloped financial markets, investment is constrained by the lack of access to credit. By increasing the internal funds available to profitable firms, the 1984 corporate tax reform in Chile played a large role in unleashing the subsequent rise in Chile's investment and economic growth. An alternative hypothesis is that most firms were not credit constrained and that the documented patterns of increases in investment and saving were due to other reforms implemented by Chile's military regime over this time period.

This section describes the major reforms that occurred in Chile in the decade leading up to the period of rapid growth: the semi-privatization of the public pension system, the liberalization and development of financial markets, and the opening to trade and capital flows.[32] Each subsection describes the major policy changes in one of these areas and makes the case that the reforms in question are, based on theory and evidence, unlikely to alter the inferences drawn so far in this paper.

To be clear, we are not arguing that these reforms did not benefit Chilean economic growth. Rather, we suspect that each of these reforms played a role by affecting Chile's steady-state levels of output and capital per worker. Convergence to these levels is a slow process for most countries and states, but in Chile, the corporate tax reform caused an investment boom and a decade of rapid convergence.

Privatization of the Public Pension System

Before 1981 Chile had an unfunded, pay-as-you-go, public pension system much like the U.S. social security system.[33] The average payroll tax rate varied significantly across firms, but was around 30 percent of wages.[34] In 1981, the Chilean government cut and standardized the payroll tax and created a new system that mandated contributions to heavily regulated but privately managed accounts. All new entrants to the labor force selected a private account into which to deposit their payments (20 percent of wages, less administrative fees and a share for disability and health insurance equivalent to 10 percent of wages), and they opted to invest these funds in one of several regulated mutual funds.[35] Those employed at the time of the reform had the option of switching into the new system or remaining in the old. The new system was immediately popular: 70 percent of private employment switched in the first year.[36]

32. See Bosworth, Dornbusch, and Laban (1994); Perry and Leipziger (1999), for detailed descriptions of the reforms implemented by the Chilean government.

33. For more complete descriptions, see Edwards (1996); Diamond (1993).

34. Exact estimates differ. See Coronado (1998); Gruber (1995); Edwards and Cox Edwards (2000). The rates were significantly higher early in the 1970s.

35. The health insurance share of the tax could be used by the payee to purchase health insurace from private providers, subject to strict regulation. Among new entrants, the participation of the self-employed was optional, and this has led to a significant problem of households' gaming some of the redistributive nature of the system by moving in and out of self-employment.

36. Coronado (1998).

Elderly workers tended to remain with the old system, and 20 percent of the self-employed opted to participate.

The new system was fully funded, with the exception that all plans were guaranteed by the government. To pay the unfunded liabilities of the old system, the government issued a large amount of new debt, termed recognition bonds, which were bought by households and slowly paid off by the government. The fiscal costs of payments for these unfunded liabilities averaged 4.7 percent of GDP in 1981–88.[37]

How might this reform be responsible for the saving and investment boom? First, as long as households do not alter their consumption behavior and government spending does not change, such a reform has no effect on aggregate national saving. In such a Ricardian world, measured household saving increases by definition, because contributions into private accounts are counted as private saving, and this increase is mirrored by the increased public spending necessary to pay the unfunded liabilities of the old system. The reform thus has no net effect on aggregate saving.

Ricardian equivalence, however, seems like a poor assumption to apply to Chile in the early 1980s. Chile had poorly developed financial markets, and it seems likely that many households and small businesses were financially constrained. Nonetheless, the impact of this reform will be exactly the same as in a Ricardian world if households cannot access or borrow against their private pension accounts. Constrained households do not change their consumption and investment, since the privatization merely replaces a government promise with a particular account that the government funds by issuing a government promise. One caveat to this argument is that this reform might alter factor prices, but this will not occur if rates of return are set by the world capital market. That is, the privatization of the pension system will not alter saving and investment if the domestic and international capital markets absorb the additional government bonds without altering the domestic real interest rate.

In practice, the privatization seems to have simply recategorized public pension contributions as private instead of public saving. Figure 6 decomposes household saving into contributions to the privatized social security system and into non–social security saving. A significant part of the trend increase in household saving (from –3.8 percent of GDP in 1975–83 to 1.7 percent of GDP in 1984–94) is due to contributions into the privatized social security accounts. The increase in measured household saving stemming from these contributions

---

37. Ortuzar (1988), quoted in Edwards (1996, table 5).

FIGURE 6.   Household Savings

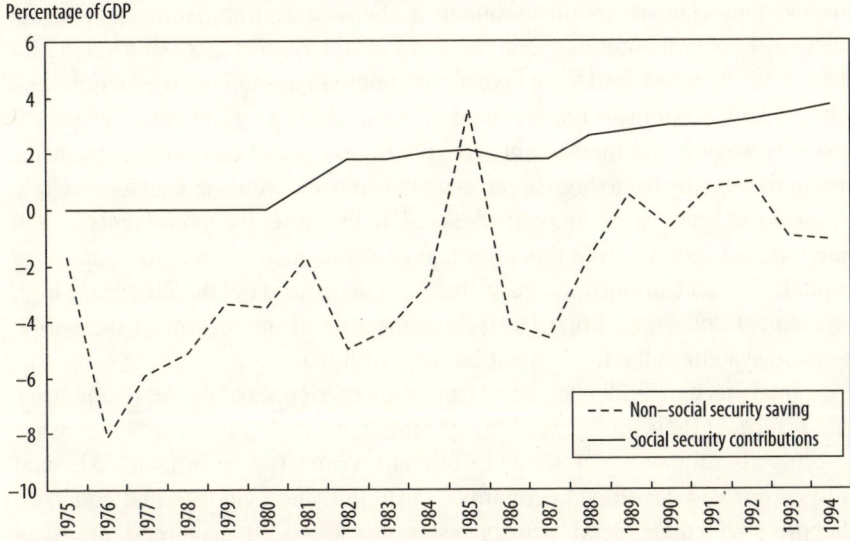

Percentage of GDP

Source: Bennett, Schmidt-Hebbel, and Soto (1999).

is mirrored by lower public saving as a result of the costs of the unfunded liabilities of the old pension system (as shown in figure 2).

Our discussion so far assumes that taxes are nondistortionary, but if private saving incentives were affected by the reform, then the privatization of social security could be partially responsible for the saving boom. For example, if payroll taxes were high and not related to benefits before the reform, then the privatization of social security would increase the incentives to earn by giving households greater benefits for greater taxes paid. An increase in labor supply could lead to an investment boom. Gruber provides evidence on this point, reporting that the incidence of payroll taxes in Chile fell fully on wages, with no effect on employment.[38] According to this evidence, payroll taxes under the old system did not create significant labor market distortions.

Another alternative channel through which privatized pension funds may have driven the investment boom is the deepening of financial markets, which could have increased both the incentives for households to save and the ease of firm access to financial capital. There is some evidence that non–social security saving increased over the relevant time period (see figure 6), but the

38. Gruber (1995).

magnitude of the increase—slightly over 3 percent of GDP from 1975–83 to 1984–94—is small relative to the increase in the aggregate saving rate. We discuss financial market development in the next section. Here we reiterate the well-known theoretical result that even if the reform increased saving, in theory this does not lead to an investment boom in a small open economy like Chile. Many economists are skeptical of this theoretical argument on empirical grounds: saving and investment rates are highly correlated across countries. But if high saving led to high investment in Chile, we would expect to see Chile exporting at least a small amount of capital. In fact, after the reform and through much of the 1980s, Chile ran significant current account deficits, importing capital. This fact strongly suggests that high saving did not directly cause high investment and, more importantly, that the role of the reform of the public pension system in the investment boom is minimal.

A final piece of evidence comes from the experiences of the set of countries that reformed their public pension systems. Samwick studies seven pension reforms in Latin America, seven reforms in Africa, two reforms in Asia, and four reforms in developed economies.[39] He finds no evidence that countries that privatized their social security systems experienced an increase in saving rates, with one exception: Chile.[40] It seems unlikely that Chile was the one exception in which the reform of a public pension system caused a large increase in saving and investment. Rather, the increase in saving in Chile is probably due to forces other than social security privatization.

Liberalization and Development of Financial Markets

The role of bank credit and publicly traded equity has expanded significantly in Chile's financial markets over the last twenty-five years.[41] Most of this financial market deepening occurred in the 1970s and 1990s, however, and the increase in financial intermediation of the 1990s seems a direct result of growth rather than the other way around.

In the first few years of the military regime, Chile focused its efforts on liberalizing the banking sector. From 1974–81, the government lifted interest rate controls, eliminated entry barriers to the banking industry, lowered liquidity

---

39. Samwick (2000).

40. Samwick (2000, p. 272) concludes that "no country other than Chile that moved to a system based more on defined contributions during the sample period experienced an increase in the trend saving rates after reform."

41. For additional details, see Gallego and Loayza (2000); Barandiarán and Hernández (1999).

FIGURE 7. Bank Credit

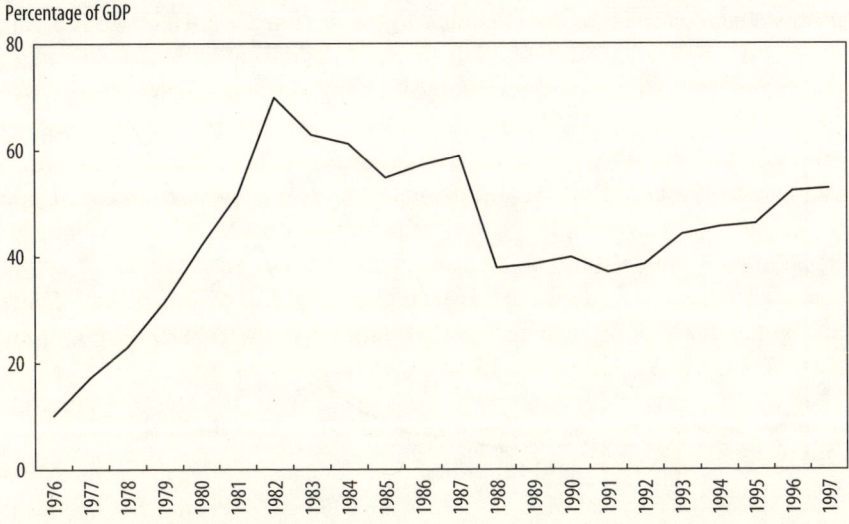

Percentage of GDP

Source: Eyzaguirre and Lefort (1999, table 3.6).

requirements for banks, eliminated quantitative controls on credit, and privatized state-owned banks. As shown in figure 7, the result was a large expansion in bank credit, which grew from 10 percent of GDP in the early 1970s to almost 60 percent of GDP by the early 1980s. This development halted with the advent of the debt crisis and the recession of 1982. After the banking crisis of 1982, the government took over most of the country's banks and undertook the process of either liquidating or recapitalizing and privatizing them, a process that took many years. Bank credit declined significantly in 1982 and continued falling during the beginning of the investment boom. Bank credit reached its low of 40 percent of GDP in 1985–86. A new banking law in 1986 established limits on the leverage positions of the banks, increased reserve requirements, and generally increased the supervisory capacity of the Central Bank over the banking sector. These restrictions kept bank credit roughly constant at 40 percent of GDP until the early 1990s. Thus, bank credit was falling as the investment boom began and did not rise as a share of output until investment and saving rates stopped growing.

The stock market played an even more minor role in Chile's financial system in the 1980s, when the market value of publicly traded equity in Chile was 30 percent of GDP. As shown in Figure 8, the Chilean stock market did not grow rapidly until the 1990s. The market value of publicly traded stocks

FIGURE 8.   **Market Value of Publicly Traded Stocks**

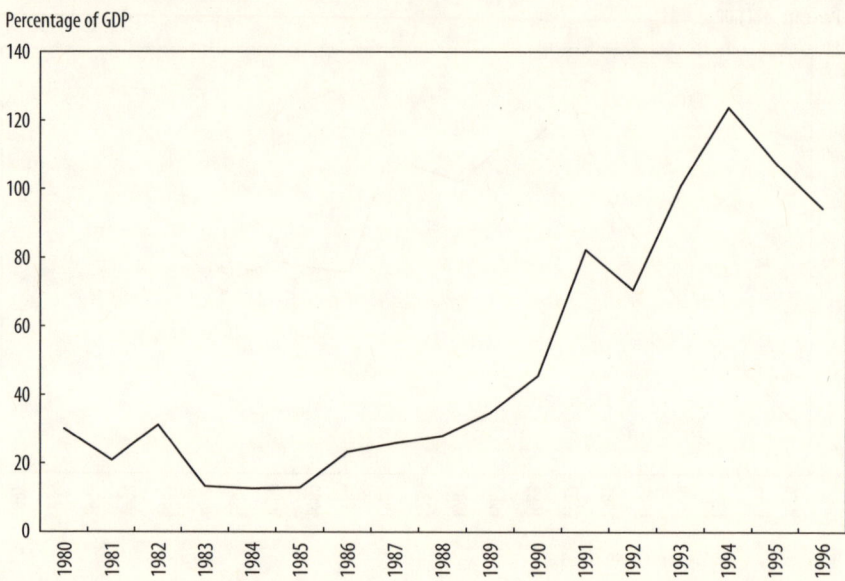

Source: Eyzaguirre and Lefort (1999).

in Chile (relative to GDP) roughly tripled from 35 percent of GDP in 1989 to 94 percent in 1996.[42] Since the growth of bank credit was limited in the 1990s, the deepening of Chile's capital markets during this decade was dispropor-tionately due to the expansion of the stock market.

These changes in Chile's financial structure could explain the investment boom if firms that were previously credit constrained were able to obtain financing for their investments as a result of the deepening of Chile's financial markets. However, the aggregate evidence indicates that the investment boom was financed not by external credit, but by retained earnings. In addition, the timing of the lending boom and the stock market boom in Chile does not support the hypothesis that the investment boom resulted from developments in Chile's financial market. The investment boom in Chile took place from 1984 to 1989, but aggregate bank credit did not increase over this period. Similarly, Chile's equity market did not increase significantly until the 1990s,

42. This increase is only partially due to an increase in the price of Chilean equity. The quantity of Chilean equity, computed by dividing the market value of Chilean stock by its price, increased by 70 percent from 1990 to 1996 (Eyzaguirre and Lefort 1999, table 3-1 and figure 3-2).

after the investment boom. The evidence suggests that the investment boom caused the development of Chile's equity market rather than the reverse.[43]

Finally, we check that our main result does not stem from the fact that credit-constrained firms increased borrowing starting in 1984. Recall that we find that the investment of likely constrained firms (measured as firms with a high correlation of investment and cash flow) increased after 1984 relative to the investment of firms that were likely unconstrained. If this boom was due to an increased access to credit, then we would expect the ratio of interest payments to capital to rise for our constrained firms relative to our unconstrained firms. To test this hypothesis, we estimate equations 3 and 4 with the ratio of interest payments to capital as the dependent variable. We find little evidence of this effect. Table 10, which presents the results that match those in table 6, contains no evidence that the constrained plants borrowed more when their investment boomed. Results using the alternative capital stock series or the alternative investment series also show, if anything, decreases in interest payments by constrained plants. However, the alternative capital and investment series together suggest statistically insignificant but economically significant increases in interest payments by these plants. The balance of the evidence is consistent not with a general increase in available debt instruments and increased access to credit for constrained plants, but rather with increased funds available from internal sources allowing plants with profitable investment opportunities to invest substantially more.

Trade Liberalization

Another major reform pursued by Chile in the late 1970s and early 1980s was the liberalization of its trade regime.[44] Chile, like many developing economies, pursued policies of import substitution in the 1960s and 1970s. By 1973, the average tariff rate exceeded 100 percent, in addition to multiple official exchange rates and quantitative restrictions on imports. One of the economic reforms pursued by the Pinochet government was international economic openness. By 1979, the average tariff rate had fallen to 12 percent, and many of the regulatory restrictions on importing and exporting had been removed.

---

43. If the investment boom was driven by the development of Chile's financial markets, then a firm's investment should become less sensitive to cash flow, not more sensitive to cash flow. Gallego and Loayza (2000) find some evidence that the investment of publicly traded companies was less sensitive to cash flow, but only after the investment boom, that is, in the 1990s relative to the 1980s.

44. See Tybout (1996); Pavcnik (2002).

TABLE 10. Interest Payments to Capital as a Function of Profit-Investment Correlations and Year[a]

Type of plant and year	Plant and year effects		Industry x year effects	
	(1)	(2)	(3)	(4)
High-correlation indicator			0.131	0.196
			(0.051)	(0.068)
High-correlation plants				
1984	−0.052	−0.138	−0.024	−0.090
	(0.086)	(0.093)	(0.109)	(0.118)
1985	−0.090	−0.180	−0.141	−0.206
	(0.088)	(0.095)	(0.111)	(0.120)
1986	−0.140	−0.232	−0.183	−0.249
	(0.090)	(0.097)	(0.114)	(0.123)
1987	−0.194	−0.288	−0.125	−0.190
	(0.092)	(0.099)	(0.116)	(0.125)
1988	0.002	−0.094	0.035	−0.031
	(0.093)	(0.101)	(0.118)	(0.126)
1989		−0.206		−0.141
		(0.102)		(0.128)
1990		−0.222		−0.166
		(0.103)		(0.129)
Medium-correlation indicator			−0.030	−0.072
			(0.050)	(0.066)
Medium-correlation plants				
1984	−0.003	0.035	0.009	0.051
	(0.083)	(0.089)	(0.106)	(0.115)
1985	0.030	0.070	0.006	0.048
	(0.085)	(0.091)	(0.109)	(0.117)
1986	−0.020	0.022	−0.028	0.014
	(0.088)	(0.094)	(0.112)	(0.120)
1987	−0.007	0.036	0.006	0.048
	(0.089)	(0.096)	(0.115)	(0.123)
1988	0.048	0.092	0.054	0.096
	(0.091)	(0.098)	(0.117)	(0.125)
1989		0.096		0.098
		(0.099)		(0.126)
1990		0.116		0.111
		(0.100)		(0.127)
No. of observations	24,631	24,631	24,631	24,631

a. Correlation categorizations are based on the three observations of investment-to-capital ratios and net-profit-to-capital ratios in 1980, 1981, and 1982. Regressions are run on data from 1982 to 1990 and include only plants that survive until at least 1984. See text for details. Standard errors are in parentheses.

From 1976 to 1981, Chilean manufacturing production grew by 25 percent, but at the same time, the balance of trade worsened and the real exchange rate appreciated significantly.

While the liberalization would seem like a boon to growth and possibly a direct cause of high investment rates, policy reversed direction during the debt crisis and the deep 1982 recession. By 1984, when the investment boom began, tariffs had been raised to an average of 36 percent, suggesting little role for tariff policy in the investment boom. Indeed, tariffs returned to an average of 15 percent only in 1988. Kasahara estimates a structural model of investment on the Chilean manufacturing census data and argues that the higher tariff rates from 1983 to 1987 actually significantly lowered investment over this period.[45]

To summarize, low tariffs lag economic growth and do not lead it. The investment boom began in 1984, when tariffs rates peaked. Openness may have been an important foundation for growth, but probably was not the precipitating factor for the investment boom and growth of the 1980s.

Conclusion

In 1984, Chile had a poorly developed financial system, with many banks under public control or poorly capitalized. Average tariff rates were double the rates of five years earlier. The semi-privatization of the public pension system had made a large amount of implicit government debt explicit. Unlike the other Latin American economies, however, Chile was experiencing the beginning of a large and persistent rise in investment and economic growth.

This paper measures the contribution of a corporate tax reform that lowered the tax on retained profits to this boom. We find that the aggregate and industry-level evidence provides clear support for the hypothesis that the reduction in the taxation of retained earnings allowed financially constrained firms to take advantage of profitable investment activities. The increase in saving associated with the investment boom was almost entirely an increase in business saving. Moreover, investment rates rose the most in industries that were the most reliant on external finance.

The plant-level evidence is less clear, however. In support of our hypothesis, we find that plants that exhibited a high correlation of investment and cash flow before the tax reform increased their investment rates the most during

---

45. Kasahara (2004).

and to some extent after the reform. In contrast, other sample splits do not reject the null hypothesis of no effect of the reform. In particular, we find no evidence that smaller plants experienced a larger increase in investment after the tax reform.

Our more general point, which is supported by the evidence from Chile's tax reform, is that in countries with poorly developed financial markets, taxation of retained profits may have a significant effect on corporate saving and can therefore be particularly harmful for growth. By taxing retained profits, the government removes internal funds from some firms in which the value of these resources exceeds the real interest rate. This argument relies on a country's having otherwise favorable macroeconomic policies and conditions. In an economy with high levels of corruption or taxation, poor property rights, poor infrastructure, and so forth, the reduction of a tax on retained profits is likely to accomplish little since the low level of investment reflects limited opportunities for profit, rather than poor financial markets. However, in developing economies with strong growth prospects, underdeveloped financial markets may be a significant factor retarding economic growth. Corporate saving is an important source of productive investment, and the Chilean experience shows that policies that increase the internal funds available to firms can have disproportionately large growth effects.

Comments

Thomas Philippon: This discussion focuses on one of the theoretical questions raised by the paper: are credit-constrained firms more sensitive to taxes on retained earnings than unconstrained firms? To assess this issue, I consider a two-period model. Capital, k, is invested in the first period and delivers profits, $f(k)$, in the second period. The firm receives an income of y in the first period. The manager of the firm decides how much to invest, k, how much to borrow, b, and how much income to distribute to current investors, d. To capture credit constraints, I assume that the cost of borrowing is increasing in the amount borrowed, according to a function $c(b)$. Finally, retained earnings are taxed at rate τ. The firm's program is therefore

$$\max_{k,b,d} \frac{f(k)}{1+r} + d - c(b),$$

subject to the resource constraint, $k = b + (1 + \tau)(y - d)$, and the constraint on distributions to current investors, $0 \leq d \leq y$. I consider several cases.

The case of no credit constraint is defined as $c(b) = b$. The solution is $d = y$, $b = k$, and $f'(k) = 1 + r$. The firm obtains a perfect tax arbitrage with a leverage of 100 percent. Investment is unaffected by taxes on retained earnings.

For the case of no borrowing, suppose that b is forced to be zero. This prevents the tax arbitrage. Provided that the marginal product is high enough relative to current income, the firm will choose $d = 0$ and $k = (1 - \tau)y$. In this case, taxes on retained earnings decrease investment. Comparing this result with the previous benchmark suggests that constrained firms should indeed be more tax-sensitive than unconstrained firms. This, however, need not be true.

The case of fake borrowing, in which $b = 0$, hides two separate issues: the presence of credit constraints and the absence of the tax arbitrage. However, it is possible to obtain the tax arbitrage even with no real borrowing. Suppose that a bank is a current investor in the firm. The firm pays $d = y$ to the bank,

41

and the bank makes a loan $b = y$ to the firm. This allows the firm to pay no taxes, while the bank has no real exposure to the firm. In this equilibrium, $k = y$. Credit constraints are completely binding, but investment does not respond to taxes on retained earnings.

Based on the above discussion, it seems to me that the correct benchmark is a model in which all firms are somewhat constrained, but some are more constrained than others. This model has two types of solutions: the interior solution and the corner solution. In the interior solution, where $d > 0$, the first-order conditions are

$$f'(k) = (1 + r)c'(b)$$

and

$$1 = (1 - \tau)c'(b),$$

provided that $d > 0$. These conditions imply that

(1) $$f'(k) = \frac{1 + r}{1 - \tau}.$$

Investment does not depend on the function $c(.)$, despite the fact that the credit constraint is binding. This is because the firm can adjust its current distributions, and the distribution margin insulates investment at the margin.

In the corner solution, with $d = 0$,

(2) $$\frac{f'(k)}{1 + r} = c'[k - (1 - \tau)y].$$

For firms that do not pay dividends, investment is sensitive to credit constraints at the margin.

The typical classification of firms into groups that are likely to be constrained and groups that are unlikely to be constrained is usually based on current income or on distributions. Suppose then that there are firms with high income, y^H, and firms with low income, y^L. High-income firms are in the interior solution, with positive dividends, while low-income firms are in the corner solution. Based on equations 1 and 2, it is not obvious that the elasticity of investment to taxes is higher for the more constrained groups. It depends on the function, $c(.)$. The answer to the initial question, therefore, is that while it is plausible that more constrained firms react more to changes in taxes on retained earnings than less constrained ones, this is not necessarily the case.

Claudio Raddatz: In 1982 Chile experienced its largest recession since the Great Depression. Real GDP declined by about 15 percent between 1981 and 1983, while unemployment increased from 10 to around 20 percent, and investment plummeted from 23 to 10 percent of GDP. Despite the magnitude of the crisis, output and especially investment recovered surprisingly fast, with the latter reaching its precrisis level three years after the crisis and increasing to about 25 percent of GDP at the end of the decade. There has long been a consensus in Chile that this investment boom was largely responsible for the performance of the economy after the crisis, but more controversy on the causes of the investment boom. Hsieh and Parker argue that this boom was largely the result of the country's 1984 tax reform, which reduced the tax on retained earnings, and that this finding provides evidence that this type of taxation is particularly harmful in economies with underdeveloped financial markets. The paper thus provides not only a possible explanation for Chile's investment boom, but also exploits the Chilean case to provide evidence on the impact of the tax system across different types of firms and the importance of financial constraints.

Although I agree with the broad argument of the paper, two issues may affect the extent to which the evidence supports its hypothesis and quantitative conclusions. First, during the period of analysis, Chile engaged in multiple structural and policy reforms, which complicates the isolation of the impact of any individual change. Second, at the time of the tax reform, Chile was just starting to recover from a big recession, which means that cyclical effects are a potential concern. I structure the rest of my discussion around these two issues.

The Case of Chile

Chile was a pioneer among developing countries in introducing a series of market-oriented reforms. In the 1970s and 1980s, Chile unilaterally reduced and simplified the existing system of tariffs, privatized a large number of state banks and companies, opened the capital account, and moved from an unfunded defined-benefit pension system to a fully funded defined-contribution system. This abundance of reforms has long represented an "embarrassment of riches" for Chilean economists. On the one hand, Chile would seem to be the perfect laboratory for studying the impact of a set of structural reforms that are relevant for developing countries. On the other hand, the bunching of reforms in a relatively short period makes it hard to separately identify the impact of each individual one.

Hsieh and Parker deal with the identification problems created by this abundance of reforms in two ways. First, they argue that the specific timing of the investment boom and other variables is unlikely to result from three major structural reforms undertaken in the 1980s—namely, the pension funds reform, the liberalization of the financial markets, and trade liberalization. Second, they exploit the theoretical prediction that the tax reform should have stimulated the investment of firms and sectors that were financially constrained.

While the discussion in the paper covers the most important structural reforms implemented in Chile around 1984, the period also featured some important changes in the conduct of macroeconomic policy. For example, the exchange rate regime underwent radical changes that resulted in a large depreciation of the nominal and real exchange rates: the peso lost 43 percent of its value between 1984 and 1986. The timing of the reform thus coincides with the depreciation, and, to the extent that this depreciation restored the international competitiveness of some Chilean firms, it could account for at least part of the investment boom attributed to the tax reform.[1] After the crisis, Chile entered a structural adjustment program with the International Monetary Fund (IMF) and the World Bank that imposed changes in the conduct of fiscal and monetary policy, and real wages declined about 20 percent. All of these events could have affected the investment rate. Moreover, several of these changes could arguably have had heterogeneous impacts on the investment rates of different industries and thus could contaminate the industry-level evidence unless properly controlled for.[2]

---

1. Morandé (1998) argues that some tradables sectors could have benefited significantly from the real depreciation, inducing them to save and invest. Meller (1996) also argues that the persistent depreciation fostered the expansion of the export sector.

2. The paper deals with the possibility that the international competitiveness of externally dependent industries could increase relatively more as a result of the real depreciation by controlling in the regressions for the net exports of an industry before the recession. Although it is not completely clear that industries that had higher net exports under an appreciated currency should experience the largest increases in competitiveness, this approach partly eases this type of concern. However, this strategy does not control for the possibility that more externally dependent sectors could have had lower levels of dollar-denominated debt. According to Meller (1996), 50 percent of bank loans were denominated in dollars before the recession.

In summary, although the evidence presented in the paper is certainly consistent with its main hypothesis and makes for a convincing case, the myriad changes happening in Chile during this period make it difficult to quantify the real importance of the tax reform for the investment boom versus alternative explanations with the available data. Some degree of skepticism with respect to the specific magnitudes reported in the paper is probably healthy.

The Cycle

The tax reform analyzed in the paper was passed in the middle of the worst recession Chile has experienced since the Great Depression. It is thus legitimate to ask to what extent the investment patterns documented in the paper are typical of the recovery phase of a big recession. I focus on the implications of the cyclicality for both the aggregate and sectoral evidence provided in the paper.

Determining the extent to which the pattern of investment documented in the paper can be attributed to a cyclical phenomenon requires assessing this episode against other relevant benchmarks. The two available options in this regard are to compare it with the pattern observed in other Chilean recessions (a within-country benchmark) and to compare it with similar episodes observed in other countries (a cross-country benchmark). Figure 9 illustrates the cyclical pattern of investment during the last three Chilean recessions (1975, 1982, and 1999). Panel A shows the evolution of investment levels in each of these episodes, normalizing the trough of the investment cycle to 100. The depth of the 1982 recession is unusual: the contraction (and recovery) of investment is much larger than in the other two episodes. To compare the patterns, however, it is better to normalize by the size of the recession (peak to trough). This is presented in panel B, which shows that the pattern observed in the 1982 recession is similar to the one seen in 1975, yet clearly different from the much milder 1999 recession. All in all, these comparisons show that the decline and recovery in investment in 1982, although more pronounced, exhibits a pattern that is common to some previous Chilean recessions.

The milder Chilean episodes discussed above may not provide a relevant benchmark, however, given the size of the 1982 recession and its systemic characteristics. If large, systemic crises are special, one may want to compare this episode with other similar crises instead. Figure 10 presents the cyclical behavior of investment in Chile in 1982, together with twenty-two cases of

F I G U R E   9 .   Comparing Cyclical Patterns of Investment in Chilean Recessions

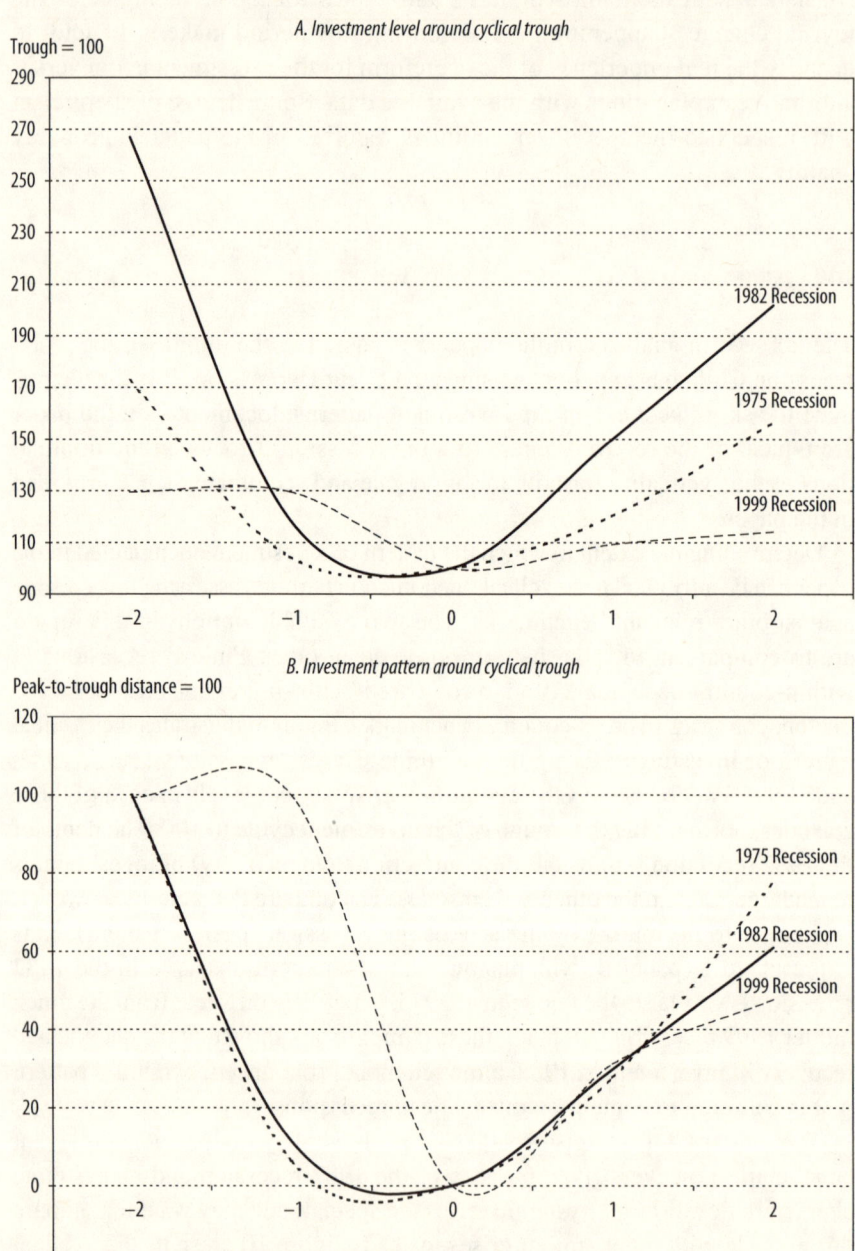

A. Investment level around cyclical trough

Trough = 100

1982 Recession

1975 Recession

1999 Recession

B. Investment pattern around cyclical trough

Peak-to-trough distance = 100

1975 Recession

1982 Recession

1999 Recession

FIGURE 10. Comparing Cyclical Patterns of Investment: Chile 1983 versus a Typical Systemic Sudden Stop Episode

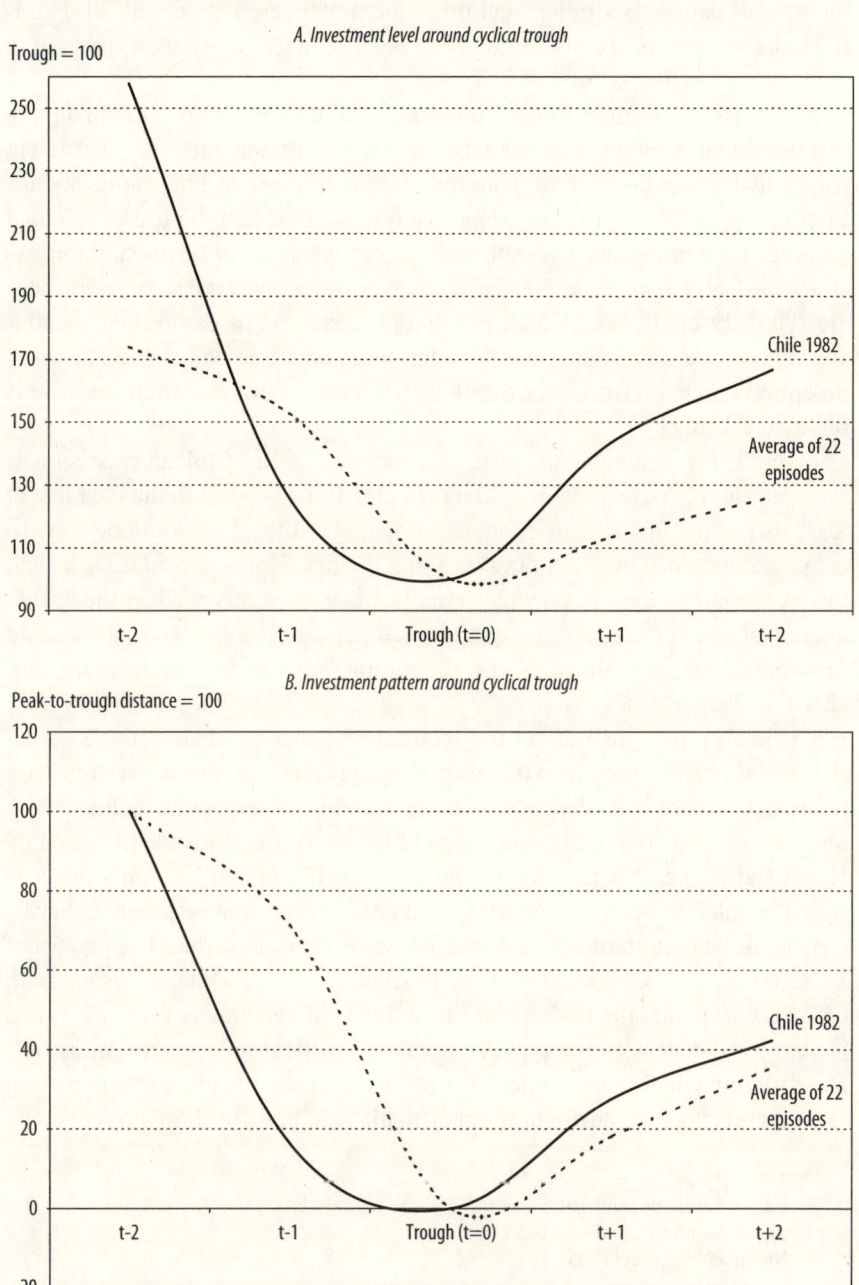

A. Investment level around cyclical trough

Trough = 100

Chile 1982

Average of 22 episodes

B. Investment pattern around cyclical trough

Peak-to-trough distance = 100

Chile 1982

Average of 22 episodes

systemic output collapses identified by Calvo, Izquierdo, and Talvi.[3] The recession experienced by Chile in 1982 is larger than the average episode, but the overall pattern is similar: real investment recovered about half of its initial value two years after the trough (43 percent in Chile versus 35 percent in the average episode).

A final aspect of the Chilean episode that could be special is the financing of investment through retained earnings. The available data are insufficient for an analysis of the sectoral patterns of corporate versus household savings in other episodes, but existing data strongly suggest that the use of retained earnings (and other internal sources of liquidity) may not be uncommon. As shown by Calvo, Izquierdo, and Talvi, the recoveries observed in these episodes are typically creditless.[4] Given that international credit is minimal by construction in these episodes, and the intermediated credit flattens out, the only potentially meaningful source of funds to finance an increase in investment is retained earnings.

Overall, the evidence suggests that the size of the Chilean recession is more unusual than its pattern, and it provides some support to the idea that at least part of the investment boom documented in the paper could be a cyclical phenomenon. This does not mean that the tax reform played no role, and the somewhat faster recovery observed in Chile may very well be the consequence of this reform. From a quantitative perspective, however, attributing the whole increase in investment and corporate savings to the reform is probably misleading.

Cyclicality may also affect the sectoral evidence presented in the paper. Braun and Larraín document that recessions have a relatively larger impact on industries that are more dependent on external finance, especially in financially underdeveloped countries (which is the flip side of the evidence provided by Hsieh and Parker).[5] The evidence provided in Braun and Larraín's paper is based on a large panel of countries, so it corresponds to a systematic characteristic of the pattern of cyclical fluctuations across industries. The pattern of industrial recoveries documented by Hsieh and Parker, while consistent with the hypothesis that the tax reform eased financial constraints for some firms, is also consistent with the typical pattern of cyclical recovery of industries. Determining whether the Chilean tax reform accentuated this cyclical pattern and quantifying its contribution is a difficult task, but a back-of-the-envelope

---

3. Calvo, Izquierdo, and Talvi (2006).
4. Calvo, Izquierdo, and Talvi (2006).
5. Braun and Larraín (2005).

calculation suggests that the size of the investment increase documented in this paper is consistent with Braun and Larraín's estimates.[6]

Cyclicality also raises issues for the firm-level evidence provided in the paper. This evidence indicates that firms that are likely to be financially constrained, based on ex ante measures of the correlation between investment and cash flow, increased investment relatively more than unconstrained firms after the reform. While this is certainly consistent with the differential effect of the tax reform, the literature on the credit channel shows that financially constrained firms experience greater cyclical fluctuations in their investment, output, and employment as a result of the cyclicality of the external financial premium than do unconstrained firms.[7] An additional issue is that the paper measures a firm's degree of financial constraints using the correlation between investment and cash flow during the contraction phase of the recession instead of in normal times. The paper argues that firms that can still invest while their income is shrinking are likely to have good access to external funds, yet these may also be firms with higher initial levels of internal and working capital, higher costs of stopping current investment projects, or a greater ability to postpone payments to suppliers to obtain liquidity.[8]

The arguments presented above suggest that at least part of the increase in investment documented in the paper at the aggregate, sectoral, and firm levels could correspond to a cyclical phenomenon. Admittedly, the Chilean

---

6. Braun and Larraín (2005) estimate that in normal times, firms in a sector at the seventy-fifth percentile of external dependence grow 1.5 percent faster than firms in an industry at the twenty-fifth percentile. Assuming for a back-of-the-envelope calculation that capital share in Chile is about 0.5 (from Chumacero and Fuentes 2005), no depreciation, no total factor productivity growth, and a common increase in employment of 75 percent (the average for 1984–89), this estimate would be consistent with a relative increase in investment of about 3.4 percent. In Hsieh and Parker, investment in industries with a high external dependence is about 2 percent higher than in industries with a low external dependence during the recovery period (obtained considering an interquartile range of external dependence of about 0.6 and the average differential investment rate after 1984 of 3 percent).

7. Gertler and Gilchrist (1994); Kashyap, Lamont, and Stein (1994); Oliner and Rudebusch (1996); Sharpe (1994).

8. See Fazzari and Petersen (1993). Additional issues with the measure of financial constraints in the paper have to do with the fact that the correlations between investment and cash flow seem to be calculated using only three years of data and without using Tobin's Q to control for investment opportunities, as is standard in the literature. Also, another explanation for the paper's results is that the correlation between profits and investment may reflect differences in expectations across firms. Firms that expected a prolonged recession may have decided to adjust their desired levels of capital. If these pessimistic firms were forced to adjust their expectations and their desired levels of capital upward after the fact, it could reproduce the patterns documented in the paper.

investment boom persisted for almost a decade, which is beyond business cycle frequencies. Nevertheless, there are two important considerations associated with the cyclicality issue. First, attributing the whole short-run expansion in investment to the reform would overestimate its overall impact even if the medium-run expansion were completely caused by it. Second, considering the possibility of cyclical effects leads me to reframe the question to ask why the boom persisted beyond 1986. While the 1984 tax reform is a possibility, some of the arguments used to disregard alternative explanations based on the specific timing of the reform and the investment boom do not apply well to this new question.

Final Remarks

Hsieh and Parker have written a very interesting paper. They address a difficult problem and present a compelling and thought-provoking argument in a clear, well-reasoned manner that should be given serious consideration. As I have discussed above, however, some remaining issues may affect the interpretation of the results, if not qualitatively, at least quantitatively. Although many of these issues cannot be properly addressed within the context of their paper, it is important for the reader to be aware of them before forming an opinion.

Another issue that arises from this discussion is the extent to which one can extrapolate the results from the Chilean experience to other countries. As mentioned above, Chile was unusual along several dimensions when the tax reform took place. The authors acknowledge this issue by qualifying their statements as applying to an economy with a sound macroeconomic environment, but this does not completely cover the particularities of the Chilean case. At least from a quantitative perspective, the authors must be careful in generating false expectations for countries willing to undertake these type of measure.

Finally, any assessment of the desirability of a reform like the one described here must take into account the potential costs associated with it. At least in the short run, a reduction in taxes will reduce government revenue, which may decrease government savings (thereby compensating the aggregate impact on investment), reduce social spending, or both. While the paper shows that this did not happen in Chile, one needs to he aware that the country was under a dictatorship during this period. Whether the same degree of fiscal austerity can result in a democratic environment is not guaranteed.

References

Agosín, Manuel R. 2001. "What Accounts for the Chilean Saving 'Miracle.' " *Cambridge Journal of Economics* 25(4): 503–16.

Agosín, Manuel R., Gustavo Crespi T., and Leonardo Letelier S. 1997. "Análisis sobre el aumento del ahorro en Chile." Research Network Working Paper R-309. Washington: Inter-American Development Bank.

Barandiarán, Edgardo, and Leonardo Hernández. 1999. "Origin and Resolution of a Banking Crisis: Chile, 1982–86." Working Paper 57. Santiago: Central Bank of Chile.

Bennett, Herman, Klaus Schmidt-Hebbel, and Claudio Soto. 1999. "Series de ahorro e ingreso por agente económico en Chile, 1960–1997." Working Paper 53. Santiago: Central Bank of Chile.

Bergoeing, Raphael, and others. 2002. "A Decade Lost and Found: Mexico and Chile in the 1980s." *Review of Economic Dynamics* 5(1): 166–205.

Bernanke, Ben, and Mark Gertler. 1995. "Inside the Black Box: The Credit Channel of Monetary Policy Transmission." *Journal of Economic Perspectives* 5(4): 27–48.

Bernanke, Ben, Mark Gertler, and Simon Gilchrist. 1999. "The Financial Accelerator in a Quantitative Business Cycle Framework." In *Handbook of Macroeconomics,* vol. 1, edited by John Taylor and Michael Woodford. Amsterdam: North-Holland.

Bosworth, Barry, Rudiger Dornbusch, and Raul Laban, eds. 1994. *The Chilean Economy: Policy Lessons and Challenges.* Brookings.

Bradford, David F. 1981. "The Incidence and Allocation Effects of a Tax on Corporate Distributions." *Journal of Public Economics* 15(1): 1–22.

Braun, Matías, and Borja Larraín. 2005. "Finance and the Business Cycle: International, Inter-Industry Evidence." Journal of Finance 60(3): 1097–128.

Budget Office. Various years. *Ley de Presupuestos del Sector Público.* Santiago: Ministry of Finance.

Budnevich, Carlos, and Alejandro Jara. 1997. "Political tributaria y ahorro de las empresas." *Revista de Análisis Económico* 12(1): 117–51.

Bustos, Alvaro, Eduardo Engel, and Alexander Galetovic. 1998. "Impuestos y demanda por capital en Chile, 1985–1995." Working Paper. Santiago: Servicio de Impuestos Internos.

Calomiris, Charles W., and R. Glenn Hubbard. 1995. "Internal Finance and Investment: Evidence from the Undistributed Profits Tax of 1936–37." *Journal of Business* 68(4): 443–82.

Calvo, Guillermo A., Alejandro Izquierdo, and Ernesto Talvi. 2006. "Phoenix Miracles in Emerging Markets: Recovering without Credit from Systemic Financial Crises." Working Paper 12101. Cambridge, Mass.: National Bureau of Economic Research.

Central Bank of Chile. 1999. *Anuario de Cuentas Nacionales, 1999.* Santiago.

———. Various issues. *Quarterly Economic and Financial Report of Chile.* Santiago.

Chumacero, Rómulo A., and Rodrigo Fuentes. 2005. "On the Determinants of Chilean Economic Growth." In *General Equilibrium Models for the Chilean Economy,* edited by Rómulo A. Chumacero and Klaus Schmidt-Hebbel. Santiago: Central Bank of Chile.

Cooper, Russell, and João Ejarque. 2003. "Financial Frictions and Investment: Requiem in Q." *Review of Economic Dynamics* 6(4): 710–28.

Coronado, Julia Lynn. 1998. "The Effects of Social Security Privatization on Household Saving: Evidence from the Chilean Experience." Finance and Economics Discussion Paper 1998-12. Board of Governors of the Federal Reserve System.

Cummins, Jason G., Kevin A. Hassett, and R. Glenn Hubbard. 1996. "Tax Reforms and Investment: A Cross-Country Comparison." *Journal of Public Economics* 62(1–2): 237–73.

Diamond, Peter. 1993. "Privatization of Social Security: Lessons From Chile." Working Paper 4510. Cambridge, Mass.: National Bureau of Economic Research.

Díaz-Alejandro, Carlos. 1985. "Good-Bye Financial Repression, Hello Financial Crash." *Journal of Development Economics* 19(1–2): 1–24.

Edwards, Sebastian. 1996. "The Chilean Pension Reform: A Pioneering Program." Working Paper 5811. Cambridge, Mass.: National Bureau of Economic Research.

Edwards, Sebastian, and Alejandra Cox Edwards. 2000. "Economic Reforms and Labor Markets: Policy Issues and Lessons from Chile." Working Paper 7646. Cambridge, Mass.: National Bureau of Economic Research.

Eyzaguirre, Nicolas, and Fernando Lefort. 1999. "Capital Markets in Chile, 1985–97: A Case of Successful International Financial Integration." In *Chile: Recent Policy Lessons and Emerging Challenges,* edited by Guillermo Perry and Danny Leipziger. Washington: World Bank.

Fazzari, Steven M., and Bruce C. Petersen. 1993. "Working Capital and Fixed Investment: New Evidence on Financing Constraints." *RAND Journal of Economics* 24(3): 328–42.

Gallego, Francisco, and Norman Loayza. 2000. "Financial Structure in Chile: Macroeconomic Developments and Microeconomic Effects." Working Paper 75. Santiago: Central Bank of Chile.

Gertler, Mark, and Simon Gilchrist. 1994. "Monetary Policy, Business Cycles, and the Behavior of Small Manufacturing Firms." *Quarterly Journal of Economics* 109(2): 309–40.

Gomes, João F. 2001. "Financing Investment." *American Economic Review* 91(5): 1263–85.

Gruber, Jonathan. 1995. "The Incidence of Payroll Taxation: Evidence from Chile." Working Paper 5053. Cambridge, Mass.: National Bureau of Economic Research.

Hassett, Kevin A., and R. Glenn Hubbard. 2002. "Tax Policy and Business Investment." In *Handbook of Public Economics,* vol. 3, edited by Alan J. Auerbach and Martin Feldstein. Amsterdam: Elsevier.

Hsieh, Chang-Tai, and Jonathan A. Parker. 2006. "Taxes and Growth in a Financially Underdeveloped Country: Evidence from the Chilean Investment Boom." Working Paper 12104. Cambridge, Mass.: National Bureau of Economic Research.

Hubbard, R. Glenn. 1998. "Capital-Market Imperfections and Investment." *Journal of Economic Literature* 36(1): 193–225.

Kasahara, Hiroyuki. 2004. "Temporary Increases in Tariffs and Machine Replacement: The Chilean Experience." University of Western Ontario.

Kashyap, Anil K., Owen A. Lamont, and Jeremy C. Stein. 1994. "Credit Conditions and the Cyclical Behavior of Inventories." *Quarterly Journal of Economics* 109(3): 565–92.

Larroulet, Cristian. 1987. "Endeudamiento interno: origenes, soluciones, y perspectives." *Estudios Públicos* 25: 77–103.

Marfan, Manuel, and Barry Bosworth. 1994. "Saving, Investment, and Economic Growth." In *The Chilean Economy: Policy Lessons and Challenges,* edited by Barry Bosworth, Rudi Dornbusch, and Raul Laban. Brookings.

Meller, Patricio. 1996. *Un siglo de economía política chilena: 1890–1990.* Santiago: Editorial Andres Bello.

Morandé, Felipe G. 1998. "Savings in Chile: What Went Right?" *Journal of Development Economics* 57(1): 201–28.

Oliner, Stephen, and Glen D. Rudebusch. 1996. "Is There a Broad Credit Channel for Monetary Policy?" *Federal Reserve Bank of San Francisco Economic Review* 1: 3–13.

Ortuzar, P. 1988. "El deficit previsional: recuento y proyecciones." In *Sistema Privado de Pensiones en Chile,* edited by S. Baeza and J. Manubens. Santiago: Centro de Estudios Públicos.

Pavcnik, Nina. 2002. "Trade Liberalization, Exit, and Productivity Improvements: Evidence from Chilean Plants." *Review of Economic Studies* 69(1): 245–76.

Perry, Guillermo, and Danny Leipziger, eds. 1999. *Chile: Recent Policy Lessons and Emerging Challenges.* Washington: World Bank.

Rajan, Raghuram G., and Luigi Zingales. 1998. "Financial Dependence and Growth." *American Economic Review* 88(3): 559–86.

Samwick, Andrew A. 2000. "Is Pension Reform Conducive to Higher Saving?" *Review of Economics and Statistics* 82(2): 264–72.

Servicio de Impuestos Internos. 1980. "Estadistica tributaria: impuesto a la renta 1980." Santiago.

Sharpe, Steven A. 1994. "Financial Market Imperfections, Firm Leverage, and the Cyclicality of Employment." *American Economic Review* 84(4): 1060–74.

Tybout, James R. 1996. "Chile, 1979–86: Trade Liberalization and Its Aftermath." In *Industrial Evolution in Developing Countries,* edited by Mark J. Roberts and James R. Tybout. Oxford University Press.

ALEJANDRO GAVIRIA

Social Mobility and Preferences for Redistribution in Latin America

This paper has two different but related parts. The first part presents an overview of the empirical evidence on intergenerational mobility levels in Latin America. This overview examines not only the objective indicators of intergenerational transmission, but also subjective opinions about both social mobility and social justice. The question of social mobility is extremely relevant in Latin America given the region's high levels of inequality. If inequality is moderate, investigating its causes may be superfluous, but when inequality is large, identifying its determinants acquires special importance. In unequal societies, more than anywhere else, social policy should be based on a detailed understanding of the root causes of inequality.

Interest in social mobility surpasses technical considerations, however. The second part of this paper reviews the relationship between social mobility and political preferences. The idea that perceptions on social mobility may affect political preferences, in general, and demands for redistribution, in particular, has been repeatedly discussed by social scientists and political commentators alike, starting with Alexis de Tocqueville.[1] Tocqueville's intuition that redistribution is indirectly related to perspectives on mobility has recently been validated, both at the aggregate and the individual level.[2] Most empirical research in this regard,

Gaviria is with the Centro de Estudios sobre Desarrollo Económico (CEDE) at the Universidad de los Andes.

I wish to thank the Inter-American Development Bank for financial support; Felipe Valencia Caicedo, María del Mar Palau, and María del Pilar López for their assistance; and Francisco Ferreira, Carol Graham, Luis Henrique Braido, Sebastian Galiani, and Carlos Eduardo Vélez for comments.

1. Tocqueville ([1835] 2003). For more recent discussions, see Lipset (1966, 1992); Piketty (1995); Alesina and Glaeser (2004); Benabou and Tirole (2005).

2. See, for example, Alesina and La Ferrara (2005); Fong (2001); Alesina and Fuchs Schuendeln (2005).

however, focuses on either developed economies or economies in transition. To my knowledge, this is one of the first studies to examine the correlates of political preferences in Latin America at the individual level—or, at the very least, one of the first systematic attempts to empirically investigate the correlation between Latin Americans' demands for redistribution and their mobility experiences.[3]

The results reported in the first part of this article show that intergenerational mobility levels are substantially lower in Latin America than in the United States. This fact is indicated not only by the previously published evidence (based on household surveys that include intergenerational data), but also by unpublished evidence first analyzed here (based on Latinobarómetro, an opinion survey carried out annually in seventeen Latin American countries). In urban areas, for example, the mean difference in schooling between children of parents without primary education and children of parents with completed higher education is six years in Latin America and only two years in the United States. Thus, if one compares a Latin American with educated parents with his or her American counterpart, the difference in years of education is minimal, but the difference becomes enormous when one compares the children of noneducated parents from Latin America and the United States.

Residents in Latin America are quite pessimistic when assessing their own mobility experiences. Almost half of those surveyed by the Latinobarómetro consider that their current socioeconomic status is the same as that of their parents. Only 20 percent consider their status higher, and the rest consider it lower. Paradoxically, respondents tend to be much more optimistic with respect to their children's possibilities for mobility: 55 percent think that the socioeconomic status of their children will be higher than their own, and only 9 percent believe the opposite. Individuals tend to be pessimistic about fairness in general. More than 70 percent of those surveyed consider that opportunities to overcome poverty are not equal for all and that success depends on connections. Over 60 percent believe poverty is unrelated to effort and ability, and more than 50 percent consider that hard work does not guarantee success. These percentages are much higher than those observed in the United States (where beliefs about equality of opportunity are widespread) and higher than those observed in Europe (where beliefs about equality of opportunity are somewhat pessimistic).[4]

3. Graham and Felton (2005) study the interplay between individual perceptions about social justice and opposition to privatization. Graham (2000) also examines the relationship between perceptions of mobility and support for reforms in Latin America.

4. See Alesina and Angeletos (2005) and Benabou and Tirole (2005) for an explanation of the differences between perceptions in the United States and Europe. Both explanations postulate feedback mechanisms between perceptions and the economic system.

Finally, the results of the second part of this paper show the existence of a systematic correlation between individual characteristics and political preferences. Demand for redistribution, for example, is higher among poor individuals, among those who did not move up the socioeconomic ladder, and among those who believe that poverty is caused by external circumstances. A similar result is obtained with respect to the approval of the market economy and the support for privatizations: the poorer and the more pessimistic regarding social justice are more prone to oppose to the former and to reject the latter. In sum, the results show that political preferences are based not only on selfish considerations about who gets what, but also on personal experiences and opinions regarding distributive justice.

This paper is organized as follows. The next section describes the data used in the study. I then summarize the evidence regarding both mobility levels and perceptions of social justice. A subsequent section reviews the correlates of the demand for redistribution and the approval of market outcomes, and the final section concludes.

Description of the Data

The main source of data used in this study is a survey of public opinion held yearly in seventeen Latin American countries, under the technical direction of the Latinobarómetro Corporation and the financial sponsorship of the Inter-American Development Bank (IDB). Sample sizes fluctuate between 1,000 and 1,200 individuals per country. Sampling methods may change from one country to another, as the sample design and data collection are contracted out to local firms. Sampling is restricted to the main urban centers, and the questions asked vary from one year to the next. The emphasis of the survey has not changed over time, however, and the questions have always focused on attitudes, preferences, and political actions.[5]

This paper uses three groups of questions. The first group corresponds to the individual's experiences and expectations of social mobility; the second, to perceptions of social justice and fairness; and the third, to political preferences, including redistribution. The paper also uses a specific question, asked in the 2000 survey, regarding the education level of the respondent parents. This question is used to assess the level of the educational mobility

---

5. The Latinobarómetro uses the World Values Survey, the General Social Survey, and the Gallup surveys on social trends (Gallup Social Audit Survey) as close references.

TABLE 1. Distribution of Respondents, by Socioeconomic Status

Quintile	Not enough, great difficulties	Not enough, difficulties	Just enough	Good enough, able to save
First	22.62	46.37	26.57	4.44
Second	15.66	42.69	36.09	5.56
Third	9.39	37.42	43.57	9.62
Fourth	6.29	28.51	51.34	13.86
Fifth	6.01	24.87	48.74	20.38

Source: Latinobarómetro (2000).

in the region.[6] The empirical exercises focus on two survey rounds (1996 and 2000), each of which has the proper combination of questions required to carry out the proposed analysis.

Surveys have an adequate socioeconomic characterization of each individual, but they do not include a precise assessment of household income or consumption. Socioeconomic classification is therefore based on questions about possession of physical assets and dwelling characteristics. I followed a three-step procedure to sort individuals into socioeconomic groups. To start, I used the first principal component to obtain a weighted average of the variables included in the estimation.[7] Individuals were then sorted on the basis of this average. Finally, I used the sorting to classify the surveyed individuals in quintiles of socioeconomic status.

In addition to objective measures, the survey includes questions regarding the subjective well-being of each individual. Table 1 shows variations by quintile of the answers to a question on whether the person's current income is enough to cover basic needs. As shown, those reporting that their income is not sufficient belong mainly to the first quintile, while those reporting greater economic ease belong mainly to the last quintile. Most respondents, however, seem reluctant to judge their situation as good, regardless of their socioeconomic position.

Table 2 shows the relationship between the educational attainment of parents and children. The results indicate that a large number of children surpass the

---

6. Text of the main questions used is presented in the appendix.

7. The principal components methodology is frequently used to estimate an individual's socioeconomic level in the absence of reliable data on income. Filmer and Pritchett (2001) argue that household assets and dwelling characteristics are observed with greater precision than consumption, and that socioeconomic level indicators based on these variables are less sensitive to temporary fluctuations of the income level.

T A B L E   2 .   **Transition Matrix of Education Attainments**

Parents' level of education	Children's level of education			
	Primary or less	Secondary or less	Technical or higher (incomplete)	Technical or higher (complete)
Primary or less	32.3	40.2	22.9	4.7
Secondary or less	4.7	42.7	43.2	9.4
Technical or higher (incomplete)	1.9	16.6	64.2	17.4
Technical or higher (complete)	2.0	11.6	57.4	29.1

Source: Latinobarómetro (2000).

education level of their parents. This fact is consistent with the advance of educational indicators in the region, and it does not necessarily imply the existence of relative mobility, defined as the change in relative positions of a dynasty in the movement from one generation to the next.[8]

Figure 1 shows the difference in the mean years of schooling between parents and children for the seventeen countries in the sample. Mean schooling is about 9.9 years for individual respondents and about 6.5 years for their parents. All countries boast a positive and substantial difference between the schooling of respondents and that of their parents. The largest difference is observed in Honduras (4.3 years) and the lowest in Chile (2.1 years). Overall, the difference is higher in countries with low attainment rates, which suggests some convergence in educational outcomes within the Latin American region.

Mobility and Social Equality: Indicators and Perceptions

Countless academic studies document the high levels of inequality in Latin America, but the reiteration of this fact has not been accompanied by systematic research on the causes of inequality. For the region as a whole, little is known about the extent to which inequality is explained by differences in opportunities or by unequal efforts and personal skills. Empirical studies that investigate the extent to which inequality in Latin America is induced by external circumstances are few and scattered.

This section presents various indicators on the distribution of educational opportunities and the levels of intergenerational mobility in Latin America.

---

8. See Behrman, Gaviria, and Székely (2001) for a systematic analysis of the correlation between educational advance and relative mobility in Latin America.

FIGURE 1.   **Difference in Years of Schooling of Parents and Children**

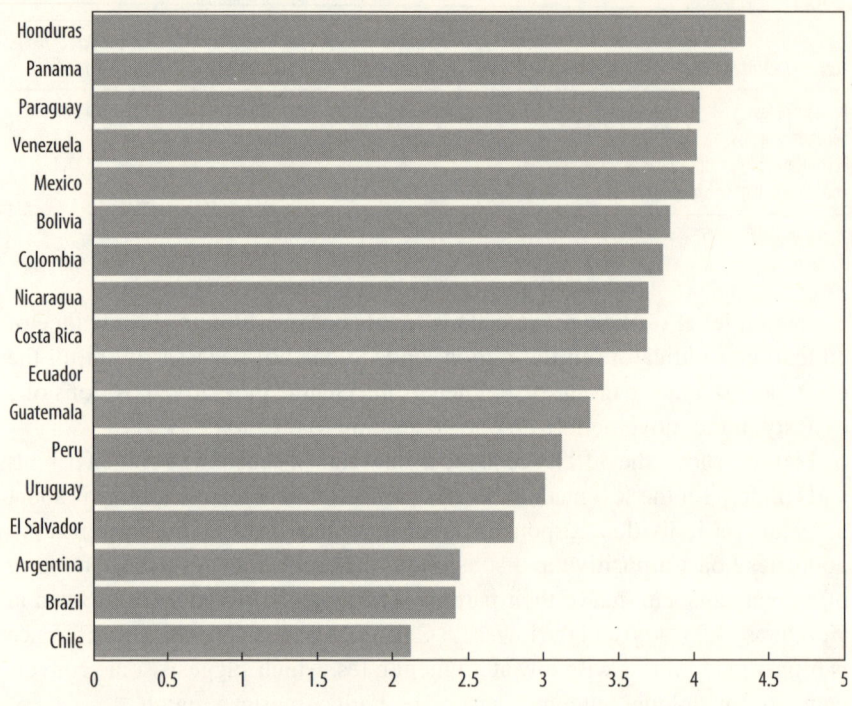

Source: Latinobarómetro (2000).

I use three types of indicators. The first is based on the correlation of the schooling of respondents and that of their parents. The second is based on respondents' perceptions of their own socioeconomic status, the observed status of their parents, and the expected status of their children. The third indicator uses a series of direct questions about social justice and the distribution of opportunities. Perceptions about social mobility are relevant in their own right because, as shown later in the paper, they have a direct effect on the demand for redistribution, in particular, and political preferences, in general.

Educational Mobility in Latin America

The lack of longitudinal surveys containing information on the socioeconomic outcomes of two generations of the same family has somewhat hampered the study of intergenerational mobility in the region. Retrospective information on parental schooling can partially circumvent the nonexistence of longitudinal

TABLE 3.   Children's Schooling as a Function of Parents' Schooling[a]

Independent variable	(1)	(2)	(3)	(4)
Schooling	0.4424	0.7059	0.7190	0.6327
	(0.0054)	(0.0187)	(0.0187)	(0.0189)
Schooling squared		−0.0180	−0.0196	−0.0163
		(0.0011)	(0.0011)	(0.0011)
Summary statistic				
R^2	0.2840	0.2950	0.3151	0.3424
Country fixed effects	No	No	Yes	Yes
Other controls	No	No	No	Yes
No. observations	16,539	16,539	16,539	16,537

Source: Author's calculations based on Latinobarómetro (2000).
a. Standard errors are in parentheses.

surveys. As mentioned in the previous section, the Latinobarómetro 2000 survey included a question on the schooling of the father of each person surveyed. This information can serve as the basis for calculating an indicator of the level of educational mobility in the region, which, in turn, can be compared to similar indicators that are available for other countries. This comparison leads to some general conclusions regarding the distribution of opportunities in Latin America vis-à-vis other regions of the world.

I used the following equation to examine the relationship between the level of schooling of children and their parents:

$$(1) \qquad S_{i,t} = \alpha + \beta_1 S_{i,t-1} + \beta_2 S_{i,t-1}^2 + w_{i,t},$$

where each period represents a generation, i represents a family dynasty, and S represents the level of schooling. A close relationship between the schooling of parents and children implies that the country or region in question has a low level of mobility. Some of the equations estimated included fixed effects by country, as well as controls for some basic individual characteristics, such as gender, age, and marital status.

Table 3 shows the estimated coefficients. If a quadratic term is not included, the estimated value of β_1 is approximately 0.44, which is substantially higher than the values observed in the United States and other developed countries.[9] The estimated value of β_2 is negative, indicating a concave relationship between the

9. Mulligan (1997, p. 200) summarizes the cross-country evidence on intergenerational educational mobility. Available estimates are approximately 0.3 for the United States and 0.2 for Germany and Malaysia.

FIGURE 2. Correlation between Schooling of Parents and Children

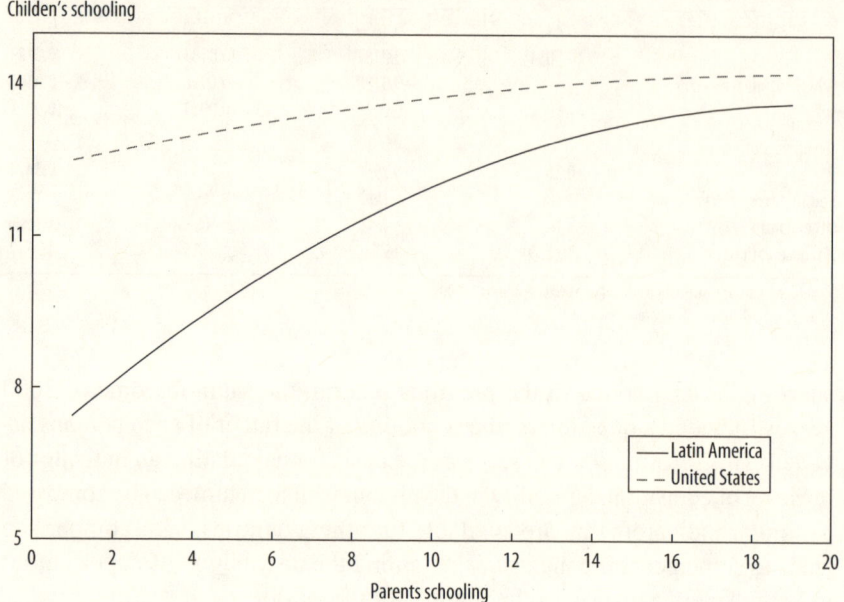

Source: Latinobarómetro (2000); General Social Survey (1990–97).

schooling of parents and children. Estimated values do not change substantially when fixed effects are added, and they only change slightly when the estimation controls for basic individual characteristics. Overall, the results show a low level of educational mobility in Latin America, at least in relative terms.

Figure 2 illustrates the relationship between the schooling of parents and children in Latin America and the United States.[10] The curves are based on the results of table 3.[11] Differences are significant for children of uneducated parents (five years), but exiguous for children of parents who graduated from college (six months). This result indicates, among other things, that educational opportunities are much more concentrated in Latin American countries than in the United States. On average, the educational achievement of an individual

10. The U.S. data are from the General Social Survey (GSS) for the 1990–97 period. Only urban data were considered. For a description of data, see Behrman, Gaviria, and Székely (2001).

11. It is reasonable to assume that the quadratic specification employed is not driven by the bounded nature of the variables. If this were the case, one would not expect a similar concavity for both Latin America and the United States, where educational attainment at the upper bound is more common.

in Latin America is strongly linked to those of his or her father. This is not the case in the United States.

Figure 3 shows the same correlation as the previous graph, but for the tenth, fiftieth, and ninetieth percentiles instead of the mean.[12] The figures show that the intergenerational transmission profiles by percentile are different for Latin America and the United States. In Latin America, profiles are concave throughout the distribution. The opposite occurs in the United States, where profiles are convex for higher percentiles. In Latin America, persistence is greater (that is, mobility is lower) among the less educated than among the more educated. In the United States, on the other hand, persistence appears to be greater among the more educated. Interestingly, persistence among the more educated follows a convex pattern in the United States: schooling grows incrementally with parental schooling.

Figure 4 illustrates the relationship between the schooling of parents and children within Latin America. For this exercise, I divided the region into three groups representing three levels of development.[13] The figure reveals little variation among the three groups. The three curves are almost identical, although the curve for group 1 starts lower and ends higher than for the other groups.

Other Sources of Evidence

The available evidence on cross-country differences in the levels of intergenerational mobility confirms the above results. Table 4 summarizes the results of some studies that directly compare the levels of mobility in Latin America and other regions, including both developed and developing countries. The studies listed are just a sample of a burgeoning literature. The first set of studies mentioned use retrospective questions about parental education (or, alternatively, questions about the education of children residing with their parents). These studies show that intergenerational connections are much stronger in Latin America than in the United States. The second set of studies compares differences in social outcomes (such as child mortality, immunizations, and

---

12. I estimated quantile regressions in each case. Deaton (1997, p. 80) discusses the usefulness of this type of analysis.

13. Specifically, I classified the countries according to their 2006 purchasing power parity (PPP) per capita GDP, defining group 1 (high) as a per capita GDP of more than US$10,000, group 2 (medium) as between US$5,000 and US$10,000, and group 2 (low) as less than US$5,000. According to this rubric, the countries in group 1 are Argentina, Costa Rica, Chile, Mexico, and Uruguay; group 2 includes Brazil, Colombia, Panama, Peru, and Venezuela; and group 3 contains Bolivia, Ecuador, El Salvador, Guatemala, Honduras, Nicaragua, and Paraguay.

FIGURE 3. Correlation between Schooling of Parents and Children: Tenth, Fiftieth, and Ninetieth Percentiles

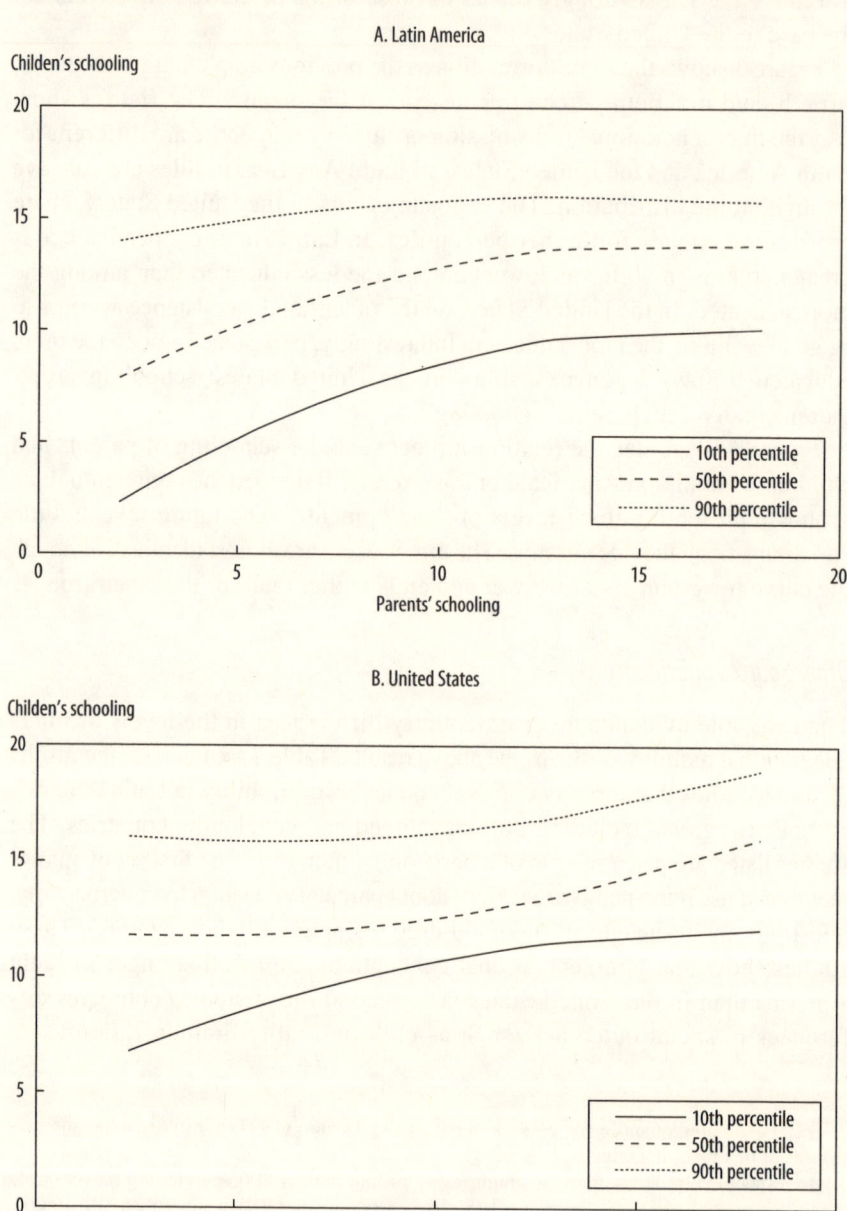

A. Latin America

Childen's schooling

Parents' schooling

- 10th percentile
- 50th percentile
- 90th percentile

B. United States

Childen's schooling

Parents' schooling

- 10th percentile
- 50th percentile
- 90th percentile

Source: Latinobarómetro (2000); General Social Survey (1990–97).

FIGURE 4.   **Intraregional Correlation between Schooling of Parents and Children, by Group[a]**

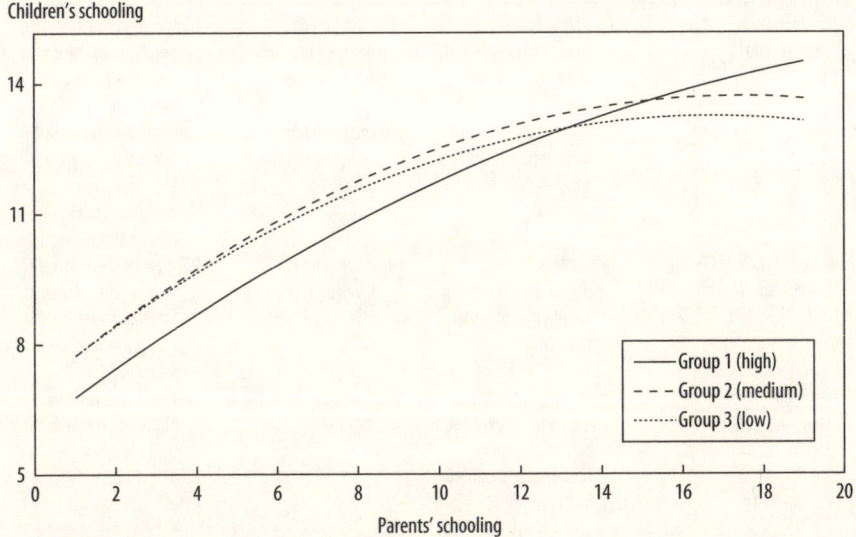

Children's schooling

Group 1 (high)
– – – Group 2 (medium)
.... Group 3 (low)

Parents' schooling

Source: Latinobarómetro (2000).
   a. Countries in the region are grouped according to their level of development, measured as 2006 purchasing power parity (PPP) per capita GDP. Group 1 (more than US$10,000) includes Argentina, Chile, Costa Rica, Mexico, and Uruguay. Group 2 (US$5,000 to US$10,000) includes Brazil, Colombia, Panama, Peru, and Venezuela. Group 3 (less than US$5,000) includes Bolivia, Ecuador, El Salvador, Guatemala, Honduras, Nicaragua, and Paraguay.

educational attainment) by socioeconomic status in Latin American countries and other developing countries. The evidence indicates that the differences are somewhat smaller in Latin America than in Africa and Southeast Asia.

For the specific case of Brazil, Bourguignon, Ferreira, and Menéndez show that share of the variance of log earnings explained by circumstances (namely, parental schooling and occupation, race, and region) appears to be much greater in Brazil than in the United States.[14] Andrade and others use instrumental variables to estimate parental earnings in the absence of direct data.[15] They then use these estimates to calculate the intergenerational relation in earnings between children and their parents. They show that, in Brazil, intergenerational links are stronger in the superior quintiles than in the inferior ones, whereas the opposite is true in Germany and the Unite States. They argue that these results, taken together, imply that intergenerational mobility has been hampered by borrowing constraints in Brazil, but not in Germany and the United States.

   14. Bourguignon, Ferreira, and Menéndez (2003).
   15. Andrade and others (2004).

TABLE 4. Studies Comparing Mobility in Latin America with Mobility in Other Countries

Study	Indicator	Countries	Conclusions
Behrman, Gaviria, and Székely (2001)	Schooling correlation between parents and children	Brazil, Colombia, Mexico, Peru, and the United States	High correlation in Mexico and Peru and much higher in Brazil and Colombia
Dahan and Gaviria (2001)	Correlation of schooling gaps between siblings residing with their parents	Sixteen Latin American countries and the United States	Correlation is between 1.8 and 3.0 times greater in Latin American countries than in the United States
Filmer and Pritchett (1998); Ferreira and Walton (2006)	Differences in social outcomes by parental wealth and parental schooling	Large sample of developing countries	Differences are relatively small in Latin America for child mortality, immunizations, and schooling
Bourguignon, Ferreira, and Menéndez (2003)	Share of the variance of log earnings explained by circumstances (parental schooling and occupation, race and region)	Brazil and the United States	Share in Brazil is much higher than that in the United States
Andrade and others (2004)	Convexity of the relationship between parents' and children's wages	Brazil, Germany, and the United States	The intergenerational persistence of wages is greater for the higher quintiles in Brazil, suggesting the existence of borrowing constraints

Perceptions of Mobility and Social Justice

The evidence presented so far, based on intergenerational correlations, indicates that educational opportunities are unequally distributed in Latin America. In what follows, I compare objective indicators with subjective measures, based on the opinions of Latinobarómetro respondents regarding the distribution of opportunities and the extent of social justice, in general. As stated earlier, these opinions are important regardless of whether they are right or wrong, since they have a measurable impact on political preferences.

The Latinobarómetro survey has frequently included several questions about perceptions of social mobility, as well as about the fairness of the prevailing socioeconomic system. In particular, the 2000 survey included three questions about mobility experiences (that is, the respondents' position relative to their parents) and mobility perspectives (that is, the future position of the respondents' children). The first question asked the respondents to place themselves on a socioeconomic scale from one to ten, with one being the lowest level and ten the highest. The second question asked the respondents to do the same for their parents (retrospective look), and the third question did the same for the respondents' children (prospective look). The average position of those surveyed is 4.4. The average for the parents (according to their children) was 4.7 and for the children (according to their parents) 5.5.

The key issue, however, is related not to the average levels, but to the observed changes with respect to one's parents and the expected changes of one's children with respect to oneself. To tackle this issue, I calculated the differences in the reported values as follows: past mobility equals personal response minus parents' response; future mobility equals children's response minus personal response. Such variables provide a subjective, but illustrative, idea of the past and future intergenerational mobility for each individual.

Figure 5 presents the results. Approximately half of the individuals surveyed (47 percent) place their parents and themselves in the same position (that is, past mobility equals zero). Only 20 percent of the respondents feel that they have been able to overtake their parent's position, while 33 percent perceive a backward movement. Overall, the results imply a pessimistic outlook on past mobility experiences.[16] In contrast, expectations of future mobility are quite optimistic: 55 percent of individuals surveyed expect their children to have a higher socioeconomic status than themselves, while only 9 percent expect a lower level for their children. In general, Latin Americans do not consider that their life histories have been a good example of mobility, but they do hope for a more favorable situation for their children.[17]

Figure 6 provides an intraregional view of past and future mobility experiences. These mobility experiences reflect the same general pattern described above: people are pessimistic about their past and optimistic about their future. Still, the figure presents some noticeable differences. Regarding past mobility, the peak for "no change" is lower for group 1 (high) than for groups 2 (medium) and 3 (low). Although most people report that they have moved backward with respect to their parents, individuals in group 1 report more forward movements than those in groups 2 and 3. With respect to future mobility, most people are optimistic, yet groups 2 and 3 have higher no change peaks than

16. Past mobility perceptions are positively correlated with educational mobility realities (measured as the difference between the years of schooling of an individual and his or her parents). The correlation is small (0.04), but statistically significant at the 5 percent level.

17. Optimism regarding future mobility seems to be, as they say, a triumph of hope over experience.

FIGURE 5.   **Perceptions of Past and Future Mobility**

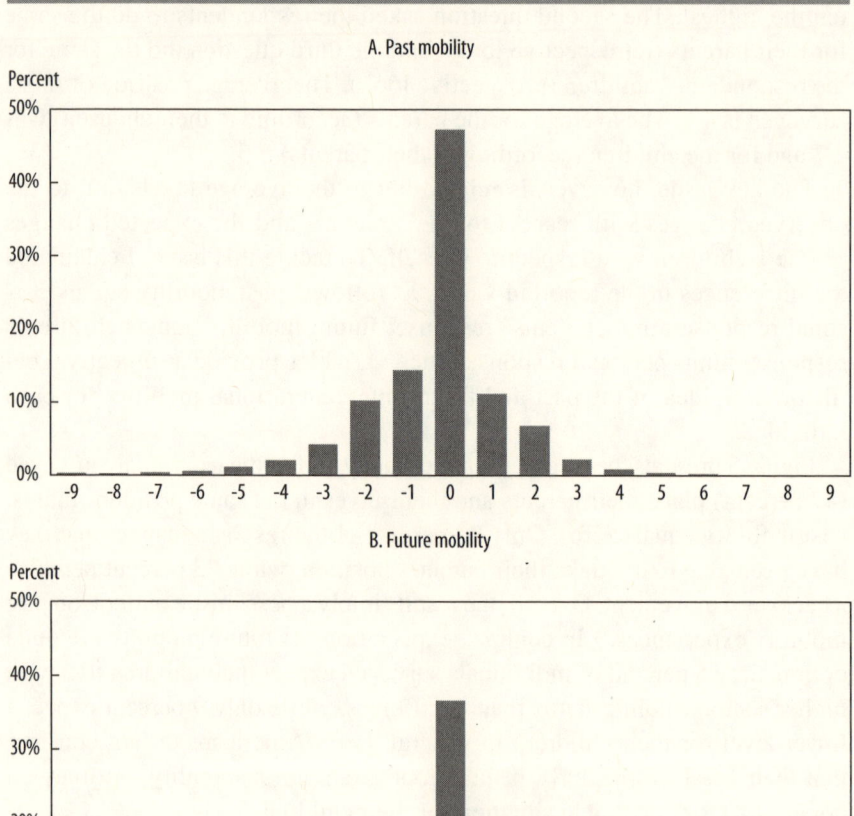

A. Past mobility

Source: Latinobarómetro (2000).

group 1. Additionally, individuals in group 1 are more optimistic about the future than those in groups 2 and 3.

The experiences of past mobility and expectations for future mobility are very independent. Correlation between these two variables is slight and negative, on average.[18] The idea of reversion to the mean appears to be widespread in the

18. The negative correlation of past and future mobility is significant and substantial (greater than 0.3) for Mexico and Venezuela.

FIGURE 6.   Intraregional Perceptions of Past and Future Mobility, by Group[a]

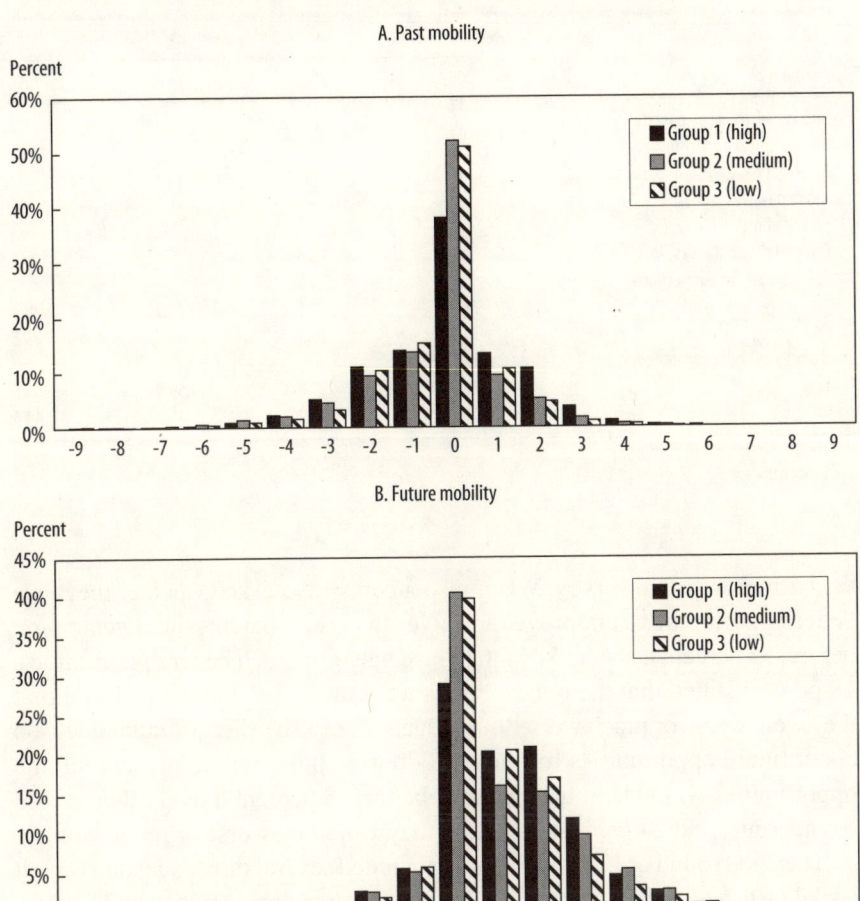

A. Past mobility

Percent

Group 1 (high)
Group 2 (medium)
Group 3 (low)

B. Future mobility

Percent

Group 1 (high)
Group 2 (medium)
Group 3 (low)

Source: Latinobarómetro (2000).

a. Countries in the region are grouped according to their level of development, measured as 2006 purchasing power parity (PPP) per capita GDP. Group 1 (more than US$10,000) includes Argentina, Chile, Costa Rica, Mexico, and Uruguay. Group 2 (US$5,000 to US$10,000) includes Brazil, Colombia, Panama, Peru, and Venezuela. Group 3 (less than US$5,000) includes Bolivia, Ecuador, El Salvador, Guatemala, Honduras, Nicaragua, and Paraguay.

minds of Latin Americans with the most abrupt histories of mobility, either upward or downward. Many seem to suspect that a substantial movement in the socioeconomic scale will be partially corrected during the following generation.

In general terms, the previous results are consistent with the answers to some direct questions about mobility perceptions included in the 1996 round of

TABLE 5. Perceptions of Social Justice
Percent

Survey question	Survey year			
	2002	2000	1998	1996
Opportunities to escape poverty				
All have equal opportunities	. . .	25.9	. . .	. . .
All do not have equal opportunities	. . .	74.1	. . .	. . .
Causes of poverty				
Lack of effort		36.5		
External circumstances		63.6	·	
Success depends on connections				
Yes	68.62	· 71.5	71.3	76.4
No	31.38	28.5	28.7	23.6
Hard work does not guarantee success				
Yes	58.11	53.8	54.9	55.6
No	41.89	46.2	45.1	44.4

Source: Latinobarómetro (various years).
. . . Not applicable.

the Latinobarómetro survey. When respondents were asked whether they face better opportunities to improve their lives than their parents did a generation before, 55 percent answered that they face better or much better opportunities, 18 percent stated that the opportunities were the same, and the rest said that they were worse or much worse. Individuals were also asked a similar question about future opportunities for their children. In this case, 58 percent felt the opportunities would be much better or better, 18 percent thought they would be the same, and 24 percent indicated they would be worse or much worse.

The 2000 round of Latinobarómetro included several direct questions about social justice (specifically, about the distribution of opportunities and the root causes of poverty). Respondents were asked whether all fellow citizens had the same opportunities to stop being poor and whether poverty is due to lack of effort or to circumstances beyond effort and ability. As shown in table 5, 74 percent stated that opportunities are not distributed equally, and 64 percent considered that poverty is caused by circumstances beyond individual skills and personal efforts.

Three Latinobarómetro surveys further asked whether connections are key for socioeconomic success and whether hard work guarantees being successful. Table 5 presents the results for 1998, 2000, and 2002. Over 70 percent agree that connections are important and more than half believe that hard work guarantees success. Percentages are stable throughout. Inside the Latin American region,

TABLE 6. **Intraregional Perceptions of Social Justice**[a]

Percent

Survey question	Group 1	Group 2	Group 3
Opportunities to escape poverty			
All have equal opportunities	23.9	28.0	25.9
All do not have equal opportunities	76.1	72.0	74.1
Causes of poverty			
Lack of effort	34.1	36.1	38.6
External circumstances	65.9	63.9	61.4
Success depends on connections			
Yes	69.3	73.0	72.2
No	30.7	27.0	27.8
Hard work does not guarantee success			
Yes	52.2	53.3	55.5
No	47.8	46.7	44.5

Source: Latinobarómetro (2000).

a. Countries in the region are grouped according to their level of development, measured as 2006 purchasing power parity (PPP) per capita GDP. Group 1 (more than US$10,000) includes Argentina, Chile, Costa Rica, Mexico, and Uruguay. Group 2 (US$5,000 to US$10,000) includes Brazil, Colombia, Panama, Peru, and Venezuela. Group 3 (less than US$5,000) includes Bolivia, Ecuador, El Salvador, Guatemala, Honduras, Nicaragua, and Paraguay.

results are almost identical across groups (table 6). Overall, the results indicate that Latin Americans tend to be pessimistic about social justice and about the relative importance of effort and ability for reaching socioeconomic success.

Figure 7 illustrates how opinions vary according to the socioeconomic status and history of the individuals surveyed. The percentage of individuals who do not believe in equality of opportunity, as well as the percentage who consider that poverty is caused by external circumstances, does not change significantly from one socioeconomic quintile to another. In other words, opinions about the distribution of opportunities (and about social justice, in general) do not seem to depend on the relative wealth of individuals. Instead, these opinions seem to be related to the individual's (self-reported or perceived) history of mobility. The figure also quantifies these opinions for individuals whose socioeconomic level decreased, remained the same, and increased relative to the perceived level of their parents.[19] The fraction of those who do not believe in equal opportunities and of those who consider that poverty is a matter of

19. Groups were classified according to the past mobility indicator described above. The first group (downward) includes individuals surveyed with values between −9 and −2. The second group (no mobility) includes those between −1 and 1, and the third group (upward) includes values between 2 and 9.

FIGURE 7. Perceptions of Social Justice, by Socioeconomic Status and History of Mobility

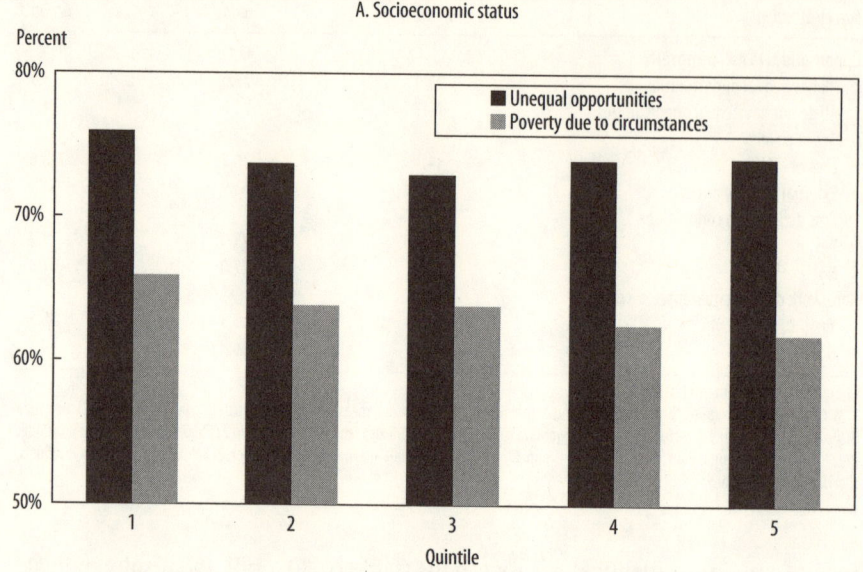

A. Socioeconomic status

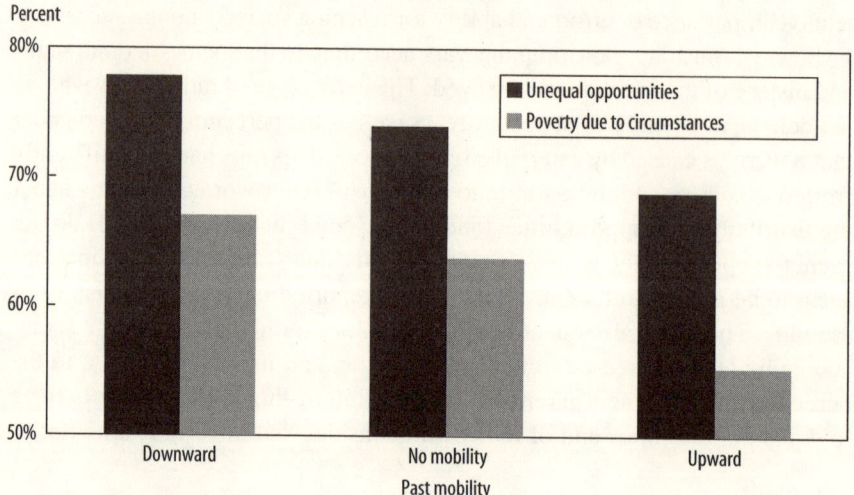

B. History of mobility

Source: Latinobarómetro (2000).

external circumstances is substantially smaller among individuals who, according to their own views, were able to surpass their parents' socioeconomic status.[20]

A similar analysis of the other two variables in question—namely, the importance of connections and the effectiveness of hard work—generates less interesting results. Neither variable changes substantially along the dimensions considered: socioeconomic quintiles and history of mobility. The fraction of individuals stating that connections are important decreases slightly as one moves from lower to higher socioeconomic quintiles, but the overriding fact of this analysis is the absence of substantial differences of opinion by either wealth or mobility.

To put the above findings into an international perspective, I compared the results with the World Values Survey (WVS). The WVS is one of the most comprehensive international surveys tracking political and sociocultural change. It covers a wide range of topics, including questions on social, cultural, political, religious, and moral views. The WVS first appeared in 1981 as the European Values Study (EVS), and it was gradually extended to encompass countries worldwide. Thus the WVS included twenty-two countries in 1990, forty-two in 1995, fifty-four in 2000, and sixty-four in 2005. A minimum of 1,000 people were interviewed per country. The survey is administered locally, so sampling methods vary across nations. For this paper, I extracted specific questions regarding socioeconomic opportunities and perceptions that resemble the questions used from the Latinobarómetro survey.

Given the differences in the questions and coverage of the WVS, the purpose of this exercise is not to conduct an external validation of the Latinobarómetro data, but rather to provide an international context for the regional results. Nevertheless, the small differences observed among the various Latin American groups indicate that the Latin American countries in the WVS constitute a representative sample of the region.[21] In any case, the results are revealing and mostly supportive of the evidence presented in the paper so far. The three issues analyzed are people's attitudes toward opportunities to escape poverty, the causes of poverty, and whether hard work guarantees success (table 7).

20. This association between individual history of mobility and political preference is consistent with Piketty (1995), who demonstrates that this sort of relationship is obtained if the importance of personal effort over socioeconomic success is unknown and if individuals use their personal histories to make the corresponding inferences.

21. The Latin American countries covered in the sample are Argentina, Brazil, Chile, Colombia, Dominican Republic, El Salvador, Mexico, Peru, Puerto Rico, Uruguay, and Venezuela.

TABLE 7. International Perceptions of Social Justice, 1994–99
Percent

Survey question	Latin America	Eastern Europe	OECD countries	Asia	United States	Africa	Total
Opportunities to escape poverty							
People have opportunities	41.7	25.7	44.7	49.9	27.3	40.0	38.2
People have very few opportunities	58.3	74.3	55.3	50.1	72.7	60.0	61.8
Causes of poverty							
Lack of effort	31.2	21.7	33.7	34.8	60.0	28.1	34.9
External circumstances	66.8	78.3	66.3	64.7	40.0	71.3	64.6
Success depends on connections							
Yes	61.5	65.0	65.2	73.2	80.5	82.1	71.2
No	38.5	35.0	34.8	26.8	19.5	17.9	28.8
Hard work does not guarantee success							
Yes							
No							

Source: World Values Survey, various years.
OECD = Organization for Economic Cooperation and Development.

With respect to the chances for getting out of poverty, respondents from Latin America are less optimistic than people from Asia and member countries of the Organization for Economic Cooperation and Development (OECD), but more optimistic than respondents from Africa, eastern Europe, and the United States. With regard to the causes of poverty, the United States registers the strongest belief in lack of effort, followed by Asia, the OECD countries, Latin America, Africa, and eastern Europe. Finally, when asked about whether hard work guarantees success, Latin Americans are the most pessimistic of all the groups. In sum, at the international level, Latin Americans are either weakly optimistic or pessimistic in their social justice outlook, as measured by their perceptions of the opportunities to escape poverty, the causes of poverty, and the relationship between hard work and success.

Political Preferences, Social Mobility, and Equality

This section describes the evidence on the demand for redistribution and other political preferences in Latin America and investigates its individual-level correlates. The intention is to empirically examine, for the case of Latin America, a model of political preferences based on two main premises: people expect individual effort and skills to be rewarded by society, but they also expect the State to intervene to correct outcomes originating in circumstances that have nothing to do with personal effort and skills. Concisely, demand for redistribution—or acceptance of market outcomes, for that matter—should be higher (lower), the more (less) pessimistic are people's perceptions about the extent of equality of opportunity, social injustice, and social mobility.

The analysis of this section can be framed in the broader discussion about the existence of social preferences. In spite of the initial reticence of many economists, the profession has gradually accepted the existence of social preferences, partly as a consequence of profuse experimental evidence. This evidence shows that individuals are often willing to assume a pecuniary cost to punish those who violate accepted rules about what is considered fair in a determined exchange.[22] Some are even willing to pay to punish those who evade the responsibility of punishing. In general, experimental evidence indicates that social preferences go further than a simple taste for equality (to use Tocqueville's expression), and they reflect a natural and a cultural inclination toward adequate rewards for personal effort and the reasonable correction of accidental circumstances (such as those related to family origin).

Empirical evidence suggests that social preferences affect political preferences in a foreseeable manner. Studies on the United States and European countries show that individuals who consider that the social order is unfair (that is, those who believe that hard work is not worth it, that connections are fundamental, and that opportunities are not properly distributed) are more likely to support redistribution and question market outcomes.[23] The following analysis examines the empirical validity of these results for Latin America.

The analysis is based on the same data from the Latinobarómetro survey described earlier. I use the 1996 and 2000 rounds of the survey, both of which included questions not only about social mobility and social justice (as described earlier), but also about redistribution and other political preferences. In 1996, respondents were directly asked whether they believe that reducing the differences between the rich and the poor is one of the main responsibilities of the state. Of the individuals surveyed, 73 percent answered "of course it is," 17 percent said "maybe yes," 6 percent responded "maybe not," and 4 percent answered "of course not." To facilitate the interpretation of the econometric

22. See, for example, Camerer (2003, chap. 2) for a summary of the evidence on the existence of social preferences in the context of the so called ultimatum game. Camerer emphasizes the role of individual characteristics in determining social preferences.

23. See Fong (2001) and Alesina and La Ferrara (2005) for the case of the United States and Corneo and Grüner (2002) for Europe.

exercises, I classified the answers into two groups: all those who answered "of course it is" and the other three responses combined.[24]

The 2000 survey asked whether respondents considered the market economy to be the most convenient for their country: 17 percent declared themselves to be very much in agreement, 40 percent in agreement, 29 percent in disagreement, and 14 percent very much in disagreement. In the same year, respondents were also asked whether privatization had been beneficial for the country. The response pattern was similar: 11 percent were very much in agreement, 27 percent agreed, 40 percent disagreed, and 22 percent were very much in disagreement. As before, I dichotomized the answers to facilitate the analysis, this time grouping the two positive answers (in agreement), on the one hand, and the two second answers (in disagreement), on the other. Finally, the 2000 survey asked the participants to place themselves on a scale from one to ten, with one being the extreme left and ten the extreme right. For the purposes of this analysis, I defined as leftist all individuals who answered one, two, or three (approximately 18 percent of the total).[25]

I estimated the following econometric model to study how political preferences (such as preferences for redistribution, attitudes toward market outcomes, and attitudes toward privatizations) relate to socioeconomic characteristics of individuals, their history of mobility, and their perceptions of social justice:

$$(2) \qquad\qquad Y_i^* = \mathbf{X}_i\beta + \varepsilon_t,$$

where Y^* is a latent variable that represents the unobserved level of support for redistribution, Y is an observed variable that equals one if $Y^* > 0$ and zero if $Y^* < 0$, and $\mathbf{X}$ is a vector with independent variables. A probit was used for the estimation, but the results do not change if alternative estimation methods are used.

Independent variables fall into four groups. The first group includes some general socioeconomic characteristics, such as age, gender, marital status, and a dummy variable for whether the person holds a regular job. Each of the three remaining groups represents a different theoretical paradigm emphasizing certain determinants of preferences for redistribution (in particular) and

24. I use dichotomization to facilitate the interpretation of results; this choice does not affect any of the conclusions.

25. The results are not dependent on this arbitrary decision. They do not change substantially if the threshold point between leftist and not leftist is defined one level above or below the chosen threshold.

opinions regarding the appropriate role of the state (in general). Specifically, the second group contains variables related to the individual's socioeconomic level. These variables are of two types. The first is subjective and is based on a direct question about the sufficiency (or insufficiency) of the household's income; the second type is objective and is based on the quintiles of socioeconomic status described earlier. Together, these variables attempt to evaluate the so-called Meltzer-Richard paradigm, according to which the demand for redistribution reflects a balance between the incentive problems imposed by higher taxes and the aspirations of the middle and lower classes.[26] According to Meltzer and Richard, selfish considerations (that is, who benefits from greater redistribution and who does not) affect the demand for redistribution, but these considerations are not absolutely blind in that they take into account the adverse effect of excessive redistribution on economic efficiency. Since redistribution negatively affects individuals with a higher socioeconomic level (whether perceived or real), the rich will be more likely to oppose it than the middle class or poor. Likewise, wealthy individuals will be more likely to support market outcomes, at least under the premise that all state interventions involve some form of redistribution.

The third group of variables includes perceptions about past mobility and expectations about future mobility. Optimism about past and future mobility should lower the demand for redistribution because individuals with high expectations of upward mobility—even if currently located at the lower end of the distribution—anticipate the losses (for themselves and for their descendants) of any future attempt to transfer income from the wealthy to the poor. Benabou and Ok emphasize the empirical relevance of this idea, known as the POUM hypothesis (that is, prospect of upward mobility).[27] According to these authors, only a quarter of the households in the United States have a real income that is above the average income, but two-thirds have an expected income above the average. Optimism about mobility may reduce the demand for redistribution through a different channel. The higher the mobility expectations, the more optimistic the individual's assessment of social justice, and thus the lower the individual demand for redistribution.

The fourth and last group of variables comprises opinions about social justice and the fairness of market outcomes. Does the respondent think that connections are fundamental? That hard work does not pay? That opportunities are poorly distributed? Or that poverty is caused by external circumstances?

26. Meltzer and Richard (1981).
27. Benabou and Ok (2001).

Alesina and Angeletos argue that social preferences, in general, and the taste for fairness, in particular, affect the demand for redistribution.[28] Overall, if individuals perceive an unfair order in which economic results do not correspond to the effort and ability of each individual, they will be more prone to support redistribution and reject market outcomes.

In conclusion, the previous discussion suggests that the poor, those who have low expectations of mobility, and those who believe that market outcomes are unfair will demand a high level of redistribution and a strong role for the state. In the following analysis, the signs of the estimated coefficients constitute an empirical basis for comparing the different theoretical paradigms mentioned in the previous paragraphs.[29]

Table 8 presents the individual determinants of the demand for redistribution. Explanatory variables are presented according to the four groups of variables mentioned above. General socioeconomic characteristics are presented first, followed by the socioeconomic measures, the mobility indicators, and the direct questions on perceptions of social justice. Two different specifications are presented, one without country fixed effects and one with. The estimations were implemented using a probit model: the table shows marginal effects (or average effects for binary variables) accompanied by standard errors corresponding to the original parameters.

Preferences for redistribution are lower among men than women, and they do not vary substantially according to age or marital status. They are lower for individuals in the higher quintiles, as well as for those who declare that their income is sufficient to satisfy all their needs. The difference between the first and the fifth quintile is more than eight percentage points. The difference between those who declare that their current income allows them to save and those who state that they have great economic difficulties is also about eight percentage points. In general, the results indicate the existence of a negative correlation between socioeconomic status and the demand for redistribution. These findings are consistent with the Meltzer-Richard paradigm mentioned above, in that individuals appear to take selfish considerations into account when expressing their support for redistribution.

The reported relationship between socioeconomic status and the demand for redistribution appears to be stronger than the relationship reported in

28. Alesina and Angeletos (2005).

29. This informal discussion of the determinants of the demand for redistribution follows a tradition in the empirical literature on the subject. See, for example, the articles already mentioned by Fong (2001), Corneo and Grüner (2002), and Alesina and La Ferrara (2005).

TABLE 8.   **Individual Determinants of Preferences for Redistribution**

Independent variable	(1)		(2)	
	Coefficient	Std. error	Coefficient	Std. error
Socioeconomic characteristics				
Man	−0.0314	0.0083	−0.0285	0.0083
Age	0.0011	0.0003	0.0012	0.0003
Married	−0.0015	0.0084	0.0000	0.0084
Employee	0.0063	0.0083	0.0113	0.0085
Socioeconomic level				
Income is not enough; difficulties	−0.0089	0.0136	−0.0122	0.0139
Income is just enough	−0.0481	0.0138	−0.0430	0.0143
Income is enough to save	−0.0808	0.0195	−0.0791	0.0200
Quintile 2	−0.0193	0.0132	−0.0216	0.0133
Quintile 3	−0.0348	0.0133	−0.0366	0.0134
Quintile 4	−0.0531	0.0136	−0.0514	0.0137
Quintile 5	−0.0840	0.0141	−0.0807	0.0143
Perceptions about mobility				
Past mobility	−0.0157	0.0044	−0.0197	0.0046
Future mobility	0.0093	0.0043	0.0036	0.0044
Opinions about social justice				
Success depends on connections	0.0690	0.0095	0.0580	0.0097
Hard work does not guarantee success	0.0226	0.0079	0.0187	0.0080
Summary statistic				
Fixed effects by country	No		Yes	
No. observations	13,223		13,223	
Pseudo R^2	0.0166		0.0402	

Source: Author's calculations, based on Latinobarómetro (1996).

studies for the United States and the Europe.[30] That is, preferences for re-distribution vary more widely with socioeconomic class in Latin America than in some developed countries. This result is consistent with the higher levels of inequality observed in Latin America.

The previous result can be examined rigorously based on data from the 1996 Latinobarómetro survey, which included a Spanish sample (2,481 observations). To compare the pattern of variation in preferences for redistribution according to socioeconomic quintiles, I re-estimated a version of equation 2. The new specification included two additional terms: a dummy variable that identified individuals living in Spain and an interaction term of this variable with each of the dummy variables designating the quintiles. Figure 8 presents the results. The comparison indicates that while Latin America displays a strong monotonic

30. Fong (2001); Alesina and La Ferrara (2005); Corneo and Grüner (2002).

FIGURE 8.   Differences in Preferences for Distribution, by Quintile

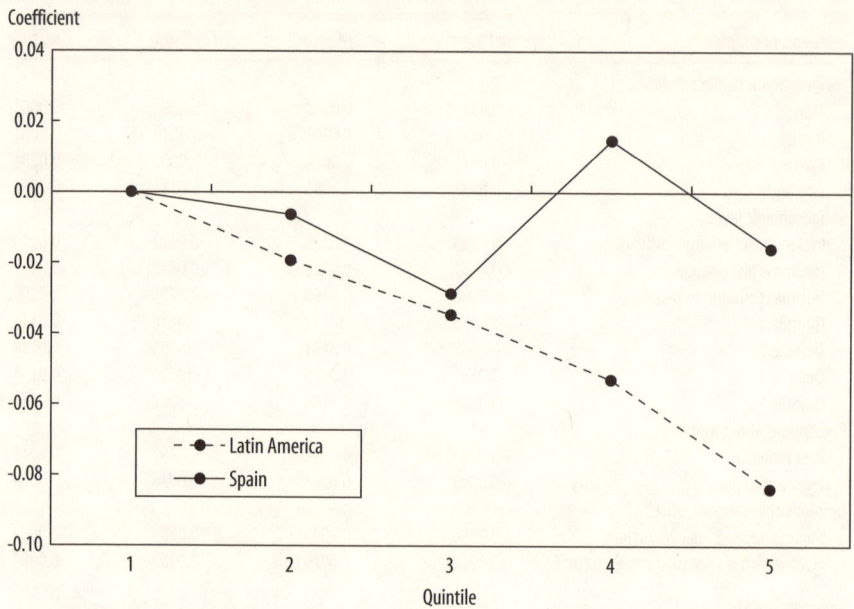

Source: Latinobarómetro (1996).

relationship between socioeconomic level and the demand for redistribution, in Spain the relationship tends to be erratic. Overall, class division appears to correlate strongly with political preferences in Latin America, but not in Spain.

Finally, the results of Table 8 are also (partially) consistent with the Alesina-Angeletos hypothesis. Individuals that experience higher mobility are less likely to favor redistribution, while those who declare that connections are fundamental (and that hard work is not rewarded) are more likely to support redistribution. The latter difference may help explain some of the variations between countries in the demand for redistribution. For example, if the percentage of individuals who believe that connections are important decreases by 30 percentage points, the percentage of those who are very much in agreement with redistribution will decrease by nearly two points.

Table 9 presents the correlates of the support for market outcomes. Independent variables are the same in the previous exercise. The results show that both men and employed individuals are more likely to declare their support for market outcomes. The same occurs with individuals belonging to the higher quintiles and those reporting that their income covers their needs. Differences

TABLE 9.   Individual Determinants of Support for Market Economy

Independent variable	(1)		(2)	
	Coefficient	Std. error	Coefficient	Std. error
Socioeconomic characteristics				
Man	0.0378	0.0090	0.0419	0.0091
Age	0.0003	0.0003	0.0006	0.0003
Married	−0.0184	0.0090	−0.0172	0.0091
Employee	0.0225	0.0091	0.0158	0.0093
Socioeconomic level				
Income is not enough; difficulties	−0.0016	0.0147	0.0131	0.0149
Income is just enough	0.0213	0.0147	0.0407	0.0151
Income is enough to save	0.0597	0.0182	0.0903	0.0183
Quintile 2	0.0199	0.0137	0.0202	0.0138
Quintile 3	0.0354	0.0137	0.0336	0.0138
Quintile 4	0.0527	0.0137	0.0493	0.0139
Quintile 5	0.0684	0.0138	0.0654	0.0140
Perceptions about mobility				
Past mobility	0.0109	0.0027	0.0152	0.0028
Future mobility	0.0141	0.0025	0.0144	0.0026
Opinions about social justice				
Success depends on connections	−0.0617	0.0100	−0.0660	0.0102
Hard work does not guarantees success	−0.0102	0.0092	−0.0223	0.0095
Summary statistic				
Fixed effects by country	No		Yes	
No. observations	13,660		13,660	
Pseudo R^2	0.0114		0.0335	

Source: Author's calculations, based on Latinobarómetro (2000).

are substantial, with seven points between the first and the fifth quintiles and six points between those who are able to save and those who report great financial difficulties. As before, the results highlight a significant gap between socioeconomic groups regarding their attitudes toward market outcomes. Class divisions correlate with political opinions, a result consistent with the Meltzer-Richard paradigm.

Support for market outcomes is also greater among those reporting greater past mobility and those expecting greater future mobility, whereas market outcomes are less likely to be supported by those who are pessimistic about the distribution of opportunities. That is, negative perceptions about the extent of social justice may erode support for market outcomes. If the percentage of those believing that opportunities are unevenly distributed increases by 30 percentage points, the percentage of those supporting market economies will decrease by a little more than two points. Again, the Alesina-Angeletos hypotheses seem to hold.

TABLE 10. Individual Determinants of Support for Privatization

| | (1) | | (2) | |
Independent variable	Coefficient	Std. error	Coefficient	Std. error
Socioeconomic characteristics				
Man	0.0131	0.0080	0.0109	0.0088
Age	−0.0003	0.0003	0.0000	0.0003
Married	−0.0162	0.0089	−0.0090	0.0090
Employee	0.0203	0.0089	0.0176	0.0090
Socioeconomic level				
Income is not enough; difficulties	0.0015	0.0145	0.0160	0.0147
Income is just enough	0.0517	0.0146	0.0806	0.0150
Income is enough to save	0.0845	0.0188	0.1274	0.0195
Quintile 2	0.0123	0.0137	0.0137	0.0138
Quintile 3	0.0249	0.0138	0.0230	0.0139
Quintile 4	0.0694	0.0140	0.0678	0.0142
Quintile 5	0.0830	0.0142	0.0790	0.0144
Perceptions about mobility				
Past mobility	0.0152	0.0027	0.0170	0.0027
Future mobility	0.0156	0.0025	0.0170	0.0025
Opinions about social justice				
Success depends on connections	−0.0894	0.0100	−0.0714	0.0102
Hard work does not guarantees success	−0.0522	0.0091	−0.0467	0.0093
Summary statistic				
Fixed effects by country	No		Yes	
No. observations	13,961		13,961	
Pseudo R^2	0.0239		0.0447	

Source: Author's calculations, based on Latinobarómetro (2000).

Table 10 presents the individual determinants of the support for privatization. The results are similar to the previous findings, and the conclusions are even more definitive. Differences among socioeconomic groups are higher in this case, as are differences associated with perceptions of past mobility and expectations of future mobility. Likewise, the connection between perceptions of social justice and support for privatization is stronger than that between perceptions of social justice and support for market outcomes. In sum, negative perceptions about mobility and equality of opportunity greatly diminish support for privatization. Once again, the Meltzer-Richard, POUM, and Alesina-Angeletos paradigms are consistent with the empirical results.

Finally, Table 11 presents the individual determinants of being leftist. Connections between this variable and the different explanatory factors are not very strong. Being leftist decreases with age and is lower among those who are satisfied with their current income level than among those experiencing

TABLE 11.   Individual Determinants of Political Preferences: Being Leftist

Independent variable	(1)		(2)	
	Coefficient	Std. error	Coefficient	Std. error
Socioeconomic characteristics				
Man	0.0169	0.0076	0.0174	0.0075
Age	−0.0017	0.0002	−0.0017	0.0003
Married	0.0045	0.0076	0.0056	0.0076
Employee	−0.0053	0.0077	−0.0040	0.0077
Socioeconomic level				
Income is not enough; difficulties	−0.0112	0.0121	−0.0114	0.0122
Income is just enough	−0.0302	0.0122	−0.0256	0.0125
Income is enough to save	−0.0422	0.0139	−0.0359	0.0144
Quintile 2	0.0113	0.0118	0.0115	0.0118
Quintile 3	0.0046	0.0117	0.0051	0.0117
Quintile 4	−0.0011	0.0117	−0.0017	0.0117
Quintile 5	−0.0076	0.0117	−0.0109	0.0115
Perceptions about mobility				
Past mobility	−0.0007	0.0023	−0.0013	0.0023
Future mobility	−0.0011	0.0021	−0.0013	0.0021
Opinions about social justice				
Success depends on connections	0.0045	0.0084	0.0105	0.0084
Hard work does not guarantees success	0.0255	0.0076	0.0258	0.0076
Summary statistic				
Fixed effects by country	No		Yes	
No. observations	11,747		11,747	
Pseudo R^2	0.008		0.0221	

Source: Author's calculations, based on Latinobarómetro (2000).

financial difficulties. Individuals who believe that poverty is caused by external circumstances are also more likely to be leftist. In general, however, this variable does not seem to have a close relationship with the different explanatory factors analyzed here.[31] Being leftist thus seems to be a less predictable political preference than those analyzed above.[32]

31. I also estimated the regressions presented in this section controlling for happiness. I constructed the variable based on a Latinobarómetro question regarding the level of satisfaction with one's life. Again, answers were dichotomized to facilitate the econometric exercises. The coefficient for the happiness dummy was either insignificant or relatively small, and the results presented in the paper are robust to the inclusion of the happiness variable.

32. I repeated the regressions that had support for the market economy, privatization, and being leftist as dependent variables using the 2005 Latinobarómetro survey data. The coefficients for subjective income generally have the same signs and significance, whereas the results for each of the socioeconomic quintiles are inconclusive. Support for privatization in Latin America has diminished substantially; it has therefore become less dependent on socioeconomic status.

Conclusions

Three general conclusions can be drawn from this paper. First, preferences for redistribution are very strong in Latin America, and support for market outcomes is weak. Second, support for redistribution, market outcomes, and privatization varies widely across social classes. For example, despite strong support for redistribution, on average, differences among rich and poor are substantial and larger than in other regions of the world. Third, individuals with pessimistic views on social justice and equality of opportunity are much more likely to support redistribution and to disagree with market outcomes and privatization. These results are consistent with the existence of social preferences and the Meltzer-Richard paradigm, and less supportive in general of the POUM hypothesis. This does not, of course, represent definitive proof of these paradigms. Rather, the results must be interpreted with caution, given the descriptive nature of the exercise.

These conclusions shed light on some of the most important social trends of the last decades in Latin America, as well as on some of the most intense current political debates. For example, the increase in social expenditure that took place in conjunction with the democratization process may be understood as the political materialization of the high demand for redistribution.[33] Likewise, the ideological polarization that affects many of the countries of the region, frequently characterized by deep class divisions, may be partially understood as the result of political differences between rich and poor. Also, political instability problems may be related to the inability of public policies to accelerate social mobility and to change pessimistic perceptions of social justice. Democracy appears to have accomplished the easy part (that is, increase social expenditures), but to have been incapable of doing the difficult part (namely, increase social justice).

In general, the results of this paper emphasize the existence of a climate of opinion similar to the one highlighted by Hirschman and Rothschild more than three decades ago.[34] According to these authors, when the majority starts doubting the possibilities for mobility, the challenges of growth and equality cannot be approached in sequence. On the contrary, when most people are impatient and pessimistic about social justice, growth and equity should be resolved simultaneously. Therein lies the biggest challenge for Latin American countries in the years ahead.

33. In Latin America as a whole, social expenditures increased from 8 percent to 13 percent of GDP between 1970 and 2000 (according to the International Monetary Fund's *International Financial Statistics*). Freedom House's index of democratic liberties doubled in the same period.

34. Hirschman and Rothschild (1973).

Appendix: Survey Questions

This appendix presents the specific questions taken from the 1996 and 2000 Latinobarómetro surveys and the 1994–99 World Values Survey (second wave). The questions were used to define the variables in this study, and the data served as the basis for running the regressions.

The 1996 Latinobarómetro Survey

The dependent variable assessing the demand for redistribution is drawn from the following question:

Do you consider that it should be the government's responsibility to . . . reduce the differences between rich and poor?

Yes, of course	1
Yes, maybe	2
Maybe not	3
Of course not	4
Unknown	8
No answer	0

Five questions from the 1996 survey were used to define independent variables, as follows.

—Subjective income:

Do your total wage and the total family income allow you to satisfactorily cover all your needs? How would you define your situation?

It is more than enough, and you can save	1
It is just enough, and you do not have great difficulties	2
It is not enough, and you have difficulties	3
It is not enough, and you have great difficulties	4
Unknown	8
No answer	0

—Past mobility:

Do you believe that the opportunities to improve your level of well-being today are much better, better, the same, worse, or much worse than the opportunities your parents had?

Much better	1
Better	2
The same	3

Worse 4

Much worse 5

Unknown 8

No answer 0

—Future mobility:

Looking into the future, do you believe that the opportunities your children will have to improve their level of well-being are currently much better, better, the same, worse, or much worse than the opportunities that your parents had?

Much better 1

Better 2

The same 3

Worse 4

Much worse 5

Unknown 8

No answer 0

—Connections and whether hard work pays off:

Do you agree with the following statements?
Success in life depends on your connections.
Hard work does not guarantee having success.

Yes 1

No 2

Unknown 8

No answer 0

—Happiness:

In general terms, would you way that you are satisfied with your life? Would you say you are . . . ?

Very satisfied 1

Quite satisfied 2

Satisfied 3

Not very satisfied 4

Don't know/No answer 0

The 2000 Latinobarómetro Survey

Two dependent variables were drawn from the 2000 Latinobarómetro survey.

—Privatization and the market economy

Do you (1) strongly agree, (2) agree, (3) disagree, or (4) strongly disagree with each of the phrases I am going to read to you:
Privatizations have been beneficial to the country.
The market economy is the most convenient economy for the country.
Strongly agree 1
Agree 2
Disagree 3
Strongly disagree 4
Unknown 8
No answer 0

—Political preferences:

We normally speak of "left" and "right" in politics. On a scale where zero is the left and ten the right, where would you place yourself?
The 2000 survey was used to develop three independent variables.

—Past and future mobility:

Imagine a staircase with ten steps, in which the poorest are on the first step and the richest are on the tenth step. Where would you place yourself? Where would you place your parents? Where do you think your children will be located?

Very poor   Very rich
1   2   3   4   5   6   7   8   9   10

Unknown 00
No answer 98
None 96

—Unequal opportunities:

Opinions differ regarding equal opportunities to escape poverty in _____(country). Some people consider that the economic situation of _____(country) gives all _____(nationality) the same opportunity to escape poverty; others consider that _____ (nationality) do not have equal opportunities to escape poverty. Which of the two is closest to your opinion?

They have equal opportunities 1
They do not have equal opportunities 2
Unknown 8
No answer 0

—Poverty caused by circumstances:

Opinions differ regarding the causes of poverty in _____(country). Some people think people are poor because they make no effort to try to improve their life conditions; others consider that people are poor because of circumstances outside their control. Which of the two is closest to your opinion?
Lack of effort 1
Due to circumstances 2
Unknown/No answer 0

The 1994–99 World Values Survey (Second Wave)

Two independent variables were drawn from the World Values Survey.

—Opportunities for escaping poverty:

In your opinion, do most poor people in this country have a chance of escaping from poverty, or is there very little chance of escaping?
They have a chance
There is very little chance
Don't know

—Hard work guarantees success:

Where would you place yourself on a scale of one to ten, in which one is the idea that "In the long run, hard work usually brings a better life" and ten is the idea that "Hard work doesn't generally bring success—it's more a matter of luck and connections"?
Don't know equals 99.

Comments

Carol Graham: This is an excellent paper on a topic that is important to Latin America's future, in general, and the sustainability of its reforms, in particular. Alejandro Gaviria makes nice use of empirical data from both Latin America and the United States, and he uses sound methodology. I agree with the general direction of the findings, and much of our own work on inequality supports that general direction. However, the story is more complex than the one that Gaviria tells, particularly with regard to preferences for redistribution. In this latter area, our findings depart quite markedly from his.

The paper lacks a discussion of what mobility indicator is most important to attitudes about redistribution, future behavior, and so on. There are many different views on this issue (as well as some empirical results), and a discussion would have enriched the paper. I personally think that attitudes about longer-term trends—and children's future—are the most important. Here I am not so sure that Latin Americans are as far from the United States as the paper suggests. While 56 percent of U.S. citizens in the General Social Survey (GSS) think that their children will live better than they, 55 percent of Latin Americans think so. That is a surprisingly small and insignificant difference. To some extent, this reflects hope and optimism as much as anything else (in that happier people tend to have higher prospects of upward mobility, and the correlation is stronger for more speculative questions about the future). Yet it also suggests that Latin Americans retain similar hope for the future mobility of their children, despite more difficult objective constraints than people in the United States.

The paper notes that almost half of Latin Americans think that their socio-economic status is the same as that of their parents, while a remarkably high 36 percent of Americans think that their status is the same as or worse than that of their parents. These differences are not that great, given the wildly different economic contexts and differences in macroeconomic stability. The two regions also seem to hold relatively similar views of the causes of poverty. In

Latin America, the paper reports that 36 percent of respondents think that poverty is caused by circumstances other than skills and personal efforts. In the U.S. GSS, 46 percent of respondents think that insufficient effort is the reason for poverty. This is different, but it not as far off as one might have guessed. Moreover, almost 80 percent of U.S. respondents think that the lack of jobs is an explanation that is somewhat or very important to poverty.

In terms of actual mobility differences between Latin America and the United States, the paper notes differences in intergenerational educational mobility. The links between parents' and children's education are strongest at the top end of the distribution in Latin America. This is not surprising, not only because of the limited supply of higher education that the paper notes, but because of all of the other barriers that members of poor households face in trying to reach university levels of education in the region. The general concavity of the distribution for the region may also reflect the previously strong incentives for completing secondary school (such as a middle-class lifestyle, stable job in the public sector, and so on), which now have changed. The kinds of jobs that used to be available to someone with just secondary education are far fewer and less desirable than they were before; the bubble in the distribution may be explained by these earlier and more generalized investments in secondary education.

Income mobility is a trickier story to tell because of data problems. Peru provides some anecdotal, but provocative, evidence. An important caveat here is that these data address intragenerational rather than intergenerational mobility, which is different from the focus of the paper although not orthogonal to the broader discussion. My coauthor and I compare mobility rates over a ten-year period for Peru and the United States, and we find more relative mobility in Peru.[1] Some of this is explained by macroeconomic volatility in Peru, but we counterbalance this effect by using expenditure rather than income data for Peru, which fluctuate less. Regardless, the results are suggestive of rather fluid short-term mobility changes. These may or may not be welfare enhancing, depending on the starting point and the direction of change, but it is hardly a story of complete stagnation. Our research also finds that perceptions of mobility are more negative than actual rates, and they are most negative for those with the most upward mobility.

Another area in which my views differ from Gaviria's involves the direct link between attitudes about redistribution and wealth. I think this has changed over time in the region. The paper relies on 1996 and 2000 data. My work

---

1. Graham and Pettinato (2002).

with Sandip Sukhtankar indicates that the link between wealth and support for market reforms has decreased over time since 2000.[2] We also find a weaker link between wealth and believing that the distribution of income is unfair than the general argument in the paper suggests. The coefficient on wealth is insignificant. Instead, we find a stronger link with perceptions of future mobility (as shown by the strong and significant coefficient on the POUMentitle variable, which asks people how long it will take to reach their desired standard of living). A counterintuitive result of our study is that the belief that taxes should be low even if welfare spending suffers is negatively correlated to wealth. The result did not change when we performed the exercise with just the top half of the distribution (that is, those who would be liable to pay taxes). These findings depart significantly from those for the United States, where income and support for redistribution are strongly and negatively correlated (as is support for redistribution and happiness).

Regardless of whether the Latin American results are due to enlightened self-interest on the part of elites or distrust of the state's capacity to redistribute fairly on the part of the poor, they do depart from the findings in the paper, and they are based on 2002 data rather than earlier data. Moreover, the early part of the decade was characterized by significant crisis, as well as reform fatigue that seems to have affected both the wealthy and the poor.

Our research on inequality and individual welfare, however, generally supports the paper's central hypothesis about what inequality signals to respondents in the region. Research with Andy Felton indicates that inequality makes the wealthy happier, on average, and the poor much less happy.[3] When we break down our wealth variable into the average wealth for the respondent's country of residence and his or her distance from the average, we find that average levels have no effect while the relative distance has a strong effect. We performed this exercise using both the average income level of the country and the average income level for cities of different sizes in the country of residence (for small, medium-sized, and large cities).

To provide a sense of the order of magnitude, we compare poor peasants in Chile and Honduras. Even though the poor Chilean is twice as wealthy as the Honduran (that is, average wealth levels are twice as high in the poorest quintile in Chile as in the same quintile in Honduras), the peasant in Chile is less happy (by half a percentage point) because his or her distance from the average is greater. The rich Honduran, meanwhile, is less wealthy than the

2. Graham and Sukhtankar(2004).
3. Graham and Felton (2006).

rich Chilean, but is happier because his or her distance from the average is greater. When we look at perceptions of inequality and future mobility, the results are even stronger. We attribute our results to what inequality signals to the average respondent in the region: persistent advantage for the rich and disadvantage for the poor.

This illustrative example supports the paper's general findings about the negative effects that inequality of income and opportunity seem to have in the region. I am not convinced, however, that they translate so clearly into support for redistribution. I think this may have changed over time. Indeed, researchers to date have only scratched the surface of the relationship between actual mobility rates, perceptions of those rates, and support for redistribution, both in the OECD and in Latin America. In the United States, perceptions of future mobility remain far more optimistic than trends in recent decades suggest they should be.[4] It is possible, although not likely, that trends in Latin America are slightly better than public opinion assesses them to be, given a history of persistent and high levels of inequality.

I conclude by reiterating that this paper provides a very sound treatment of an important subject. I would argue, though, for further discussion of what kind of mobility (own experience, children's, and so on) matters most and links most closely to attitudes about redistribution, as well as more attention to how time trends in the region may have changed these attitudes in a way that is not reflected in the paper.

Luis H. B. Braido: This short note presents a few thoughts on the work by Alejandro Gaviria. In its first part, Gaviria's paper presents evidence suggesting that intergenerational mobility is much lower in Latin America than in some developed countries, such as the United States. It identifies a positive correlation between the educational level of parents and their children in Latin America. On average, children whose parents have completed college present approximately equal years of schooling in both Latin America and the United States. This picture changes completely, however, when one compares children whose parents have not completed primary school. Latin American children whose parents were not formally educated seem to be much more likely to remain uneducated than their counterparts in the United States.

These findings confirm the anecdotal evidence on the subject. From a normative point of view, public policies intended to equalize educational opportunities for all children should be a priority for the region. One impor-

4. See Sawhill (2007).

tant point must be noted, however. Most policy studies use literacy and years of schooling as proxies for education, so many educational policies across the world focus primarily on these two aspects of the problem. Despite the importance of those policies, educational quality remains significantly hetero-geneous across the schools available for children with different family back-grounds. The school environment and quality of teachers are not homogeneous across neighborhoods, partly because educated parents spend more time super-vising the education of their children.

Gaviria's initial results also suggest that Latin Americans are very pessimistic about their own mobility experience, but relatively optimistic about the social mobility opportunities for their children. This evidence is based on qualitative data, which are naturally subject to the usual criticisms regarding how to compare subjective answers that depend on personal perceptions. Nevertheless, these findings may reflect recent social programs that have been implemented in the region, which improved the welfare and educational opportunities of children. Programs such as *Escola para Todos* and *Bolsa Família* in Brazil, *Oportunidades* (formerly *Progresa*) in Mexico, *Programa de Asignación Familiar* (PRAF) in Honduras, the Programme of Advancement through Health and Education (PATH) in Jamaica, and *Bono de Desarrollo Humano* in Ecuador, among others, might have raised Latin American expectations about social mobility for future generations.

The second part of Gaviria's paper identifies correlations between individ-uals' socioeconomic characteristics and their preferences for different public policies. The paper reports that some individuals—namely, those who are poor, or have not yet experienced social upgrades, or believe that socioeconomic success depends on external circumstances and connections—typically present stronger demands for redistributive government policies and are more likely to oppose the privatization programs recently conducted in the region.

These results also confirm casual observation, but they are hard to interpret. From the individual perspective, it seems natural that those who have more to benefit from social programs and those who are more pessimistic about social justice are more likely to support governmental redistributive inter-ventions, while taxpayers are more likely to worry about the long-run impact of these programs. However, since the data used come from different regions and countries, one should worry about the extent to which these correlations reflect different socioeconomic equilibria, in which case beliefs may be self-reinforcing and the direction of causality may thus be harder to ascertain.

Consider, for instance, the model analyzed in Alesina and Angeletos, in which agents combine capital and labor effort to produce goods by means of a stochastic production function.[1] Redistribution policies, if desired, must be financed by distortionary taxes. The authors explore two possible economic equilibria. In the first case, agents believe that the competitive equilibrium is fair and do not support redistribution policies. In equilibrium, most of the individual income depends on the amount of capital and effort employed in production (as opposed to the stochastic shock). The society's original rejection of redistributive policies is thus adequate in this equilibrium. A second possibility occurs when agents originally believe that competition is unfair. In this case, they support insurance policies that redistribute income after the productivity shock is realized. In equilibrium, there are weaker incentives to invest in capital and labor effort, and most of the production depends on luck (that is, on the productive shock). Consequently, the society's original support for insurance (that is, redistributive policies) is also justified.

Data from different locations in Latin America may reflect different socio-economic equilibria. For instance, popular support for redistributive polices and the amount of public resources available for them vary considerably across areas with different characteristics, such as the degree of urbanization (that is, metropolitan versus rural areas) and the main economic activity (industry versus service economies). Therefore, interpreting the positive correlation between individuals' characteristics and demand for social policies is not straightforward.

1. Alesina and Angeletos (2005).

References

Alesina, Alberto, and George-Marios Angeletos. 2005. "Fairness and Redistribution." *American Economic Review* 95(4): 960–80.

Alesina, Alberto, and Nicola Fuchs Schuendeln. 2005. "Good-bye Lenin (or Not?): The Effect of Communism on People's Preferences." Working Paper 11700. Cambridge, Mass.: National Bureau of Economic Research.

Alesina, Alberto, and Edward Glaeser. 2004. *Fighting Poverty in the U.S. and Europe: A World of Difference.* Oxford University Press.

Alesina, Alberto, and Eliana La Ferrara. 2005. "Preferences for Redistribution in the Land of Opportunities." *Journal of Public Economics* 89(5–6): 897–931.

Andrade, Eduardo, and others. 2004. "Do Borrowing Constraints Decrease Inter-generational Mobility? Evidence from Brazil." São Paulo: Banco Nacional de Desenvolvimento Econômico e Social (BNDES).

Behrman Jere R., Alejandro Gaviria, and Miguel Székely. 2001. "Intergenerational Mobility in Latin America." *Economía* 2(1): 1–44.

Benabou, Roland, and Efe A. Ok. 2001. "Social Mobility and the Demand for Redistribution: The POUM Hypothesis." *Quarterly Journal of Economics* 116(2): 447–87.

Benabou, Roland, and Jean Tirole. 2005. "Belief in a Just World and Redistributive Policies." Working Paper 11208. Cambridge, Mass.: National Bureau of Economic Research.

Bourguignon, François, Francisco H. G. Ferreira, and Marta Menéndez. 2003. "Inequality of Outcomes and Inequality of Opportunities in Brazil." Working Paper 630. University of Michigan, William Davidson Institute.

Camerer, Colin F. 2003. *Behavioral Game Theory: Experiments in Strategic Inter-action.* Princeton University Press.

Corneo, Giacomo, and Hans Peter Grüner. 2002. "Individual Preferences for Political Redistribution." *Journal of Public Economics* 83(1): 83–107.

Dahan, Momi, and Alejandro Gaviria. 2001. "Sibling Correlations and Intergenerational Mobility in Latin America." *Economic Development and Cultural Change* 49(3): 537–54.

Deaton, Angus. 1997. *The Analysis of Households Surveys.* Johns Hopkins University Press.

Ferreira, Francisco H. G., and Michael Walton. 2006. "Inequality of Opportunity and Economic Development." Policy Research Working Paper 3816. Washington: World Bank.

Filmer, Deon, and Lant Pritchett. 1998. "The Effects of Household Wealth on Educational Attainment around the World: Demographic and Health Survey Evidence." Washington: World Bank, Development Economics Research Group (DECRG).

———. 2001. "Estimating Wealth Effects without Expenditure Data or Tears: An Application to Education Enrollments in States of India." *Demography* 38(1): 115–32.

Fong, Christina. 2001. "Social Preferences, Self-Interest, and the Demand for Redistribution." *Journal of Public Economics* 82(2): 225–46.

General Social Survey. Various years. University of Chicago, National Opinion Research Center, National Data Program for the Sciences (www.norc.org/GSS+Website).

Graham, Carol. 2000. "The Political Economy of Mobility." In *New Markets, New Opportunities? Economic and Social Mobility in a Changing World,* edited by Nancy Birdsall and Carol Graham, pp. 225–67. Brookings.

Graham, Carol, and Andrew Felton. 2005. "Life Satisfaction in Seventeen Latin American Countries." Brookings. Mimeographed.

———. 2006. "Inequality and Happiness: Insights from Latin America." *Journal of Economic Inequality* 4(1): 107–22.

Graham, Carol, and Stefano Pettinato. 2002. *Happiness and Hardship: Opportunity and Insecurity in New Market Economies.* Brookings.

Graham, Carol, and Sandip Sukhtankar. 2004. "Does Economic Crisis Reduce Support for Markets and Democracy in Latin America? Some Evidence from Surveys of Public Opinion and Well-Being." *Journal of Latin American Studies* 36(2): 349–78.

Hirschman, Albert O., and Michael Rothschild. 1973. "The Changing Tolerance for Income Inequality in the Course of Economic Growth." *Quarterly Journal of Economics* 87(4): 544–66.

Latinobarómetro. Various years. Santiago: Latinobarómetro Corporation (www.latino barometro.org).

Lipset, Seymour M. 1966. "Elections: The Expression of the Democratic Class Struggle." In *Class, Status, and Power,* edited by Reinhard Bendix and Seymour M. Lipset. New York: Free Press.

———. 1992. "Foreword: The Political Consequences of Social Mobility." In *Social Mobility and Political Attitudes: Comparative Perspectives,* edited by Frederick C. Turner. New Brunswick: Transaction Publishers.

Meltzer, Allan H., and Scott F. Richard. 1981. "A Rational Theory of the Size of Government." *Journal of Political Economy* 89(5): 914–27.

Mulligan, Casey B. 1997. *Parental Priorities and Economic Inequality.* University of Chicago Press.

Piketty, Thomas. 1995. "Social Mobility and Redistributive Politics." *Quarterly Journal of Economics* 110(3): 551–84.

Sawhill, Isabel. 2007. "Do Open Borders Produce Greater Happiness? An Under-analyzed Question." In *Brookings Trade Forum 2006: Global Labor Markets?* edited by Susan Collins and Carol Graham, pp. 245–50. Brookings.

Tocqueville, Alexis de. [1835] 2003. *Democracy in America.* New York: Penguin Classics.

World Values Survey. Various years. Stockholm: World Values Survey Association.

MAURICIO MESQUITA MOREIRA
EDUARDO MENDOZA

Regional Integration: What Is in It for CARICOM?

Economic and political integration has long been a painful issue on the Caribbean agenda. As one analyst states, "The recognition of the seminal truth that only a unified Caribbean, politically and economically, can save the region from its fatal particularism is at least a century old."[1] Despite this early awareness, the first ambitious and wide-reaching policy initiative was only implemented in 1958, with the short-lived West Indian Federation. The collapse of this initiative in 1962 did not mean, however, the end of the integrationist ideal, which flared up again six years later in the form of the less ambitious Caribbean Free Trade Association (CARIFTA). Countries in the region have since raised the stakes, aiming at deeper, broader, and more complex forms of integration. In 1973, they established the Caribbean Community and Common Market (CARICOM), which sought to establish a customs union and policy and functional cooperation. In the 1990s, a number of culturally and economically diverse nations joined the agreement, and ambitious targets were set to create a single market and economy with full factor mobility and harmonization of economic policies (namely, the CARICOM Single Market and Economy, or CSME).

All this integrationist zeal begs the question of whether politics or economics (or both) is the driving force behind the movement. Exploring the underlying forces may provide clues to the rationality of the process and, therefore, its chances of success. Politicians and economists alike have already made numerous efforts to clarify these issues and to draw lessons from the region's experience with over three decades of integration. Even so, some gaps of

Moreira and Mendoza are with the Inter-American Development Bank, Department of Integration.

We thank Andrés Rodríguez, Irene Brambilla, and Stephen Meardon for their very helpful comments.

1. Lewis (1968, p. 363).

understanding remain about motivation, rationality, and results. Given that politicians in the region are building in the midst of what may arguably be the deepest and most comprehensive process of integration in the western hemisphere, the time could not be more opportune for a concerted effort to fill these gaps.

The rest of the paper is divided into three sections: the next section draws on the literature on trade, growth, and regional agreements to discuss the motivation behind the Caribbean drive for integration. We argue, with the help of an empirical growth model, that the traditional gains from regional integration are bound to be limited for three reasons: the Caribbean economies' openness, the relatively small common market, and the countries' similar factor endowments. We also argue, however, that integration may produce substantial gains in the area of nontradables.

The subsequent section uses descriptive data and a gravity model to discuss the results of integration over the last three decades in the light of the issues raised earlier. The analysis of descriptive data indicates that regional preferences have had a positive, though modest, impact on intraregional trade, with most of the gains happening before CARICOM was signed. The gravity model confirms the trade-creating nature of the preferences, but suggests that the gains have been declining since the 1970s, despite (or because of) the trade-creating reforms of the 1990s.

The final section summarizes the main findings and conclusions, with a focus on what is arguably the main message of this paper. Specifically, integration can generate significant benefits in nontradables as a result of regional cooperation in the countries' social and physical infrastructure, and these gains are likely to dwarf the traditional gains from trade.

Motivation

The literature on regional agreements suggests that such pacts are inspired by the interplay of political and economic arguments.[2] The political motivations range from regional security to bargaining power. That is, countries sign regional agreements because they believe integration will reduce political and military rivalry among member countries (as in the case of the European Union and the Southern Common Market, or MERCOSUR), reduce the political and military threat of countries outside the agreement (for example, the Association

2. World Bank (2000); IDB (2002).

of Southeast Asian Nations, or ASEAN), and increase their bargaining power in international negotiations.

None of these political arguments seems to have carried much weight in the case of the Caribbean—or, to be more precise, of the Anglo-Saxon Caribbean—with the possible exception of the bargaining argument in later stages of CARICOM integration. That does not mean, however, that politics did not play a part. In fact, regional integration appears to have emerged as a tool for political independence. Both the colonizer (Great Britain) and the colonies (West Indies) at some point shared the belief that, given the small size of the administrative units, political independence was only viable under the form of a federation, namely, the West Indian Federation established in 1958.[3]

Behind this political motivation lay an economic understanding that there is a minimal size below which countries or governments cannot be economically viable. It did not take long, however, for the larger units of the federation (namely, Jamaica and Trinidad and Tobago) to realize that the size constraints on political emancipation were not that binding. This realization, combined with a skeptical view of the benefits of regional integration, led to the collapse of the federation in 1962. Nevertheless, politicians appear to have held on to the underlying idea that size is an important constraint—not as an impediment to statehood, but as a limitation on economic development—and this perception appears to have been the main driver behind renewed attempts at regional integration, including CARIFTA in 1968, CARICOM in 1973, and the CSME in the late 1990s.

Some Caribbean analysts, while acknowledging that economic motivation has played a leading role in the integration process, argue that "the real basis and impetus for our integration is cultural."[4] That may well be the case, but the overriding motivation for regional agreements has been to reduce some of the disadvantages of small size.[5] Countries join forces to create economies of scale, which allow them to increase productivity, diversify their output, and ultimately boost growth.

Economic theory, since the writings of Adam Smith, supports the notion that size matters for welfare and growth. Smith, for instance, explains that the extent of the market limits the division of labor and any benefits thereof in terms of productivity and output diversification. More recently, the literature on trade argues that economies of scale play a key role in shaping trade

3. Lewis (2002).
4. Farrell (1981). Ross-Brewster (2000) makes a similar point.
5. Venables (2003).

patterns, particularly between countries with similar factor endowments, and also have a bearing on the gains from trade.[6] Likewise, the endogenous growth theories suggest that large countries are likely to grow faster than small countries because growth depends on innovation, which is intensive in scale effects.[7]

Other arguments in the literature go beyond the impact of size on trade and growth. Alesina and Spolaore, for instance, speak of size advantages that are perhaps more closely related to the concerns that led to the West Indian Federation.[8] They argue that larger countries have lower per capita costs in the provision of public goods (including infrastructure, defense, regulation, health, and police services); can better internalize cross-regional externalities by centralizing the regulation of externality-prone activities (such as environmental regulation); can provide better insurance against region-specific shocks (for example, recessions and natural disasters); and can attenuate regional disparities with redistributive schemes. All these advantages are essentially advantages to developing the country's social and physical infrastructure, with the former defined as "the institutions and government policies that determine the economic environment within which individuals accumulate skills and firms accumulate capital and produce output."[9]

Such arguments resonate deeply in a region where all but three countries (namely, Jamaica, Trinidad and Tobago, and Haiti) are classified by the United Nations as microstates.[10] In fact, this type of reasoning has led some analysts, from the Caribbean and elsewhere, to elaborate on the specific vulnerabilities of small island states, a category that suffers from both economic and geographical disadvantages and that encompasses most Caribbean states.[11] Some of the alleged economic disadvantages of the small island states are based on the arguments reviewed above (for example, high export concentration and vulnerability to natural disasters), whereas others are specific neither to islands nor to small countries (for example, remoteness, energy dependence, and financial dependence) and still others cannot even be considered disadvantages at all (for example, trade openness).[12]

---

6. Helpman and Krugman (1986).
7. See, for example, Grossman and Helpman (1991); Rivera-Batiz and Romer (1991).
8. Alesina and Spolaore (2003).
9. Hall and Jones (1999).
10. Countries with a population of one million or less.
11. See, for example, Witter, Brigulio, and Bhuglah (2002); CARICOM Secretariat (2005, chap. 7).
12. See Srinivasan (1986) for a critical review of these arguments.

Inconsistencies aside, the very existence of this type of literature confirms the strong perception among Caribbean states that their limited size generates economic disadvantages. While this helps explain why economics and not politics appears to be driving integration in the region, it also suggests a paradox: if the Caribbean states are so size conscious, why did they not move earlier and faster toward deeper, more complex forms of regional integration?

Part of the answer lies in the politics of sovereignty, but the costs and benefits of size also play a role. As Alesina and Spolaore argue, if size had only benefits (and no costs), the world would be organized as a single political entity.[13] This is particularly true for the Caribbean, where most countries are quite small. Size also has costs, however, mainly in the form of heterogeneous preferences. That is, the larger the country, the more difficult it is to devise policies and produce public goods that satisfy everybody's preferences, particularly since larger populations and territories tend to have more heterogeneous preferences. Countries that are considering joining some sort of political union or even a common market thus face a trade-off between the benefits of size and the costs of heterogeneous preferences. In the Caribbean, the equilibrium between these costs and benefits has thus far translated into very small countries and limited forms of integration. Either the Caribbean countries value their distinct preferences very highly (despite the supposed shared cultural identity) or they perceive the size benefits of integration to be small. Both forces are likely to be operating.

We can only speculate about preferences, but the region's history of political independence and integration suggests that they are indeed a major issue. As Doumenge points out, small island states are known to be highly protective of their sovereignty rights: "Islanders are never happier with insularity than when asserting that they are completely different from their neighbors, particularly with regard to language, customs, laws, legal and administrative regulation, currency, system of government, and all other symbols which demonstrate the small self-contained universe. Consequently, small islands tend to band together only under the influence of external forces."[14]

Size benefits are easier to estimate than preferences, and they seem to provide good reason for the region not to be enthusiastic about integration. Whereas the theory behind the advantages of country size seems to be robust, the empirical evidence falls well short of supporting its conclusions. As a number of authors point out, there is no systematic evidence showing that small countries are

13. Alesina and Spolaore (2003).
14. Doumenge (1983), quoted in Srinivasan (1986, p. 212).

poorer or grow more slowly than larger countries, even after the analysts control for a number of factors, including natural resources.[15] This seems to hold even for the Caribbean alone. A quick look at the data suggests, if anything, that smaller countries grow faster than larger countries and are wealthier. The coefficients of correlation between size and growth and size and wealth for the region are −0.6 and −0.5, respectively.[16] These results may well be reversed after we control for all possible omitted factors. Nevertheless, size constraints, if they are really binding, have not prevented a significant number of very small countries in the Caribbean from outperforming their larger counterparts.

Thus, while the theory looks sound, the data do not offer any significant support. Nevertheless, before jumping to the conclusion that size does not matter for development, Caribbean policymakers should be aware that the theory has induced analysts to overrate the disadvantages of size by not drawing attention to the distinction between the political size of the country and the size of its market. This point is convincingly made by Alesina and Spolaore, who point out that the two do not necessarily coincide in an open economy.[17] Even if the area and population of a country are small, access to world markets can imply that the actual size of the country's market is many times that of its domestic market. Trade, then, can be a powerful instrument for attenuating size restrictions, and it can effectively shift the trade-off between the associated costs and benefits.

This insight suggests that the Caribbean paradox may not be a paradox at all. As shown in table 1, all countries in the region, with the exception of Haiti, have trade-to-GDP ratios that are well above the world and Latin American averages. Increased openness, fueled by unilateral preferences granted by the United Kingdom and later by the European Union, the United States, and Canada, has probably attenuated the size handicap, reducing the appeal of regional integration without reducing its heterogeneity costs.

Openness to capital flows, which in the Caribbean are largely made up of foreign direct investment (FDI) and aid, may also have played a role in relaxing size constraints and making integration less of an imperative. The Caribbean's

15. For example, Easterly and Kraay (1999); Alesina, Spolaore, and Wacziarg (2005); Rose (2006).

16. We calculate the coefficient of correlation between size and growth using the countries' average population and their average real rate of per capita gross domestic product (GDP) growth in the 1971–2003 period. The level of significance is 5 percent. For size and wealth, we use population and purchasing power parity (PPP) per capita GDP for 2003. The level of significance is 10 percent. Data for both coefficients are from the Penn World Table version 6.2

17. Alesina and Spolaore (2003).

TABLE 1.   Average Aid per Capita, FDI, and Trade-to-GDP Ratio, 1970–2003[a]

Country or region	Aid	FDI	Openness
Barbados	27.2	2.8	107.5
Belize	96.9	2.4	119.2
Dominica	171.5	5.5	116.7
Grenada	97.9	6.0	104.5
Guyana	68.2	3.9	199.0
Haiti	23.3	0.4	50.1
Jamaica	42.8	3.0	92.4
St. Kitts and Nevis	115.4	9.7	117.2
St. Lucia	91.2	10.0	98.5
St. Vincent and the Grenadines	86.3	6.3	109.5
Suriname	148.8	n.a.	66.2
Trinidad and Tobago	6.7	5.5	96.5
Latin America and the Caribbean	7.6	1.5	44.4
Sub-Saharan Africa	19.7	1.2	65.4
East Asia and the Pacific	3.4	1.7	68.5
World	7.8	1.1	38.3

Source: World Bank, *World Development Indicators.*
   a. "Aid" is measured in constant 1982–84 U.S. dollars. "FDI (foreign direct investment)" is averaged over the period, in percent. "Openness" is measured for 2002, in percent.

inflows of aid per capita in the last three decades reached levels well above those of sub-Saharan Africa or Latin America as a whole, particularly among the smaller countries that form the Organization of Eastern Caribbean States (OECS) (see table 1). Most countries in the region also received substantial amounts of foreign direct investment as a percentage of their GDP, often reaching levels well above the averages for Latin America and East Asia.

The Specifics of a South-South Caribbean Integration

Even if greater openness had not alleviated size constraints, the Caribbean states would still have good reason to question the enlarged market effect or the benefits of integration, in general. South-south agreements, in general, and CARICOM, in particular, are subject to important structural limitations, most notably size constraints and factor endowments.

SIZE CONSTRAINTS. Although one of the objectives of south-south agreements is to overcome the disadvantages of small size, the enlarged market created by such arrangements (assuming the inclusion of a full customs union) often does not allow for substantial scale gains. This is particularly true for CARICOM, where the combined GDP of all member countries in 2003 (US$29.2 billion) ranked above the world's median country (US$14.4 billion), but was not that much different from small Latin American countries such as Ecuador (U.S.$27.2 billion). In terms of population, CARICOM also ranked above the world median country in 2003 (15 million versus 6.4 million), but was smaller than Latin American countries such as Chile (15.6 million).

To gauge the magnitude of this market-size effect, we use Alesina, Spolaore, and Wacziarg's empirical framework to simulate the impact of the enlarged CARICOM market on the region's growth rates.[18] The exercise includes two stages: we first estimate the relationship between long-term growth rates, size, and openness, controlling for other key growth determinants such as investment and human capital, and then use this estimated relationship to simulate shocks in some of the key variables to measure their impact on the growth of the four Caribbean countries for which data are available (namely, Barbados, Guyana, Jamaica, and Trinidad and Tobago).

The empirical framework for the first stage uses the following general growth specification:

$$(1) \qquad \ln\left(\frac{y_{it}}{y_{it-\tau}}\right) = \beta_0 + \beta_1 \cdot \ln\left(y_{it-\tau}\right) + \beta_2 \cdot \ln\left(S_{it}\right) + \beta_3 \cdot O_{it}$$

$$+ \beta_4 \cdot \left[O_{it} \times \ln\left(S_{it}\right)\right] + \beta_5' \cdot \mathbf{Z}_{it} + \varepsilon_{it},$$

where $i = 1, \ldots, n$ denotes country i; $t = 1, \ldots, T$ denotes time t; y represents per capita income; S is a measure of country size (real GDP or population); O is a measure of openness (trade to GDP in current prices of purchasing power parity); and $\mathbf{Z}$ is a vector of control variables that are determinants of the steady-state level of per capita income, including human capital (the average years of secondary schooling in the total population over age twenty-five) and the ratios of investment and government consumption to real per capita GDP.

As in Alesina, Spolaore, and Wacziarg, we run the model using both seemingly unrelated regressions (SUR) and three-stage least squares (3SLS).[19] SUR is essentially a flexible form of the random-effects panel estimator; the estimation procedure involves formulating one equation per decade, constraining the coefficients to equality across periods, and running SUR on the resulting system of equations. The 3SLS estimator alleviates the possible endogeneity of openness and GDP growth; as in Frankel and Romer, we use

18. Alesina, Spolaore, and Wacziarg (2005).
19. Alesina, Spolaore, and Wacziarg (2005).

geographical variables as instruments (namely, dummies for small country, island, small island, and landlocked country).[20]

The data are structured in a panel comprising four periods of ten-year averages (1960–69, 1970–79, 1980–89, 1990–99) and up to eighty-two countries, which includes Barbados, Guyana, Jamaica, and Trinidad and Tobago.[21] Table 2 presents the results of the regressions, with different measures of size and openness. The magnitude, sign, and significance of the coefficients across specifications are similar to those of Alesina, Spolaore, and Wacziarg and generally robust to the two econometric techniques used.[22] The fact that the coefficient of the interaction term is negative and significant confirms the argument that the positive impact of size is tempered by the countries' openness.

In the second stage of the exercise, we use the coefficients of the most robust specification (namely, population and current openness) to simulate CARICOM's size effect on growth (that is, we raise each country's population, i, to the size of CARICOM's total population). We then compare it with other growth-enhancing shocks, such as bringing the countries' openness, stock of human capital, investment, and government consumption to the level of Hong Kong, arguably one the most successful small economies before being returned to mainland China. This type of comparison is always somewhat arbitrary because it is not clear what sort of shock would be comparable to full integration. Nevertheless, it serves to illustrate the order of magnitude of the impacts. Table 3 shows the magnitude of the shocks per variable per country. In the case of government consumption, the shock implies reducing the above-average Caribbean levels to Hong Kong's modest levels. Since government consumption is negatively correlated with growth, a reduction brings about a positive impact. As shown in figure 1, CARICOM's effect compares unfavorably with the other shocks, delivering a small, negative impact on growth, which probably reflects the fact that openness in these countries is already above the world average and that an increase in size would have a stronger effect on costs (such as policymaking costs in the face of heterogeneous preferences) than on benefits.

While these results seem to rule out size as a major constraint for growth in the Caribbean, they should not be interpreted as definitive proof that there are no relevant scale benefits to be reaped from regional integration in the

20. Frankel and Romer (1999).

21. Alesina, Spolaore, and Wacziarg (2005) do not include the four countries mentioned. See the appendix for a list of our data sources and country sample.

22. Alesina, Spolaore, and Wacziarg (2005).

TABLE 2. Size and Openness in a Growth Model, 1960–99[a]

| | Size measured as population | | | | Size measured as real GDP | | | |
| | Current openness | | Real openness | | Current openness | | Real openness | |
Explanatory variable	SUR	3SLS	SUR	3SLS	SUR	3SLS	SUR	3SLS
Size * Openness	−0.006**	−0.008**	−0.007	−0.011*	−0.003*	−0.002	−0.007**	−0.014***
	(0.00)	(0.00)	(0.00)	(0.01)	(0.00)	(0.00)	(0.00)	(0.00)
Size	0.467***	0.680***	0.258*	0.466**	0.484***	0.838***	0.450***	0.903***
	(0.14)	(0.17)	(0.13)	(0.18)	(0.13)	(0.20)	(0.13)	(0.19)
Openness	0.104***	0.138***	0.111**	0.191**	0.095*	0.100	0.193**	0.399***
	(0.03)	(0.04)	(0.05)	(0.08)	(0.04)	(0.07)	(0.07)	(0.11)
Initial per capita GDP	−0.859***	−0.849***	−1.023***	−1.129***	−1.109***	−1.725***	−1.224***	−1.780***
	(0.18)	(0.19)	(0.19)	(0.21)	(0.19)	(0.24)	(0.21)	(0.25)
Human capital	0.524***	0.488***	0.592***	0.580***	0.496***	0.495**	0.523***	0.498**
	(0.14)	(0.14)	(0.14)	(0.15)	(0.14)	(0.16)	(0.15)	(0.16)
Investment (percentage of GDP)	0.109***	0.102***	0.110***	0.104***	0.099***	0.083***	0.097***	0.078***
	(0.02)	(0.02)	(0.02)	(0.02)	(0.02)	(0.02)	(0.02)	(0.02)
Government consumption (percentage of GDP)	−0.038***	−0.041***	−0.037**	−0.040***	−0.036**	−0.043***	−0.038**	−0.050***
	(0.01)	(0.01)	(0.01)	(0.01)	(0.01)	(0.01)	(0.01)	(0.01)
Intercept	0.944	−2.855	5.852*	3.282	−1.400	−5.986	0.618	−6.127
	(2.92)	(3.54)	(2.80)	(3.41)	(3.31)	(5.07)	(3.27)	(4.60)
Intercept 1970–79	0.462	−3.422	5.397	2.753	−1.952	−6.770	0.058	−6.892
	(2.96)	(3.59)	(2.84)	(3.46)	(3.35)	(5.12)	(3.32)	(4.67)
Intercept 1980–89	−0.725	−4.671	4.251	1.599	−3.187	−8.176	−1.084	−8.015
	(2.97)	(3.60)	(2.84)	(3.46)	(3.35)	(5.13)	(3.31)	(4.66)
Intercept 1990–99	−0.629	−4.670	4.376	1.680	−3.171	−8.514	−0.952	−7.981
	(2.95)	(3.61)	(2.82)	(3.45)	(3.35)	(5.13)	(3.29)	(4.63)
No. of observations per period	82	82	82	82	82	82	82	82

Source: Authors' calculations.
*Statistically significant at the 10 percent level.
**Statistically significant at the 5 percent level.
***Statistically significant at the 1 percent level.
a. The dependent variable is the growth rate of real per capita income. Standard errors are in parentheses.

TABLE 3.   Magnitude of the Shocks per Variable
Percent change

Country	Size (population)	Openness	Human capital	Government consumption
Barbados	2,220	146	11	−43
Guyana	667	29	186	−83
Jamaica	144	137	123	−77
Trinidad and Tobago	386	213	63	−62

Source: Authors' calculations.

FIGURE 1.   Impact of CARICOM's Market Size Effect on Growth in Four Countries[a]

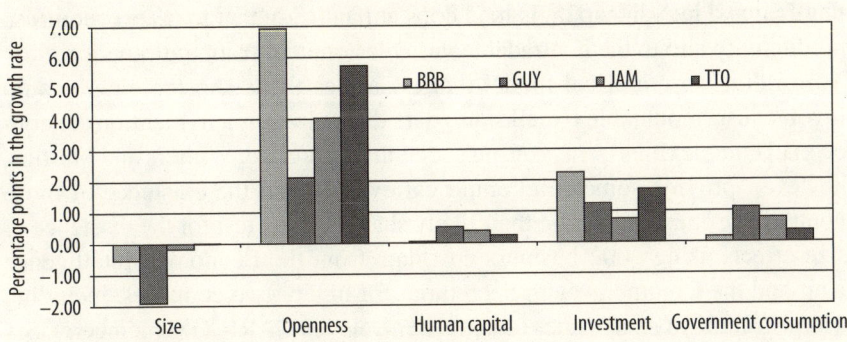

BRB = Barbados; GUY = Guyana; JAM = Jamaica; TTO = Trinidad and Tobago.
a. For change in size, we raised each country's population to the level of the Caribbean Community and Common Market (CARICOM) as a whole. For change in openness, human capital, and government consumption, we equalized each country's levels to Hong Kong's level in the last year of the sample. See the text and appendix for details.

Caribbean. There are least two good reasons to be careful about ruling out those benefits. First, these results reflect mainly empirical regularities across countries and time and do not necessarily capture all the specific conditions of the Caribbean economies involved. In particular, lack of data prevented the inclusion of the smaller economies, which in theory could be the main beneficiaries of these gains.

Second, Alesina, Spolaore, and Wacziarg do not incorporate nontradables into the production function, although their theoretical discussion suggests that larger countries face lower costs in the provision of public goods and other nontradables.[23] To get a complete picture of the size effects, the model would to have to take into account the interaction of size with this input and

23. Alesina, Spolaore, and Wacziarg (2005).

the interaction of this input with the other variables, particularly investment in human and physical capital.

Nontradables can be treated as an input whose complementarity with other inputs makes a direct contribution to growth, or they can be viewed as affecting growth mainly through total factor productivity (for example, improving information flows, reducing uncertainty via better institutions, and generating agglomeration economies).[24] Either way, improvements in the social and physical infrastructure brought about by, say, economies of scale at the regional level are bound to raise the profitability of the other factors and promote their accumulation. This level effect (as opposed to the productivity effect) cannot be captured if, as in the Alesina-Spolaore-Wacziarg model, investment in physical and human capital is held constant and assumed to be exogenous to productivity and to the nontradable variables omitted from the equation.

Building an empirical model that addresses those shortcomings would involve insurmountable (small state) data difficulties, not to mention the conceptual complexities of measuring social infrastructure. Winters and Martins, however, provide some solid empirical evidence on the existence of those nontradable gains, including their likely shape.[25] They test for the existence of size effects using 2002 business cost data from the Economist Intelligence Unit and the Commonwealth Secretariat for ninety-two countries, including a large sample of small states (among them, eleven CARICOM members). Six of the dependent variables are directly related to the countries' infrastructure (namely, airfreight, sea freight, telephone, electricity and water charges, and the cost of personal air travel) and, therefore, of direct interest to this argument about the relevance of nontradable gains.

For air and sea freight, they find a U-shaped relationship between cost and population, with a turning point for airfreight between 1.5 million and 3.5 million people (which is larger than all CARICOM countries except Haiti and Jamaica) and a turning point for sea freight that is well beyond any existing country size. For the other infrastructure variables, they find a linear, negative, and statistically significant relationship between costs and country size. The authors also estimate the cost disadvantages that arise from these size effects for representative small countries vis-à-vis a median-sized country (defined as 10 million people, which is close to CARICOM's 15 million total population). The results

---

24. See Canning, Fay, and Perotti (1994) on how to interpret the contribution of physical infrastructure to growth. Gwartney, Holcombe, and Lawson (2006) discuss the whole of the social infrastructure.

25. Winters and Martins (2004).

point to severe cost disadvantages for micro (12,000 people) and very small states (197,000 people), ranging from an average of 31 percent in airfreight to 158 percent in sea freight. The threshold (1.6 million people) and small countries (4 million people) have lower, but still substantial cost disadvantages, ranging from 15 percent in sea freight to 30 percent in electricity usage.

The magnitude of these cost disadvantages supports our claim that CARICOM faces relevant scale gains in nontradables and that those gains might have a significant impact on productivity and capital accumulation, something that is not entirely captured by the Alesina-Spolaore-Wacziarg empirical model.[26] The precise magnitude of those gains in CARICOM, as well as their overall impact on growth, is anybody's guess because the required data are just not available. By definition, these nontradable effects cannot be mitigated by openness, and they are likely to be nonlinear since they are mainly associated with fixed costs and tend to lose importance once a country reaches a certain size. In other words, they are likely to be particularly relevant to countries such as the CARICOM members, which are in the bottom of the size distribution. This reasoning, combined with the results of the Alesina-Spolaore-Wacziarg model and the magnitude of gains estimated by Winters and Martins, suggests that nontradable gains are much more promising for the region than traditional trade gains.

FACTOR ENDOWMENTS. The second limitation on south-south agreements such as CARICOM is the similarity of the member countries' technology and factor endowments. Similar factor endowments and technology imply that the countries' array of comparative advantages tend to overlap, suggesting that a great deal of their trade would necessarily come from outside the agreement. This, in turn, increases the agreement's exposure to trade diversion and agglomeration.[27]

The costs and benefits of trade diversion are well known and inherent in any preferential agreement.[28] The losses are mainly associated with replacing efficient, extraregional suppliers with inefficient, regional ones, while the benefits include scale and learning gains accruing from the replacement of

26. Alesina, Spolaore, and Wacziarg (2005). A recent World Bank (2005) report on the Caribbean infrastructure similarly recommends that a regional approach can lead to higher economies of scale, lower regulatory costs, higher bargaining power in procurement, and greater efficiency gains through competition in areas such as telecommunications, water, and energy. Some countries in the region are already reaping some of those benefits, as in the case of the Eastern Caribbean Regulatory Authority (ECTEL), a regional telecommunication advisory body established by the OECS countries.

27. See, for example, Venables (2003).

28. See, for example, de Melo and Panagariya (1993).

extraregional producers with regional producers. The key to the net result lies in the level of the agreement's protection against the rest of the world. High levels of protection could impose severe costs on member countries that are consumers of the diverted good, whereas the scale and learning gains linked to the production of this good are likely to be compromised by the size constraints discussed above.

The process of agglomeration is also relevant for the understanding of the full consequences of trade diversion. When countries share similar technology and factor endowments, the centripetal forces of agglomeration—that is, the forces that encourage firms to locate close to each other—can be overwhelming.[29] Since the advantages of size are not balanced by significant differences in factor prices (such as capital and labor), the most likely result is the agglomeration of economic activities in the large countries of the agreement (in this case, Jamaica and Trinidad and Tobago), assuming that there are no major differences in factors such as macroeconomic management and the quality of institutions. This is particularly true for activities that are intensive in scale and sensitive to labor and technological externalities, such as manufacturing. In the context of free trade, agglomeration may not be cause for concern since it can reduce costs in the region as whole, raising welfare. In the context of a regional agreement, however, agglomeration may be driven beyond optimal levels by the forces of trade diversion. The benefits of trade diversion could thus be concentrated on the largest countries, with the costs being borne by the smaller, poorer partners.

Looking Back: Integration Policies and Results

The previous sections provided an overview of what to expect from agreements such as CARICOM. This section looks at the actual results of the integration initiatives to date. The aim is not to make a comprehensive evaluation of all economic implications, which is virtually impossible given methodological and data constraints. Rather, we concentrate on what is widely seen as the main channel through which economic integration affects member countries' economic performance, namely, intra- and extraregional trade flows. Data restrictions forced us to tighten the focus of the analysis to exclude trade in services. This would not be a cause for concern in most regions in the world, but it does limit our analysis of CARICOM since the majority of the member countries (particularly the smaller ones) have a major stake in the export of services.

29. Venables (2003).

That characteristic does not invalidate an analysis based purely on goods, however, for a number of reasons. First, the ability to expand and diversify the production and export of goods has been a key motivation (implicitly or explicitly) in all integration initiatives in the region since the West Indian Federation. Second, the limitations of south-south agreements in general (such as market size and the similarity of factor endowments) and CARICOM in particular (namely, openness) also apply to trade in services, so the inclusion of services probably would not change either the direction or the magnitude of the impacts on trade flows, particularly intraregional trade flows. Finally, even though countries such as the members of the OECS do not have a significant stake in the production of goods, their welfare depends heavily on the price and quality of the goods they consume, including capital, intermediate goods, and consumer goods. In sum, while we would have preferred to include services, their exclusion does not invalidate the analysis and probably does not change its main conclusions.

Intraregional Trade, Trade Costs, and the Distribution of Benefits

Figure 2 offers a broad picture of intra- and extraregional merchandise trade flows in CARICOM in 1970–2003. We excluded trade in oil products because it was not subject to relevant trade barriers at any time during the period, and its high share of intraregional trade (an average of 37 percent over the period) and high price volatility would cloud the analysis. Since the first integration initiative was in 1958 with the West Indies Federation, we would have liked to examine trade and tariff data starting in the 1950s. This would provide a better perspective of trade flows before and after the first preferences were granted. Data constraints, however, force the analysis to begin in 1970, three years before CARICOM was signed, and to be limited to trade flows. It seems reasonable to assume that at that time, a number of trade preferences were already in place among most Caribbean countries; for instance, the CARIFTA agreement speaks of immediate free trade among member countries. Nevertheless, it is difficult to assess how important they were, since there were many exceptions and differential treatment for less developed countries.[30]

Figure 2 shows that intraregional trade grew much faster than extraregional trade in the first half of the 1970s, even before CARICOM was signed.

---

30. See the Dickenson Bay Agreement (available online at www.sice.oas.org/Trade/CCME/dikson.asp) and CARICOM Secretariat (2005). CARIFTA included all present CARICOM members except Suriname and Haiti. The Eastern Caribbean Common Market included all OECS members.

FIGURE 2.   CARICOM's Non-Oil Intra- and Extraregional Trade Flows, 1970–2003[a]

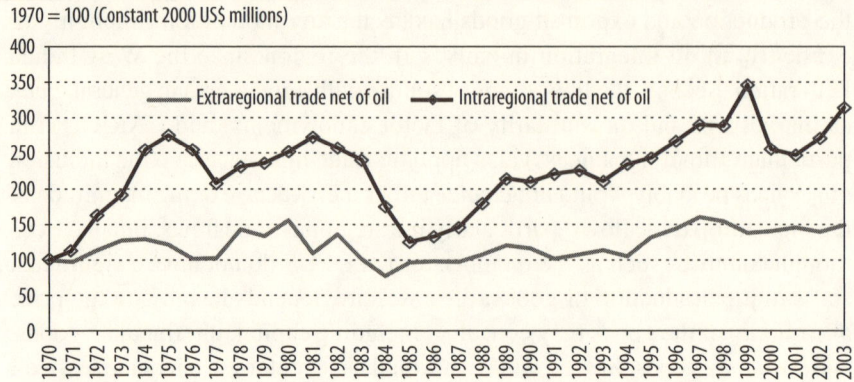

1970 = 100 (Constant 2000 US$ millions)

Source: United Nations Commodity Trade Statistics Database (COMTRADE); Caribbean Community and Common Market (CARICOM) Secretariat.
a. Oil products are SITC 3 V.1. Haiti is not included.

CARICOM is widely seen as a landmark in the integration process, since it represented the member countries' decision to upgrade CARIFTA's free trade zone to a common market.[31] From the strict perspective of trade costs, however, it is not clear whether the new treaty markedly changed the status quo. CARIFTA's two main characteristics were inherited by CARICOM and prevailed into the early 1990s: first, CARIFTA was an incomplete free trade zone that incorporated several exceptions and differential treatment for countries, sectors, and regions; and, second, the agreement imposed relatively high tariffs on extraregional trade.[32] The customs union, which was the innovation introduced by CARICOM, was not seriously enforced until the late 1990s. The fact that intraregional trade grew slightly faster after 1973 but soon hit a ceiling seems consistent with the hypothesis that the status quo did not change. However, many factors may explain this behavior, including the structural limitations of the agreement discussed earlier and the debt crisis that affected the region in the 1980s.

OPEN REGIONALISM.   Whatever the underlying factors, the bottom line is that the peak reached by intraregional trade in 1975, in constant dollars, was only

31. See the Treaty of Chaguaramas (available online at www.sice.oas.org/Trade/CCME/CCME2.asp).

32. Information about the member countries' tariffs in the 1970s and 1980s is sketchy, but most analysts describe this period as one of import substitution. Caldentey (2005), for instance, estimates the average nominal protection for manufactured goods in the 1980s (including tariffs and surcharges) at 50 percent in Trinidad and Tobago, 43 percent in Barbados, and 41 percent in Jamaica.

surpassed twenty-two years later, in 1997 (figure 2). The new increase in trade followed a series of reforms that started with the decision to establish the CSME in 1989 and were institutionalized by the revised Treaty of Chaguaramas signed in 2001. These reforms improved the discipline and implementation of the free trade zone and customs union, and they reduced protection against extraregional imports at both the country and the regional levels. A common external tariff was finally agreed in 1992, but it took another ten years to be fully implemented by most member countries. The common external tariff simple average thus fell from 20 percent in the early 1990s to 10 percent in 2003.[33]

An examination of actual tariff levels (measured as tariff revenue divided by the value of imports) across countries and sectors shows, however, that some of the problems of the agreement still lingered in 2003–04. Interregional tariffs were close to zero in most countries, but the picture changes markedly when import taxes are taken into account.[34] Average import taxes ranged from 7.0 to 8.0 percent in countries such as Dominica, Grenada, and Saint Lucia, and they were as high as 19.3 percent in Suriname. Moreover, extraregional actual tariffs still showed considerable variation across countries, ranging from 7 percent in Jamaica to 15 percent in Suriname, and sectors, leaving considerable room for trade diversion. In manufacturing, for instance, preferences ranged from 7 to 18 percentage points and in agriculture they reached 20 percentage points for some goods.[35]

The reforms of the 1990s gave intraregional trade a new boost, but it was not enough to generate a robust performance. Figure 2 shows that the declining trend that set in during the debt crisis of the 1980s was reversed, but so far the share of intraregional trade excluding oil remains around the modest levels achieved in the late 1970s, at 5.6 percent in 2003 (the latest figure available). The situation looks better when oil is included, with the share of interregional trade reaching all-time highs in the 1990s and finishing at 7.6 percent in 2003. Trade in oil has little to do with trade liberalization, however, given that it is guided by supply and price dynamics. Nevertheless, even if we overlook these issues and consider all trade, intraregional trade remains indisputably marginal.

33. See Jessen and Vignoles (2005).

34. Import taxes are introduced for a variety of reasons, but their main purpose is to prop up fiscal revenue without undermining common market discipline. Since governments cannot change tariffs, they create other taxes on imports to replace the lost revenue.

35. Data are from the countries' customs administration, collected by the Inter-American Development Bank's project on "Fiscal Impact of Integration and Trade Liberalization Efforts in the Caribbean." For details, see the working paper version of this study (Moreira and Mendoza 2006).

TABLE 4.   CARICOM Member Countries' Share of Intraregional Trade, 1970–2003[a]
Percent

	Total exports				Non-oil exports[b]			
Country	1970	1980	1990	2000–03	1970	1980	1990	2000–03
Non-OECS countries	81.9	73.2	68.7	74.2	92.9	82.1	86.6	88.7
Barbados	15.2	17.7	16.8	18.9	8.3	13.9	13.1	13.0
Belize	0.9	0.9	3.5	1.4	1.6	2.5	1.4	2.3
Guyana	25.5	15.5	9.7	10.1	17.6	8.9	6.7	11.3
Jamaica	21.2	14.8	27.3	35.4	17.6	18.7	10.8	7.0
Trinidad and Tobago	19.1	24.4	11.4	8.4	47.9	38.2	54.6	55.3
OECS countries	18.1	26.8	31.3	25.8	7.1	17.9	13.4	11.3
Antigua	3.3	6.1	4.7	4.0	1.5	2.1	0.8	0.7
Dominica	2.1	3.5	3.7	3.2	0.7	3.0	3.8	3.7
Grenada	3.4	3.9	5.3	4.7	0.4	1.2	1.3	1.4
Montserrat	0.6	1.0	0.8	0.3	0.0	0.1	0.0	0.1
St. Kitts and Nevis	0.8	2.5	3.0	2.9	0.5	1.0	0.4	0.3
St. Lucia	4.6	6.0	8.6	6.3	2.8	4.6	2.8	2.4
St. Vincent and the Grenadines	3.2	3.8	5.1	4.4	1.2	6.0	4.3	2.7
CARICOM	100.0	100.0	100.0	100.0	100.0	100.0	100.0	100.0

Source: United Nations Commodity Trade Statistics Database (COMTRADE); Caribbean Community and Common Market (CARICOM) Secretariat.
OECS = Organization of Eastern Caribbean States.
a.   The CARICOM sample does not include Suriname and Haiti, which joined the bloc later in the period.
b.   Excludes SITC 3 rev.1.

While the protracted implementation of the free trade zone and customs union probably contributed to those meager results, it is not the sole explanation. Given the limitations of size and factor endowment discussed earlier, it is unlikely that a swift, faultless process would have created more trade. The share of intraregional trade in the bloc is not much different from that of other south-south agreements that share similar limitations. For instance, intraregional trade peaked in 1998 at just over 11 percent of total trade in MERCOSUR and not more than 13 percent in the ANDEAN community.[36]

INTRAREGIONAL TRADE COMPOSITION AND THE DISTRIBUTION OF GAINS.
Other issues worth examining include the distribution and composition of intraregional trade. Table 4 shows how the market is distributed among member countries and how this distribution has evolved. Export shares changed drastically over the sample period even among the non-OECS countries, with Jamaica more than halving its participation and Barbados nearly doubling

36. Own calculation, based on COMTRADE data.

its share. The OECS members gained considerable ground in the 1970s, but their share of intraregional non-oil exports then shrank significantly, with the exception of Dominica.

Disaggregated export data are available starting in the 1980s. They confirm the concentration of export activity, both within and across country groups, and reveal the contours of the intraregional division of labor (see table 5). Trinidad and Tobago seems to be reinforcing its dominant position in the region as the main agricultural and manufacturing producer, in addition to mining. Other trends include the collapse of Jamaica's position and a decline in the OECS' share, with the exception of ores and metals.

While these figures are too crude to support a conclusive inference on the distributive impact of regional integration, it seems safe to assume that trade diversion has played a nonnegligible role, given the size of the preferences, the asymmetries in country size, and the similarities in factor endowments. This hypothesis is confirmed by the gravity model presented below. Without time-series data on preferences, however, it is impossible to determine the exact size of this effect, particularly at the sectoral level.[37]

THE EXTERNAL POSITION. As in the case of intraregional flows, the impact of integration on extraregional trade does not appear to have been significant. To be sure, non-oil extraregional exports showed signs of improvement in the 1990s, an event that coincided with the bloc's deepening (see figure 3). Since 1998, however, non-oil extraregional exports have fallen sharply, which raises doubts about any long-term positive impact. This declining trend is particularly worrying considering that the annual average of extraregional exports in 2000–03 was only 28 percent above the 1970s average. This contrasts sharply with the trend for Latin America and the Caribbean as a whole, where the average in 2000–03 was 240 percent above the 1970s average.

The distribution and composition of extraregional exports among countries are very similar to those of intraregional exports, although the movements are less pronounced (table 6). We find limited signs of dispersion toward the OECS countries in manufacturing in the 1990s, but this trend was reversed in

---

37. An important caveat is that, as mentioned earlier, the analysis does not include services, and this is by far the dominant activity for the small OECS countries. The inclusion of services probably would not change our results significantly, however. The bulk of these countries' services exports (namely, tourism) are to markets outside the region, which does not affect their share of intraregional trade. Integration may have accelerated the growing specialization of these countries in tourism, but this would reinforce our argument. The dominant share of services in these economies undoubtedly reduces the cost of any structural adjustment, but as consumers of goods, these countries remain exposed to trade diversion.

TABLE 5. Country Share of CARICOM Intraregional Exports by Sector: 1980s, 1990s, and 2000–03

Period average, in percent

Country	Agriculture			Manufacturing			Fuels			Ores and metals		
	1980s	1990s	2000–03	1980s	1990s	2000–03	1980s	1990s	2000–03	1980s	1990s	2000–03
Non-OECS countries	77.3	87.8	90.5	87.8	90.9	92.2	100.0	100.0	99.9	98.0	93.6	88.3
Barbados	9.0	11.8	9.8	24.7	19.6	17.4	2.8	0.8	1.9	8.0	13.5	3.9
Belize	8.5	3.9	3.5	0.1	0.2	0.9	0.0	0.0	0.0	0.0	0.2	0.4
Guyana	20.3	13.8	19.1	5.9	3.8	2.5	0.0	0.0	0.0	8.2	14.1	35.8
Jamaica	15.7	9.9	7.8	24.9	11.0	6.3	2.6	1.8	0.2	63.2	35.2	18.4
Trinidad and Tobago	23.8	48.4	50.2	32.2	56.3	65.1	94.5	97.4	97.8	18.6	30.8	30.2
OECS countries	22.7	12.2	9.5	12.2	9.0	7.8	0.0	0.0	0.1	1.9	6.2	11.3
Dominica	1.4	0.7	0.6	4.7	5.9	5.4	0.0	0.0	0.0	1.3	4.1	7.4
St. Kitts and Nevis	0.9	0.6	0.4	1.0	0.1	0.1	0.0	0.0	0.1	0.5	0.1	0.8
St. Lucia	6.0	3.1	3.7	4.3	1.9	1.4	0.0	0.0	0.0	0.0	0.0	2.2
St. Vincent and the Grenadines	14.3	7.8	4.9	2.3	1.2	0.9	0.0	0.0	0.0	0.2	2.0	0.9
CARICOM	100.0	100.0	100.0	100.0	100.0	100.0	100.0	100.0	100.0	100.0	100.0	100.0

Source: United Nations Commodity Trade Statistics Database (COMTRADE) (SITC, rev. 1).

OECS = Organization of Eastern Caribbean States.

FIGURE 3.   **CARICOM's Extraregional Total and Non-Oil Exports, 1970–2003**[a]

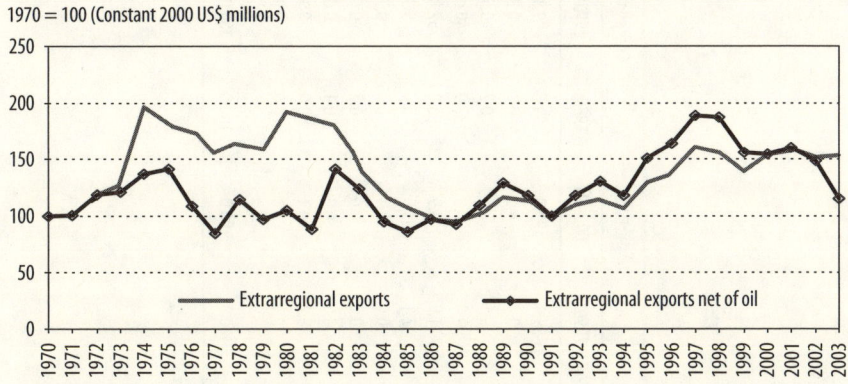

1970 = 100 (Constant 2000 US$ millions)

Source: United Nations Commodity Trade Statistics Database (COMTRADE); Caribbean Community and Common Market (CARICOM) Secretariat.

a. Oil products are SITC 3 V.1. Haiti is not included.

the 2000s. Overall, extraregional exports remain heavily concentrated among larger members. Trinidad and Tobago, in particular, has consistently captured increasing shares of both agriculture and manufacturing, although total exports in these sectors have barely grown in the last three decades.

The Gravity Test

We have raised a number of hypotheses about the impact of regional integration in the Caribbean based only on theory and descriptive statistics. In this subsection, we take a more rigorous approach and use a gravity model to test some of those hypotheses. This is not the first time the gravity model has been used to assess CARICOM's impact. Égoumé-Bossogo and Mendis pioneered this effort, and they reach very positive conclusions using data for forty-four countries over the period 1980–99.[38] They find that CARICOM is trade creating and that this positive impact increased throughout the period, especially after the member countries agreed to reduce the common external tariff in the early 1990s.

These results should be considered with some skepticism, however. Gravity models are notorious for overestimating the impact of trade agreements, and this clearly seems to be the case with Égoumé-Bossogo and Mendis's work.[39]

38. Égoumé-Bossogo and Mendis (2002).
39. Égoumé-Bossogo and Mendis (2002). See Anderson and van Wincoop (2004) for a review.

TABLE 6. Country Share of CARICOM Extraregional Exports by Sector: 1980s, 1990s, 2000–03
Period average, in percent

Country	Agriculture			Manufacturing			Fuels			Ores and metals		
	1980s	1990s	2000–03	1980s	1990s	2000–03	1980s	1990s	2000–03	1980s	1990s	2000–03
Non-OECS countries	85.0	86.0	91.3	94.2	93.1	93.7	99.6	99.4	99.9	99.6	99.3	98.5
Barbados	4.8	3.4	4.0	13.0	3.2	2.7	0.2	0.2	4.6	0.1	0.8	0.6
Belize	7.8	12.5	16.0	2.1	1.7	1.6	0.0	0.1	0.6	0.2	0.5	0.7
Guyana	26.6	22.0	25.8	3.2	1.9	2.6	0.0	0.0	0.0	37.9	40.0	38.8
Jamaica	36.9	33.5	33.7	50.3	52.0	36.6	0.8	1.9	0.9	56.0	52.8	49.1
Trinidad and Tobago	8.9	14.5	11.9	25.5	34.3	50.3	98.6	97.1	93.8	5.4	5.3	9.3
OECS countries	15.0	14.0	8.7	5.8	6.9	6.3	0.4	0.6	0.1	0.4	0.7	1.5
Dominica	3.5	2.9	1.7	1.2	2.2	1.1	0.1	0.2	0.0	0.2	0.6	0.9
St. Kitts and Nevis	1.6	1.0	0.9	3.4	1.2	1.9	0.2	0.0	0.0	0.1	0.0	0.1
St. Lucia	6.3	5.7	2.9	0.7	1.4	0.7	0.0	0.3	0.1	0.0	0.1	0.1
St. Vincent and the Grenadines	3.5	4.4	3.2	0.6	2.1	2.6	0.1	0.1	0.0	0.0	0.0	0.3
CARICOM	100.0	100.0	100.0	100.0	100.0	100.0	100.0	100.0	100.0	100.0	100.0	100.0

Source: United Nations Commodity Trade Statistics Database (COMTRADE) (SITC, rev. 1).
OECS = Organization of Eastern Caribbean States.

For instance, their estimates suggest that CARICOM has led member countries to trade between five and forty-eight times more than would have been predicted based on their size and geographical characteristics. These estimates simply are not plausible given the theoretical limits of intra-CARICOM trade discussed earlier and the patterns shown in the descriptive data. One possible explanation is that the only small-island countries in the authors' sample are from CARICOM, which may lead the regional dummy to pick up geographical effects that have nothing to do with the agreement. Moreover, the authors do not control for country-specific effects or sample selection bias.

The empirical strategy used here tries to mitigate these problems by putting together a data set that consists of a panel of 152 countries (including fourteen Caribbean countries and twenty-eight other small economies), for the period 1970–2003 (see the appendix for information on the sample). The period is not long enough to include intraregional preferences dating back to the formation of CARIFTA in 1968, but it does include three years prior to the signing of the CARICOM agreement and all the changes over the course of its existence. To address the issues of unobserved country characteristics and sample selection bias, we draw on recent advances in the gravity literature.[40]

Our specification takes the following form:

$$(2) \quad \ln M_{ij} = \alpha + \beta_1 \ln Y_i + \beta_2 \ln Y_j + \beta_3 \ln N_i + \beta_4 \ln N_j + \beta_5 \ln L_i$$
$$+ \beta_6 \ln L_j + \beta_7 LK_i + \beta_8 LK_j + \beta_9 I_i + \beta_{10} I_j + \beta_{11} \ln D_i$$
$$+ \beta_{12} COL_{ij} + \beta_{13} CON_{ij} + \beta_{14} LANG_{ij} + \sum_k INT_k \cdot \left(P_{ki} \cdot P_{kj} \right)$$
$$+ \sum_k IM_k \cdot \left[P_{ki} - \left(P_{ki} \cdot P_{kj} \right) \right] + \sum_k EX_k \cdot \left[P_{kj} - \left(P_{ki} \cdot P_{kj} \right) \right] + \varepsilon_{ij},$$

where where $i = 1, \ldots, I$ denotes the reporting country; $j = 1, \ldots, J$ denotes the partner country; $k = 1, \ldots, K$ denotes a trade agreement; M denotes the flow of imports (in current U.S. dollars); Y denotes GDP (in current U.S. dollars); N denotes population; L denotes the land area; LK is a dummy variable taking the value of one if the country is landlocked, and zero otherwise; I is a dummy variable taking the value of one if the country is an island, and zero otherwise; D denotes the simple geodesic distance between the most important cities in each country; COL is a dummy variable taking the value of one if the countries

40. See, in particular, Soloaga and Winters (2001); Feenstra (2002); Rose (2004); Helpman, Melitz, and Rubinstein (2007).

involved share a colonial relationship, and zero otherwise; *CON* is a dummy variable taking the value of one if the countries involved share a border, and zero otherwise; *LANG* is a dummy variable taking the value of one if the countries involved share the same language, and zero otherwise; *P* is a dummy variable taking the value of one if the country is a member of the trade agreement *k,* and zero otherwise; and ϵ is the error term, assumed to be log-normally distributed.

As in Soloaga and Winters, we decompose the total effect of each trade agreement, *k,* into three separate effects: the impact on the members' intraregional trade (both exports and imports), measured by the coefficients INT; the impact on the members' imports from the rest of the world, measured by the coefficients IM; and the impact on the members' exports to the rest of the world, measured by the coefficients EX.[41] Soloaga and Winters' primary concern is with the marginal impact of the agreement on trade and welfare. They therefore define net trade creation as a situation in which INT is positive and IM is negative, and the sum of the two coefficients is positive. That is, the agreement's positive impact on the propensity to import from the region outweighs its negative impact on the propensity to import from outside the region. Net trade diversion, in turn, is defined as a situation in which the sum of the coefficients is negative. If both coefficients are positive, these authors assume that there is only trade creation (on the margin). The purpose of this last EX variable is to measure the agreement's marginal impact on the region's exports to the rest of the world.

Another way of interpreting these coefficients is to compute their absolute impact on their respective trade flows.[42] Net trade creation is then defined as the difference between the amount of trade diverted from nonmembers (obtained by applying the coefficient IM to the observed extraregional trade flows) and the amount of trade created between members (obtained by applying the coefficient INT to observed intraregional trade flows).[43]

In our estimation procedure, we use separate fixed effects for exporters, importers, and years.[44] Using exporting and importing country fixed effects

41. Soloaga and Winters (2001).
42. This approach is closer to Viner (1950).
43. As de Melo, Panagariya, and Rodrik (1993) point out, Viner's conclusion that trade creation is always welfare improving and trade diversion always welfare diminishing is less general than initially proposed and involves a number of caveats. Nevertheless, most analysts consider that agreements generating a net trade creation are likely to improve the members' welfare.
44. This approach follows Feenstra (2002) and Rose (2004).

helps us control for the countries' idiosyncratic and asymmetric behavior as exporters and importers (in that every country pair can be represented twice, with imports from i to j and imports from j to i). At the same time, it eliminates the possibility of identifying the agreement dummy throughout the sample period, rather than just after the agreement was signed. If such an agreement dummy were introduced, its effect would not be distinguishable from those of the country fixed effects because the dummy and the fixed effects would be perfectly collinear. Including the dummy in all years would provide the extra security of knowing if the effects captured by the coefficient were already present before the agreement for some "abnormal" reason, as Soloaga and Winters put it.[45] However, given that the implementation of CARICOM has been protracted (with marked changes in both intra- and extraregional tariffs) and, in fact, has yet to be completed, the variation of the agreement dummy coefficient throughout the various phases of the agreement can provide relevant information about the sign and trend of the effects.

Fixed effects improve the accuracy of the estimation but do not address the sample selection problem. That is, the model only takes into account bilateral relationships with positive trade flows. Nor does it control for the fact that policies that affect trade costs have an impact not only on the intensive margin of trade (that is, firms that already export), but also on its extensive margin (or the number of exporting firms). Using a gravity equation derived from a general equilibrium model of trading countries with heterogeneous firms, Helpman, Melitz, and Rubinstein show that when the analysis does not control for changes in the extensive margin, "the coefficient, γ, on distance (or any other coefficient on a potential trade barrier) can no longer be interpreted as the elasticity of a firm's trade with respect to distance (or other trade barriers). . . . Instead, the estimation of the standard gravity equation confounds the effects of trade barriers [including trade agreements] on firm-level trade with their effects on the proportion of exporting firms, which induces an upward bias in the estimated coefficient, γ."[46]

To address these two types of bias, we closely follow Helpman, Melit, and Rubinstein's proposed solution. We use a two-stage strategy, in which the

45. Soloaga and Winters (2001). For instance, if the regression estimates a positive and significant coefficient for the CARICOM dummy in 1968 (five years before the agreement was signed), then this would indicate that the dummy is picking up more than just the agreement itself. It would also provide a benchmark for assessing the impact of the agreement after it was signed. The true impact would be given by the difference between the coefficients before and after the agreement.

46. Helpman, Melitz, and Rubinstein (2007 p. 11).

first stage consists of a probit equation that uses an indicator variable (equal to one if there is a positive flow of trade and zero otherwise) to estimate the probability of country j exporting to country i as a function of observable variables (namely, the same independent variables used in the gravity equation above). All the information available in the data set is used in this stage, so we consider all the possible bilateral relationships between the countries involved (that is, 152 reporting countries * 151 partners * 34 years = 780,368 possible relationships). The intuition here is that the same variables that affect export volume from country j to country i also affect the probability that country j exports to country i. The probit procedure provides enough information to decompose these two effects.

We then use the predicted probabilities of the probit equation to build two variables for all country pairs with positive trade flows. The first $(\hat{\eta})$ is the variable used in the standard Heckman correction for sample selection (namely, the inverse Mills ratio).[47] It controls for the bias produced by having only country pairs that trade in the sample. The second variable $(\hat{W})$ is built under the assumption (derived from the theoretical model) that we can use the predicted probabilities to estimate a latent variable, Z_{ij}, which is the ratio of the variable export profits of the most productive firm to the fixed costs of exporting from country j to country i. Positive exports are only observed if $Z_{ij} > 1$, and a higher value for Z_{ij} implies a larger number of exporting firms. The inclusion of $(\hat{W})$ in the gravity model helps control for the effect of trade frictions and country characteristics on the proportion of exporters: the extensive margin effect.[48]

The second stage consists of estimating the gravity equation with the same independent variables plus the two variables calculated in the first stage. Since the reduced form of the gravity equation is nonlinear in $(\hat{W})$, we use a maximum likelihood (ML) estimation procedure. All stages include separate fixed effects for exporters, importers, and years to ensure consistency.

Table 7 presents the main results, including a simpler version of the model using ordinary least squares (OLS) and fixed effects. As expected, the difference between the OLS and ML estimations are confined to the magnitude of the coefficients, so we concentrate our analysis on the latter. We present two specifications. The first follows equation 2, while the second allows the

47. Heckman (1976).
48. The formula for the second variable is $\hat{\omega}_{ij} = \ln\{\exp[\delta(z_{ij} + \hat{\eta}_{ij})] - 1\}$, where z_{ij} is the latent variable defined as $z_{ij} = \phi^{-1}(\hat{p}_{ij})$, with ϕ denoting the cumulative normal distribution function and $\hat{p}_{ij}$ denoting the predicted probabilities estimated by the probit equation. The variable, $\hat{\eta}_{ij}$, represents the Mills ratio. See Helpman, Melitz, and Rubinstein (2007) for a formal derivation of this formula.

T A B L E 7.   **Gravity Equation with Trade Agreements, 1970–2003**[a]

Explanatory variable	OLS		ML	
	(1)	(2)	(3)	(4)
GDPi	0.538	0.539	0.429	0.429
	(0.020)***	(0.020)***	(0.022)***	(0.022)***
GDPj	0.553	0.554	0.444	0.446
	(0.021)***	(0.021)***	(0.023)***	(0.023)***
Population$i$	0.507	0.463	0.452	0.415
	(0.057)***	(0.059)***	(0.058)***	(0.060)***
Population$j$	0.001	−0.030	−0.134	−0.161
	(0.073)	(0.074)	(0.077)*	(0.078)**
Land area$i$	−0.060	−0.054	0.039	0.044
	(0.023)**	(0.023)**	(0.027)	(0.027)
Land area$j$	0.266	0.281	0.285	0.298
	(0.044)***	(0.044)***	(0.044)***	(0.045)***
Landlocked$i$	−1.917	−1.805	−2.214	−2.120
	(0.272)***	(0.275)***	(0.273)***	(0.275)***
Landlocked$j$	−4.439	−4.472	−3.509	−3.540
	(0.223)***	(0.224)***	(0.236)***	(0.235)***
Island$i$	−0.415	−0.214	−1.824	−1.645
	(0.353)	(0.359)	(0.387)***	(0.390)***
Island$j$	−2.682	−1.995	−1.753	−1.457
	(0.375)***	(0.424)***	(0.379)***	(0.409)***
Distanceij	−1.358	−1.357	−0.917	−0.918
	(0.019)***	(0.019)***	(0.047)***	(0.046)***
Colonyij	0.474	0.472	0.271	0.270
	(0.051)***	(0.051)***	(0.053)***	(0.053)***
Shared borderij	0.580	0.583	0.891	0.893
	(0.096)***	(0.096)***	(0.096)***	(0.096)***
Languageij	0.631	0.630	0.418	0.417
	(0.039)***	(0.039)***	(0.045)***	(0.045)***
CARICOM (intraregional)	1.150		0.336	
	(0.154)***		(0.187)*	
CARICOM (imports)	−0.662		−0.855	
	(0.078)***		(0.081)***	
CARICOM (exports)	−0.856		−0.928	
	(0.080)***		(0.080)***	
$\hat{\eta}$			0.299	0.302
			(0.084)***	(0.082)***
$\hat{\delta}$			0.745	0.742
			(0.089)***	(0.087)***
Summary statistic				
No. of observations	403,481	403,481	403,481	403,481
R^2	0.6977	0.6979		

Source: Authors' calculations.
    CARICOM = Caribbean Community and Common Market; MERCOSUR = Southern Common Market; NAFTA = North American Free Trade Agreement; SPARTECA = South Pacific Regional Trade and Economic Cooperation Agreement.
    *Statistically significant at the 10 percent level.
    **Statistically significant at the 5 percent level.
    ***Statistically significant at the 1 percent level.
    a. In the table, i denotes the reporting country and j the partner country. The dependent variable is ln(IMPORTSij). Specifications 2 and 4 estimate the coefficients of the CARICOM set variables by year (not reported in the table). See figures 4 and 5 for exporter, importer, and year fixed effects (not reported in the table). The trade agreements included (coefficients not reported) are the Andean Community, ASEAN, European Union, MERCOSUR, NAFTA, and SPARTECA. Robust standard errors (clustering by country pair) are in parentheses.

coefficient of the CARICOM dummies to vary over time to capture changes in the agreement's impact over the period. Our estimation confirms Égoumé-Bossogo and Mendis's result of CARICOM's having a positive impact on intraregional trade (column 3), but the level of magnitude is much more plausible and, certainly, more in line with theory and the way the agreement has been implemented.[49] Our results imply that CARICOM has increased intraregional trade by about 40 percent, or [exp (0.336) − 1]*100, on average over the period.

Our results also point to a negative impact on extraregional imports, which contrasts with Égoumé-Bossogo and Mendis's findings. This implies a net trade diversion as suggested by our analysis of the descriptive data, both on the margin, as defined by Soloaga and Winters (that is, the sum of the INT and IM coefficients is negative), and in absolute terms (that is, IM is considerably higher than INT, and it affects a much larger extraregional base).

The introduction of CARICOM dummies by year in the second specification (column 4) sheds some light on how the agreement's impact evolved over the period and how it might behave in the future. The yearly results are particularly important given that the barriers to intra- and extraregional trade changed considerably over the period. As discussed earlier, this instability reflects the difficulties encountered in implementing a fully operational common external tariff, the numerous exceptions to the free trade zone and common external tariff granted to the smaller and poorer countries, and an overall lack of discipline in implementing agreed rules. Given the lack of data on these constant changes, the evolution of the agreement's coefficients is our best shot at tracking down CARICOM's trade impacts.

· The results, which are plotted in figure 4, suggest that the agreement's heyday was on the early 1970s, right after it was signed. Since implementation moved slowly, the positive impact on intraregional trade in those years may reflect the preferences established under CARIFTA in 1968 or even some idiosyncrasy of trade in the region, though the latter option is not likely to have played a significant role given the fixed effect controls used in the estimation. As the agreement moved into the late 1970s and 1980s, the positive impact on intraregional trade decreased abruptly. This may have resulted from the increase in intraregional barriers to trade imposed by import substitution policies in the larger countries in the 1970s and, later, by the debt crises in the 1980s. The reforms of the 1990s seem to have stopped the free fall of the agreement's benefits, but they were clearly unable to reverse the declining trend.

---

49. Égoumé-Bossogo and Mendis (2002).

FIGURE 4.   CARICOM's Estimated Coefficients, 1973–2003

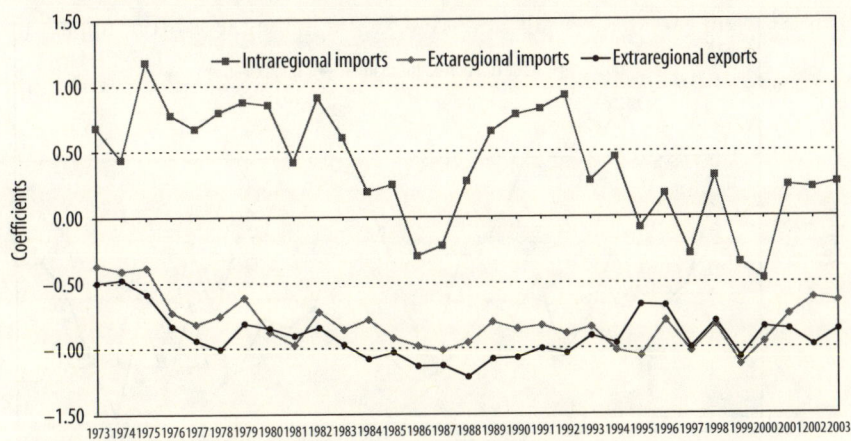

Source: Data from table 6, column 4. Time-variant CARICOM coefficients are available on request.
CARICOM = Caribbean Community and Common Market.

The impact on extraregional trade is estimated to be negative right from the start of the series. It worsens in the 1970s and 1980s, probably as a result of the increase in extraregional protection triggered by the same shocks experienced by intraregional trade. It then undergoes a slight improvement after the reforms in the early 1990s, when members reached an agreement on implementing a considerably lower common external tariff.[50] The behavior of the coefficient on extraregional exports follows a similar pattern, failing to show any positive impact on the region's competitiveness.

Figure 5 shows how trade creation and diversion evolved during the period, using the marginal and absolute concepts discussed earlier. In absolute terms, the agreement was net trade diverting over the whole period, increasingly so in the late 1970s and 1980s and less so in the 1990s. The drop in external protection apparently was not sufficient to minimize the negative impact on external imports, while factors such as the limited size of the common market and the similarity of factor endowment did not provide enough fuel for trade creation. The marginal concept followed a similar negative trend; the only marked difference was a brief period of net trade creation in the early 1970s.[51]

50. The previous CET was never fully implemented.
51. In the working paper version of this study (Moreira and Mendoza 2006), we use a smaller database (sixty-nine countries, for the period 1970–2003) and a panel with country-pair random effects; we reached similar results in terms of the trends of CARICOM's impacts.

FIGURE 5.   CARICOM's Trade Creation, 1973–2003[a]

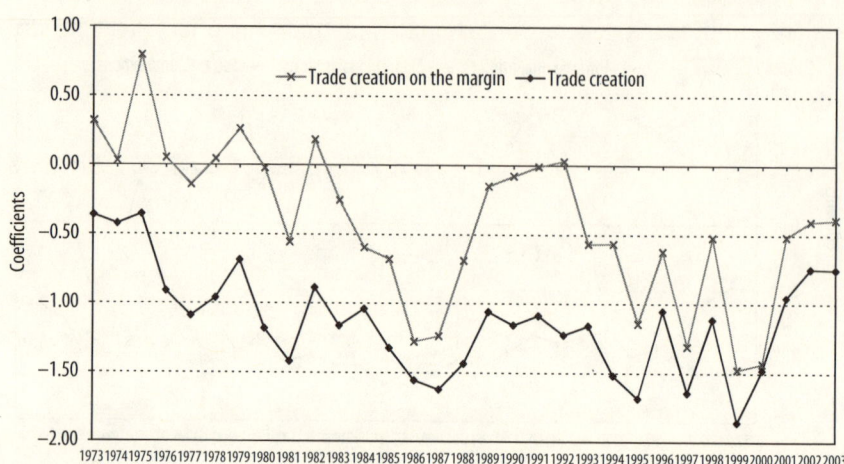

Source: Data from table 6, column 4. Time-variant CARICOM coefficients are available on request.
CARICOM = Caribbean Community and Common Market.
a. Trade creation on the margin is the sum of the coefficient of the intraregional (INT) and extraregional (IM) import dummies. Trade creation is the sum of the value of intraregional and extraregional imports that stand above the level predicted by geographical variables and country fixed effects, normalized by the value of total observed imports.

What has been happening in the region is arguably trade destruction rather than trade diversion, since the negative impact on trade abroad has not been matched by the creation of trade at home. The region imports less from the rest of the world, but since it does not have the necessary skills and endowment to substitute for those imports, it stops consuming those goods altogether or, more likely, starts buying them from smugglers. This picture contrasts heavily with the rosy scenario described by Égoumé-Bossogo and Mendis, and it confirms the agreement's limitations in generating traditional trade gains.[52] The fact that the agreement failed to boost trade even after the reforms of the 1990s suggests that the trade-creating prospects of the CSME are not at all encouraging.

Policy Implications and Conclusions

In the Caribbean, where all but three countries are classified by the United Nation as microstates, the motivation behind regional integration arises from a deep-rooted economic perception about size constraints on development.

52. Égoumé-Bossogo and Mendis (2002).

Economic theory lends qualified support to this concern, but the theory does not contend that the advantages of size are absolute. Large size carries costs in the form of heterogeneous preferences, and trade can often attenuate size restrictions. These insights are particularly useful for understanding the dynamics of Caribbean integration The costs and benefits of size help explain why, despite their profound awareness of their size limitations, Caribbean countries have long resisted deep forms of political and economic integration. The high degree of openness that marks most economies in the region, the countries' nonreciprocal preferential access to markets in the United States and the European Union, and the substantial inflows of aid and FDI to the region have probably attenuated the size handicap, thereby reducing the appeal of regional integration without lowering the associated heterogeneity (or sovereignty) costs.

Our growth accounting exercise, which simulates the impact of the enlarged CARICOM market on the growth rates of Barbados, Guyana, Jamaica, and Trinidad and Tobago, illustrates these points. The results show that changes in size—the so-called market-size effect—have little impact on these countries' growth rates, particularly when compared to changes in other growth determinants such as openness, investment, and human capital. These results seem to reflect the fact that these economies are already more open than the world average, and an increase in size would carry more costs (in the form of heterogeneous preferences) than benefits.

The interaction between size, openness, and preference costs also seems to be behind the timing of the CSME initiative. Two of the main pillars of CARICOM's openness—namely, unilateral preferences for CARICOM exports to world markets and inflows of international aid and FDI—are being rapidly eroded by the proliferation of preferential agreements and unfavorable rulings by the World Trade Organization (WTO), together with the growing competition for aid and FDI. Thus, while globalization is expanding the world market, the Caribbean's export markets are shrinking because of the idiosyncrasies of their insertion into the world economy. To put it in another way, globalization is tightening the region's size constraints.

So, how can the CSME help Caribbean countries redress the balance between size and openness and thereby improve the region's growth prospects? Policymakers should have no illusions about the traditional trade gains of integration, for three key reasons: policy barriers to intraregional trade are, on average, already low; the countries' factor endowments are generally very similar; and the region as a whole fits into the description of small country. Our descriptive analysis of the region's trade flows supports these claims. Three decades of integration have not done much to bolster intraregional trade, and the CSME is unlikely to change this picture. True, the period analyzed covers different levels of discipline and implementation of the free trade zone and common market, and the analysis of actual tariffs and tax burdens on imports suggests that removing those trade costs will lead to additional gains. On average, though, these costs are not high enough that their removal would substantially change the rather modest performance of intraregional trade.

We also performed a more rigorous analysis using a gravity model. The results confirm that the agreement has had a positive impact on intraregional trade over its three decades of existence. At the same time, the trade-creating benefits are much lower than previously estimated and have been declining since the early 1970s, despite the reforms of the 1990s. Moreover, the agreement has been net trade diverting, on average, and the recent changes in the common external tariff were not enough to change that. Finally, the impact on extraregional exports is, if anything, negative.

The signs of trade diversion are particularly troubling considering that the production of goods is clearly moving toward one of the largest countries in the region. To avert a politically unsustainable scenario in which larger and wealthier countries receive all the benefits of integration, it is important to design policies that favor the smaller and poorer partners, beyond further reductions in the common external tariff. CARICOM has already taken a key initiative in this direction with the creation of the Regional Development Fund. Other possibilities include giving smaller, poorer countries the possibility of offering more generous fiscal and credit incentives than their larger counterparts, within the context of a much needed harmonization of investment policies, and adopting a distribution criterion of the common tariff revenue that would favor the more vulnerable partners.

The free movement of labor, which also figures among the objectives of the CSME, is also likely to spread the benefits of integration more evenly. It allows labor to follow spatial changes in the allocation of investment, creating job options for workers that live in countries or regions that might eventually lose from integration. It also prevents wages and incomes among member countries from following a politically unstainable divergence path. Liberalization in this area has to be gradual, however, to avoid large and rapid movements of labor across borders, a phenomenon that could cause a political backlash. An intraregional work visa scheme with quotas for unskilled workers might be an efficient way to start this process.

The prospects of trade-related gains are thus modest and conditional on common market rules' being strictly enforced (and distributional risks' being managed). The advantages of size go well beyond the production of tradable goods, however, and the real payoff of integration may come in non-trade-related areas. Size matters in the production of goods and services that make up the countries' social and physical infrastructure. The empirical evidence on infrastructure costs in small states supports this claim, and there is no reason for these gains to be limited to physical infrastructure. Other nontradable sectors such as education and all the institutions of government are likely to have a minimum efficient scale that is far larger than most states in the Caribbean. Reaping those gains can have very concrete implications for growth if it stimulates investment in human and physical capital, as suggested by the empirical growth model reviewed.

This point has not gone unnoticed by CARICOM governments and officials, who list "functional cooperation" as one of their goals, and the region already has a number of important initiatives in areas such as education, disaster management, and foreign policy coordination. Nevertheless, the text of the treaties and their implementation seem to give functional cooperation an ancillary role to the traditional, trade-related areas of CARICOM. Functional integration is even described as the "noneconomic" side of integration, when, in fact, integration gains in nontradables are likely to dwarf the traditional gains from trade. To maximize those nontradable gains, the region must broaden the focus of integration and undertake more ambitious efforts than have been seen so far. The key to those gains is to find nontradable goods and services whose joint provision on a regional basis reduces costs—and, therefore, the fiscal burden on firms and individuals—while improving their availability.

Appendix: Data Sources and Country Samples

We used the following data sources in constructing our version of the growth regression:

—Growth rate of real per capita income, population, GDP, real per capita GDP, investment, and government consumption: Penn World Table version 6.2.[53]
—Human capital: Barro and Lee (2001).
—Small country, island, small island, and landlocked country (geographic dummy variables): source: authors' calculations.

53. Heston, Summers, and Aten (2002).

The countries included in the growth exercise are as follows:

—Industrial countries: Australia, Austria, Belgium and Luxembourg, Canada, Denmark, Finland, France, Greece, Ireland, Italy, Japan, the Netherlands, New Zealand, Norway, Portugal, Spain, Sweden, Switzerland, the United Kingdom, and the United States.

—Africa: Algeria, Benin, Botswana, Cameroon, Congo, Gambia, Ghana, Kenya, Lesotho, Malawi, Mali, Mauritius, Mozambique, Niger, Rwanda, Senegal, South Africa, Togo, Uganda, Zambia, and Zimbabwe.

—Asia: Bangladesh, Fiji, Hong Kong (China), India, Indonesia, Korea, Malaysia, Nepal, Pakistan, Papua New Guinea, Philippines, Sri Lanka, and Thailand.

—Developing Europe: Iceland and Turkey.

—Middle East: Iran, Israel, Jordan, and Syria.

—Latin America and the Caribbean: Argentina, Bolivia, Brazil, Chile, Colombia, Costa Rica, the Dominican Republic, Ecuador, El Salvador, Guatemala, Honduras, Mexico, Nicaragua, Panama, Paraguay, Peru, Uruguay, and Venezuela.

—Caribbean Community and Common Market (CARICOM): Barbados, Guyana, Jamaica, and Trinidad and Tobago.

Table A-1 lists the countries included in our gravity tests, together with their respective regional trade agreements. Our data sources for this exercise are as follows:

—Import flows (in current U.S. dollars): United Nations Commodity Trade Statistics Database (COMTRADE); CARICOM Secretariat.

—GDP (in current U.S. dollars) and population: World Bank, *World Development Indicators* (WDI); Penn World Table, version 6.2.

—Land area, geodesic distance between the cities, colonial history, geographical characteristics, and language: the Centre d'Etudes Prospectives et d'Informations Internationales (CEPII) database.

TABLE A-1. Gravity Model: Countries and Agreements in Sample[a]

	Country	Agreement		Country	Agreement		Country	Agreement
1	Afghanistan		30	Comoros		59	Haiti	
2	Algeria		31	Congo		60	Honduras	
3	Antigua and Barbuda	CARICOM	32	Costa Rica		61	Hong Kong	
4	Argentina	MERCOSUR	33	Cuba		62	Hungary	EU
5	Australia	SPARTECA	34	Cyprus		63	Iceland	
6	Austria	EU	35	Côte d'Ivoire		64	India	
7	Bahamas	CARICOM	36	Democratic People's Rep. Korea		65	Indonesia	
8	Bahrain		37	Democratic Rep. Congo		66	Iran	
9	Bangladesh		38	Denmark	EU	67	Iraq	
10	Barbados	CARICOM	39	Dominica	CARICOM	68	Ireland	EU
11	Belize	CARICOM	40	Dominican Republic		69	Israel	
12	Benin		41	Ecuador		70	Italy	EU
13	Bermuda		42	Egypt		71	Jamaica	CARICOM
14	Bhutan		43	El Salvador		72	Japan	
15	Bolivia		44	Equatorial Guinea		73	Jordan	
16	Botswana		45	Ethiopia		74	Kenya	
17	Brazil	MERCOSUR	46	Fiji	SPARTECA	75	Kiribati	
18	Brunei Darussalam		47	Finland	EU	76	Kuwait	
19	Burkina Faso		48	France	EU	77	Lao People's Democratic Rep.	
20	Burundi		49	Gabon		78	Lesotho	
21	Cambodia		50	Gambia		79	Liberia	
22	Cameroon		51	Germany	EU	80	Macao	
23	Canada	NAFTA	52	Ghana		81	Madagascar	
24	Cape Verde		53	Greece	EU	82	Malawi	
25	Central African Republic		54	Grenada	CARICOM	83	Malaysia	
26	Chad		55	Guatemala		84	Maldives	
27	Chile	MERCOSUR	56	Guinea		85	Mali	
28	China		57	Guinea-Bissau		86	Malta	
29	Colombia		58	Guyana	CARICOM	87	Mauritania	

(continued)

T A B L E A - 1. Gravity Model: Countries and Agreements in Sample[a] (Continued)

	Country	Agreement		Country	Agreement		Country	Agreement
88	Mauritius		110	Poland		132	Suriname	CARICOM
89	Mexico	NAFTA	111	Portugal	EU	133	Swaziland	
90	Micronesia		112	Qatar		134	Sweden	EU
91	Mongolia		113	Republic of Korea		135	Switzerland	
92	Morocco		114	Romania		136	Syrian Arab Republic	
93	Mozambique		115	Rwanda		137	Thailand	
94	Namibia		116	Saint Kitts and Nevis	CARICOM	138	Togo	
95	Nepal		117	Saint Lucia	CARICOM	139	Tonga	SPARTECA
96	Netherlands Antilles		118	Saint Vincent and the Grenadines	CARICOM	140	Trinidad and Tobago	CARICOM
97	Netherlands	EU	119	Samoa	SPARTECA	141	Tunisia	
98	New Zealand	SPARTECA	120	São Tomé and Príncipe		142	Turkey	
99	Nicaragua		121	Saudi Arabia		143	Uganda	
100	Niger		122	Senegal		144	United Arab Emirates	
101	Nigeria		123	Seychelles		145	United Kingdom	EU
102	Norway		124	Sierra Leone		146	United Rep. of Tanzania	
103	Oman		125	Singapore		147	United States	NAFTA
104	Pakistan		126	Solomon Islands	SPARTECA	148	Uruguay	MERCOSUR
105	Panama		127	Somalia		149	Vanuatu	SPARTECA
106	Papua New Guinea	SPARTECA	128	South Africa		150	Venezuela	
107	Paraguay	MERCOSUR	129	Spain	EU	151	Zambia	
108	Peru		130	Sri Lanka		152	Zimbabwe	
109	Philippines		131	Sudan				

CARICOM = Caribbean Community and Common Market; EU = European Union; MERCOSUR = Southern Common Market; NAFTA = North American Free Trade Agreement; SPARTECA = South Pacific Regional Trade and Economic Cooperation Agreement.

a. Agreements are listed on the basis of data availability and identification.

Comments

Stephen Meardon: The gist of Mauricio Mesquita Moreira and Eduardo Mendoza's answer to the question posed in their title is persuasive. I grant their main argument: the CARICOM members' "prospects of trade-related gains are modest and conditional on common market rules being strictly enforced." It is harder to grant the parenthetical point at the end of that sentence: "(and distributional risks being managed)." That is not to say that a concern with the possible distributional consequences of the CARICOM is necessarily misplaced. The distribution of industry among countries, and of income among countries and classes, clearly has consequences. One may worry about those consequences either for moral reasons or for fear of popular resentment and its repercussions on economic policy. But Moreira and Mendoza have in mind a particular "distributional risk" that is overstated. This may seem a narrow point in the context of their expansive article, but it is worth making because their note of concern is not heard just once: it is carried throughout the paper. Yet it seems discordant with reason and evidence.

The distributional risk that preoccupies the authors is that of "the agglomeration of economic activities" in the big and rich CARICOM countries at the expense of the small and poor ones. The authors state that the larger members, particularly Trinidad and Tobago, have benefited from CARICOM's diversion of trade, to the extent that their shares of intraregional (as well as extraregional) manufacturing exports are increasing. Concerted action is required before the larger and wealthier countries crowd out the smaller countries altogether.

The preoccupation is amiss for three reasons. First, in CARICOM, smaller does not mean poorer, and larger does not necessarily mean wealthier. The authors know this well—hence their avoidance of using common categories like less-developed countries and more-developed countries interchangeably with their chosen categories of OECS countries, which are generally small, and non-OECS countries, which are generally large. In the Caribbean, however, the association of size and wealth should arguably not just be avoided, but rather reversed.

Generally, small OECS countries, like St. Lucia and St. Kitts and Nevis, are modestly to moderately prosperous. Generally, large non-OECS countries are a mix, including a moderately prosperous country (namely, Trinidad and Tobago), a less prosperous one (Guyana), and an even less prosperous one that also happens to be one of the largest (Jamaica). All of the OECS countries had higher per capita income levels in 2003 than Guyana and Jamaica. Moreover, based on figure 1 in the paper, the smaller countries, most of which are in the OECS, appear at least vaguely to have seen higher growth rates of per capita income from 1971 to 2003 than the larger countries. Moreira and Mendoza themselves call attention to this fact early in the paper. Consider what this implies for their distributional fears!

Second, inasmuch as agglomeration is occurring in one particular big and prosperous country (Trinidad and Tobago), it is a stretch to say that what is being agglomerated there are "economic activities." In some instances, Moreira and Mendoza speak more precisely of the agglomeration of manufacturing industry or "the production of goods," but the alarm of the other formulation continues to ring in one's ears.

The production and export of tangible goods, especially manufactured goods, is fetishized. It is hard to see why. The intraregional division of labor appears to favor a pattern of production and trade that can be characterized simply, if a little crudely, like this: among non-OECS countries, Trinidad and Tobago exports fuels and manufactured goods both intraregionally, to the likes of St. Lucia and St. Kitts and Nevis, and extraregionally, to the United States; Jamaica and Guyana struggle. Among OECS countries, St. Lucia and St. Kitts and Nevis export tourist services extraregionally to the United States and Europe. Judging from the data already surveyed, the pattern appears to be serving St. Kitts and Nevis very well—and St. Lucia, too, in terms of growth rates of income if not yet levels. Instead of giving manufactured goods the privileged place among economic activities and worrying on behalf of the OECS about their agglomeration in Trinidad and Tobago, one might more reasonably give the privileged place to tourist services and worry on behalf of Jamaica and Guyana about their agglomeration in the OECS.

Third, however, even if it is legitimate to worry about the effects on other countries of the agglomeration of manufacturing in Trinidad and Tobago—at least inasmuch as the agglomeration is the result of trade diversion that is costly to the other countries' taxpayers—the concern with the OECS countries still seems misplaced. Trade diversion, the authors show in figure 6, was not much of an issue until the late 1970s. It grew throughout most of the 1980s, reaching its most serious point in 1986–87, and then subsided in the late 1980s and vanished ("at the margin") by 1992. It then reappeared in 1993 and persisted through 2003. To the extent that the trade diversion is related to manufactures, and Trinidad and Tobago is the beneficiary, one might expect the country's share of CARICOM intraregional exports of manufactures to have grown from the 1980s to the 1990s and again from the 1990s to the 2000s. A glance at table 4 reveals that this expectation is validated: Trinidad and Tobago's share grew from 32.1 percent in the 1980s to 56.3 percent in the 1990s and 65.1 percent in the early 2000s. But which intraregional partners were importing their wares, and in what values? Although the tables do not say precisely, table 3 outlines the changes in CARICOM countries' shares of intraregional imports of goods. As Trinidad and Tobago's share declined by nearly two-thirds, or 16 percentage points, from 1980 to 2000–03, the largest increase was in Jamaica's share, which more than doubled as it rose over 20 percentage points. The collective share of the OECS countries hardly budged. This does not establish decisively that Jamaican taxpayers, rather than OECS ones, have borne the price of CARICOM's trade diversion, but it hints at that conclusion.

Concern about the distributional consequences to small and poor countries of establishing trade preferences vis-à-vis big and rich countries is an old trope that may still be valid in some cases. For at least a few reasons, it is probably not so in the particular case of CARICOM. Among the many virtues of Moreira and Mendoza's article is this: the evidence they offer is enough to bring one to reject the trope, even if the authors cannot bring themselves to do it.

Irene Brambilla: A big part of the discussion by Moreira and Mendoza centers on country and market size. This is only natural. Regional integration is, to some degree, about becoming a larger economy. It is about increasing the extent of the market and having more negotiating power in international forums. In the case of the Caribbean, some of the countries involved are among the smallest countries in the world—three of them with a population below 100,000.

Size can refer to different aspects of the economy, however. One question related to size is whether CARICOM members have access to a larger market because of the agreement. In classical trade models, market size does not matter; gains from trade are derived from the change in relative prices. Nevertheless, firms benefit from larger markets under imperfect competition and scale economies, when they are able to slide down their average cost curves. Aggregate resources are used more efficiently. The gains from having access to a bigger market are even larger under interfirm technological externalities and dynamic learning by doing. Exports per se do matter.

So, has CARICOM led to an increase in market size for its members? Moreira and Mendoza are skeptical, arguing that the CARICOM member countries already had access to a large export market prior to signing CARICOM. As former colonies of the United Kingdom, they had preferential access to the U.K. market that was later extended to preferential access to the European Union. The United States also granted unilateral preferential access to CARICOM members.

There is a lot of intuition and some verifiable truth to this argument. Data from the U.N. Commodity Trade Statistics Database (COMTRADE) indicate that only 18 percent of CARICOM exports went to other CARICOM members in 2000. This is a relatively small share compared, for example, with the United States and the North American Free Trade Agreement (NAFTA): 34 percent of U.S. exports went to NAFTA that same year.

The interpretation of time series is not as straightforward. One problem is the lack of a clear-cut definition of the periods before and after CARICOM that could serve as a basis for evaluation. CARICOM was signed in 1973, but integration attempts in the region go back as early as the 1950s. At the same time, member countries still apply considerable import taxes to inter-CARICOM imports.

Moreira and Mendoza identify two key time periods for their before-and-after comparisons: the early 1970s, when CARICOM was signed, and the 1990s and early 2000s, when a series of reforms led to significant advances in the implementation of free trade and a common external tariff. Figure 3 in the paper shows the evolution of inter- and intraregional trade from 1970 onward. The graph shows that the two reform periods coincide with an increase in intraregional trade that does not take place at the expense of interregional trade. While this is not enough evidence to establish a direct causality from CARICOM to trade flows, it does suggest that CARICOM signatories did indeed take advantage of the new trade opportunities.

Other relevant issues are related not to market size, but to the size of the trade bloc. Large economies can affect the terms of trade, and they can also exert more influence in multilateral negotiations. Although Moreira and Mendoza do not directly address these issues, they indirectly disregard them by arguing that the combined size of the CARICOM bloc is still small, with a population comparable to Chile and a GDP comparable to Ecuador. This is certainly true on aggregate, yet the CARICOM countries are important producers of a few products, such as sugar cane and rum. The major exporter of rum within the CARICOM is Jamaica, with a share of 5.7 percent of world exports in 2004. The combined share of the CARICOM bloc is 14 percent, which is hardly insignificant. These are only a few isolated products, but they are significant within such small economies.

Increasing the size of a bloc also opens the door to agglomeration externalities, especially (but not only) under free movement of factors of production. Moreira and Mendoza point out that these forces could lead to regional inequality if Jamaica and Trinidad and Tobago, the largest members of CARICOM, were to capture the bulk of manufacturing sectors that are sensitive to agglomeration externalities.

The discussion about size serves as a starting point for a more systematic empirical evaluation. The authors run a growth regression with decadal panel data at the country level. The main explanatory variables are size, measured as either population or GDP, and openness, measured (imports plus exports) over GDP. The result, as expected, is positive, but the insight is that the positive effect of size is decreasing in openness, meaning that more open economies benefit less from being larger—or that large economies benefit less from being open. The regression results are then used to simulate a change in size in the four CARICOM countries included in the regression, whereby the actual population of each CARICOM country is replaced by the total CARICOM population. The estimated impact on the growth rate is negative for three of the four countries.

The premise of the simulation exercise and the interpretation of the results are somewhat unclear. The idea behind the exercise is that full integration is equal to an increase in size as measured by population. But does population size refer to market size, which is associated with the exploitation of scale economies, or to bloc size? Surely it does not fully capture market size. First, as argued in the paper, international markets also count for market size, and this is partly captured by the openness variable. Second, CARICOM was signed in 1973 and spans three of the four decades of data (so the simulation is not really counterfactual), meaning that the CARICOM countries already had an expanded market as a result of CARICOM during this period. Moreover, even if the data were pre-CARICOM, CARICOM (or any other preferential trade agreement) does not represent a movement from autarky to free trade; the CARICOM market would have been partially available to its members even in the absence of a free trade agreement. Such a big change in population overstates the change in market size generated by CARICOM. Third, full integration implies a change in openness, which is, however, kept constant in the simulation exercise. Should the exercise then be interpreted as a change in bloc size while keeping market size constant (through the openness variable)? What are the channels through which size is expected to operate in the exercise?

One of the paper's conclusions is that CARICOM countries were already very open economies before signing CARICOM, so they did not benefit much from the agreement and the agreement was not trade creating. This leads to the discussion of two more points: trade creation versus trade diversion; and the integration in nontradables. In some cases, trade creation and diversion need to be specifically defined. This is one such case. In the textbook scenario, when countries sign a preferential trade agreement, either domestic production is replaced by imports that are produced more efficiently by the signing partner (trade creation), or efficiently produced imports from the rest of the world are replaced by the less efficient production from the partner (trade diversion). In the case of CARICOM, long-term negotiations resulted in a reduction of the average common external tariff from 20 percent to 10 percent, thereby allowing for efficient imports from the rest of the world to replace domestic production. This situation is not contemplated in the textbook analysis of trade creation and trade diversion, but it is not uncommon among countries that sign preferential trade agreements amidst liberalization episodes and broad structural reform programs.

There is no undisputed procedure to measure aggregate trade creation and diversion empirically, and most studies, including this one, rely on gravity regressions that use bilateral trade data. The portion of bilateral trade that is not explained by "natural forces" such as income and distance is attributed to "institutional forces"—in this case, the CARICOM agreement. The results of this reduced-form analysis reflect the net effect of changes in trade policy, including both the reduction of intra-CARICOM tariffs and taxes and the reduction in the common external tariff.

The ideal gravity exercise is one in which data are available before and after the CARICOM agreement. This is important for two reasons. First, in this ideal scenario, identification comes from both the time and cross-country dimensions; second, it allows for the inclusion of country-pair fixed effects that capture unobserved predispositions for bilateral trade. As noted above, the periods before and after CARICOM are not clear-cut, and, more importantly, there are no pre-CARICOM data. This leaves Moreira and Mendoza with the deviations from natural forces as the sole source of identification of the CARICOM effects and no possibility to control for country-pair unobservables.

They estimate several specifications, some of them correcting for sample selection issues, some allowing for importer and exporter unobservables, and some allowing for trade creation and diversion coefficients that vary over time. They find that trade creation was greatest in the early stages of the CARICOM and that trade diversion dominated later in the period.

Moreira and Mendoza's view of the trade-related aspects of CARICOM is not rosy. They argue, however, that the CARICOM initiative and further integration through the single-market economy (CSME) offer the potential for economies of scale in nontradables sectors: "Integration gains in nontradables are likely to dwarf the traditional gains from trade." This is an important point, although they do not pursue it in detail. The paper's central message is that policymakers would do well to shift the CARICOM integration efforts from trade policy to other aspects.

References

Alesina, Alberto, and Enrico Spolaore. 2003. *The Size of Nations.* MIT Press.

Alesina, Alberto, Enrico Spolaore, and Romain Wacziarg. 2005. "Trade, Growth, and the Size of the Countries." In *Handbook of Economic Growth,* vol. 1, edited by Philippe Aghion and Steven Durlauf. Amsterdam: Elsevier.

Anderson, James E., and Eric van Wincoop. 2004. "Trade Costs." *Journal of Economic Literature* 42(3): 691–751.

Barro, Robert J., and Jong-Wha Lee. 2001. "International Data on Educational Attainment: Updates and Implications." *Oxford Economic Papers* 53(3): 541–63.

Caldentey, Esteban Pére. 2005. "Export Promotion Policies in CARICOM: Main Issues, Effects, and Implications." International trade series 56. Santiago: Economic Commission for Latin America and the Caribbean.

Canning David, Marianne Fay, and Roberto Perotti. 1994. "Infrastructure and Growth." In *International Differences in Growth Rates: Market Globalization and Economic Areas,* edited by Mario Baldassarri, Luigi Paganetto, and Edmund S. Phelps. New York: St. Martin's Press.

CARICOM Secretariat. 2005. *CARICOM: Our Caribbean Community.* Kingston, Jamaica: Ian Randle Publishers.

De Melo, Jaime, and Arvind Panagariya. 1993. "Introduction." In *New Dimensions in Regional Integration.* Cambridge University Press for the Center for Economic Policy Research.

Doumenge, François. 1983. *Viability of Small Island States.* Geneva: United Nations Conference on Trade and Development.

Easterly, William, and Aart Kraay. 1999. "Small States, Small Problems?" Policy Research Working Paper 2139. Washington: World Bank.

Égoumé-Bossogo, Philippe, and Chandima Mendis. 2002. "Trade and Integration in the Caribbean." Working Paper WP/02/08. Washington: International Monetary Fund.

Farrell, Trevor. 1981. "Five Major Problems for CARICOM." In *The Caribbean Community: Beyond Survival,* edited by Kenneth O. Hall. Kingston, Jamaica: Ian Randle Publishers.

Feenstra, Robert C. 2002. "Border Effects and the Gravity Equation: Consistent Methods for Estimation." *Scottish Journal of Political Economy* 49(5): 491–506.

Frankel, Jeffrey A., and David Romer. 1999. "Does Trade Cause Growth?" *American Economic Review* 89(3): 379–99.

Grossman, Gene, and Elhanan Helpman. 1991. *Innovation and Growth in the Global Economy.* MIT Press.

Gwartney, James D., Randall G. Holcombe, and Robert A. Lawson. 2006. "Institutions and the Impact of Investment on Growth." *Kyklos* 59(2): 255–73.

Hall, Robert, and Charles I. Jones. 1999. "Why Do Some Countries Produce So Much More Output per Worker than Others?" *Quarterly Journal of Economics* 114(1): 83–116.

Heckman, James J. 1976. "The Common Structure of Statistical Models of Truncation, Sample Selection, and Limited Dependent Variable and a Simple Estimator for Such Models." *Annals of Economic and Social Measurement* 5(4): 475–92.

Helpman, Elhanan, and Paul Krugman. 1986. *Market Structure and Foreign Trade.* MIT Press.

Helpman, Elhanan, Marc Melitz, and Yona Rubinstein. 2007. "Estimating Trade Flows: Trading Partners and Trading Volumes." Working Paper 12927. Cambridge, Mass.: National Bureau of Economic Research.

Heston, Alan, Robert Summers, and Bettina Aten. 2002. "Penn World Table Version 6.2." University of Pennsylvania, Center for International Comparisons.

IDB (Inter-American Development Bank). 2002. *Beyond Borders. The New Regionalism in Latin America.* Washington: Johns Hopkins University Press for the Inter-American Development Bank.

Jessen, Anneke, and Christopher Vignoles. 2005. "CARICOM Report No 2." Washington: Inter-American Development Bank, Institute for the Integration of Latin America and the Caribbean (INTAL).

Lewis, Gordon K. 1968. *The Growth of the Modern West Indies.* Kingston, Jamaica: Ian Randle Publishers.

Lewis, Patsy. 2002. *Surviving Small Size: Regional Integration in Caribbean Ministates.* Kingston, Jamaica: Stephenson's Litho Press.

Moreira, Mauricio Mesquita, and Eduardo Mendoza. 2006. "Regional Integration: What Is in It for CARICOM?" Working Paper 29. Washington: Inter-American Development Bank, Institute for the Integration of Latin America and the Caribbean (INTAL).

Rivera-Batiz, Luis A., and Paul Romer. 1991. "Economic Integration and Endogenous Growth." *Quarterly Journal of Economics* 106(2): 531–55.

Rose, Andrew K. 2004. "Do We Really Know That the WTO Increases Trade?" *American Economic Review* 94(1): 98–114.

———. 2006. "Size Doesn't Really Matter: In Search of a National Scale Effect." Working Paper 12191. Cambridge, Mass.: National Bureau of Economic Research.

Ross-Brewster, Havelock R. H. 2000. "Identity, Space, and the West Indian Union." In *Contending with Destiny: The Caribbean in the 21st Century,* edited by Kenneth Hall and Denis Benn. Kingston, Jamaica: Ian Randle Publishers.

Soloaga, Isidro, and L. Alan Winters. 2001. "Regionalism in the Nineties: What Is the Effect on Trade?" *North American Journal of Economics and Finance* 12(1): 1–29.

Srinivasan, T. N. 1986. "The Cost and Benefits of Being a Small, Remote, Island, Landlocked, or Ministate Economy." *World Bank Research Observer* 1(2): 205–18.

Venables, Anthony J. 2003. "Regionalism and Economic Development." In *Bridges for Development: Policies and Institutions for Trade and Integration,* edited by Robert Devlin and Antonio Estevadeordal. Washington: Inter-American Development Bank.

Viner, Jacob. 2005. *The Customs Union Issue.* New York: Carnegie Endowment for International Peace.

Winters, L. Alan, and Pedro Martins. 2004. "When Comparative Advantage Is Not Enough: Business Costs in Small Remote Economies." *World Trade Review* 3(3): 347–83.

Witter, Michael, Lino Brigulio, and Assad Bhuglah. 2002. "Measuring and Managing the Economic Vulnerability of Small Island Developing States." Paper prepared for the UNDP Global Roundtable on Vulnerability and Small Island Developing States: Exploring Mechanisms for Partnerships. United Nations Development Program, Montego Bay, Jamaica, 9–10 May.

World Bank. 2000. *Trade Blocs.* Oxford University Press for the World Bank.

———. 2005. "Institutions, Performance, and the Financing of Infrastructure Services in the Caribbean." Working Paper 58. Washington: World Bank.

ADRIANA CUOCO PORTUGAL
MAURÍCIO BUGARIN

Electoral Campaign Financing: The Role of Public Contributions and Party Ideology

D emocracy has made impressive progress over the last thirty years in Latin America. Since the beginning of the so-called third wave of democratization in 1978, the UNDP's index of electoral democracy has risen from below 0.3 in 1977 to above 0.9 in 2002, confirming that most citizens in the region live in highly electoral democratic countries.[1] That positive situation, however, has repeatedly been upset by political challenges. Over the thirteen-year period 1990–2002, Latin America registered twelve cases of elections with significant irregularities.[2] Moreover, cases of illicit political funding through hidden accounts or covert line items have ignited several crises and placed many a president and former president in situations of impeachment or even imprisonment, including Brazil's Fernando Collor de Mello, Ecuador's Jamil Mahuad, Guatemala's Alfonso Portillo, Nicaragua's Arnoldo Alemán, and Venezuela's Carlos Andrés Pérez.[3]

The concern about political corruption in Latin America has called attention to electoral campaign finances. Academics and policymakers have renewed the debate on the appropriate form of campaign financing regulation.[4] On the policy front, Transparency International analyzes seven Latin American countries from July 2002 to June 2003 (namely, Argentina, Brazil, Chile, Costa Rica,

Portugal is with the University of Brasília; Bugarin is with Ibmec São Paulo.

We thank Ian Ayres, Mirta Bugarin, Marco Bonomo, Ernesto Dal Bó, Rafael Di Tella, Eduardo Engel, Francisco Ferreira, Carlos Melo, André Oliveira, Rodrigo Peñaloza, Mattias Polborn, and Roberto Rigobon for helpful comments on earlier versions of this article. We also gratefully acknowledge the financial support of the National Council for Scientific and Technological Development (CNPq), Office for the Coordination of Higher Education Development (CAPES), and the Foundation for Scientific and Technological Initiatives (FINATEC).

1. UNDP (2004).
2. UNDP (2004).
3. Griner and Zovatto (2005).
4. Poiré (2005).

Guatemala, Nicaragua, and Peru).[5] Four of the seven countries modified their political campaign financing law in that short period (Argentina, Brazil, Chile, and Peru). Moreover, Costa Rica witnessed a clear call for such reform, leading the Constitutional Court to rule that "the movements and balances of current accounts held by political parties in state or private commercial banks or in any other nonbank financial entity can, in principle, be accessed by anybody."[6] Thus, five of the seven countries studied in the report made significant changes to their electoral campaign financing procedures.

While Latin America stands out as a region of frequent campaign legislation reforms, more traditional democracies also display their share of procedural changes. Public financing of electoral campaigns was implemented in the United Stated in 1904, and several additional rules have since been established, mainly motivated by fundraising scandals (such as the Watergate investigations) or the increasing cost of electoral campaigns. An important recent change was the 2003 Bipartisan Campaign Reform Act, which prohibits transfers from parties to candidates (soft money) if the money was obtained from illegal sources.[7]

Germany initiated public electoral financing in 1959, but the system was reformed in 1992 in response to a concern that public financing might reduce incentives for financial support from party members and sympathetic citizens.[8] The original Parties Financing Act set government disbursement levels for parties based on the number of votes received. A 1994 revision to the Law established that public financing is based on party membership and private contributions, as well as the number of votes received.[9] Moreover, anonymous

5. Transparency International (2004).

6. Transparency International (2004, p. 183). The report further states that "Investigations into the source of financing for the two main political parties, the National Liberation Party (PLN) and Social Christian Unity Party (PUSC), during the 2002 presidential election campaigns, uncovered a myriad of irregular funding tools—currently the subject of a congressional probe—and highlighted the need to tighten political finance legislation" (Transparency International, 2004, p. 182).

7. See Félix Ulloa, "A Framework for Political Party Financing," at www.aceproject.org/main/english/ei/eix_a040.htm and at www.cbc.ca/news/features/campaign_contributions030128.html (accessed July 2007).

8. See Félix Ulloa, "A Framework for Political Party Financing," at www.aceproject.org/main/english/ei/eix_a040.htm (accessed July 2007).

9. See www.germany-info.org/relaunch/info/publications/infocus/Elections/Political_parties.html.

private donations must not exceed U.S.$500, and detailed information must be provided on donors of more than U.S.$10,000.[10]

In 2003 Canada's House of Commons passed a bill limiting corporate and union donations to political parties to a maximum of US$1,000 and allowing them only at the riding association level, not at the level of direct donations to federal parties. Individual donations were also limited, with a maximum of US$5,000 per person. A new system of public funding has been established to compensate for the funding shortfall, based on the number of votes received by a party in the previous election, in the form of US$1.75 per taxpayer subsidy.[11]

In Latin America, Brazil's recent history presents a clear example of the region's electoral reform. In 1971, Law 5682 imposed a total ban on direct private political donations to parties and created a public fund for supporting electoral campaigns. Eighty percent of the total amount of the fund resources were distributed among existing parties according to their proportional representation in congress, while the remaining 20 percent was shared equally among all parties.[12] In late 1992, the congress impeached Brazilian President Fernando Collor de Mello after a long trial characterized by strict respect for the established institutions and popular pressure. One of the main arguments for the impeachment was that the president was unable to explain campaign donations he received illegally.[13] The Collor scandal highlighted the fact that it is basically impossible to ban private political donations. New campaign financing legislation was therefore passed in 1995, allowing private financing (Law 9096). The legislation also established new norms for the working of the public fund, known as the Parties' Fund (Fundo Partidário). According to the new rules, the treasury transfers to the Fund every year an amount equivalent to R$0.35 times the number of registered voters in December of the previous year. Of these resources, 99 percent is distributed among parties according to their congressional representation, while the remaining 1 percent

10. See www.cbc.ca/news/features/campaign_contributions030128.html (accessed July 2007).

11. See www.cbc.ca/news/features/campaign_contributions030128.html (accessed July 2007).

12. The distribution of public resources according to the parties' proportions in the legislature seems to be the most common way of distributing public resources to finance campaigns. Countries using this system include Belgium, France, Italy, and Spain.

13. A parliamentary inquiry committee found over U.S.$350 million of unexplained funds. See *Veja Online,* "Fique de Olho," in "O Esquema PC," April 2000, available at veja.abril. uol.com.br/idade/corrupcao/pc/caso.html (accessed December 2007).

is shared equally among all parties. Although private financing became legal after the 1995 law, the huge variation in candidates' declared donations suggests that there might still be an important market for illegal contributions.[14] The Brazilian congress is currently reviewing several projects for a new electoral law. A project passed in the Senate in April 2001 and still under discussion in the House of Representatives eliminates private donations and increases the amount of the treasury transfer from R$0.35 to R$7.00 per registered voter.[15] The proportional rule for the distribution of public funds among parties remains unchanged.[16]

The above examples suggest that the effect of different types of electoral financing have not yet been clearly sorted out in the applied policy debate. In the theoretical literature's seminal paper, Baron models an electoral competition in which candidates may favor interest groups to receive campaign contributions and, consequently, influence uninformed voters.[17] He introduces public financing by means of an equal lump sum given to each candidate. This financing leads, first, to a reduction of an original policy bias in favor of interest groups and, second, to a more egalitarian electoral competition. Baron's mechanism, however, is highly unlikely to exist in practice, as it suggests that the same amount of public money should be given to all parties, regardless of size. Zovatto studies eighteen Latin American countries and finds that all fifteen nations that adopted direct public financing of electoral campaigns allocate at least part of the resources based on party size in the previous elections.[18] In our model, therefore, we assume this type of public financing proportional to party representation.

---

14. The 1998 election provides a clear example of the variation in campaign resources. The winning governor of the state of Paraíba, José Maranhão, declared having spent U.S.$110,400 on his campaign, whereas the winning governor of the nearby (and smaller) state of Sergipe, Albano Franco, declared a campaign budget of U.S.$1.1 million. The runner-up candidate for the presidency that year, Luiz Inácio "Lula" da Silva, declared a budget of U.S.$3.4 million, whereas the winner, Fernando Henrique Cardoso, declared more than eleven times that amount (U.S.$37 million). See "O Caixa Dois de Volta à Luz," *Veja* (no. 1,676), 20 November 2000; the amounts in reals were converted to dollars based the exchange rate in July 1998.

15. Brazilian Senate Projects 151/99 and 353/99, passed on 26 April 2001 (Project 4593/01 in the House of Representatives).

16. The House of Representatives recently established a special commission to study this and other issues, but the proposal to increase the per capita voter transfer from R$0.35 to R$7.00 remains in the new 2003 project (Project 2679/03), which is still under discussion.

17. Baron (1994).

18. Zovatto (2003). The fifteen countries are Argentina, Bolivia, Brazil, Colombia, Costa Rica, the Dominican Republic, Ecuador, El Salvador, Guatemala, Honduras, Mexico, Nicaragua, Panama, Paraguay, and Uruguay.

Roemer analyzes two different public financing institutions in a model in which each lobbyist group contributes only to a specific party.[19] In one of the institutions, each informed voter receives a voucher worth k dollars to be donated to the party of his or her choice; in the other, public funds match private contributions. The study finds that parties propose policies that are closer to the preferences of the informed voters under the former public financing system, and that the distortion caused by private financing is magnified under the latter matching system. Public financing may thus succeed in reducing policy distortion when it is based on a system that resembles the party's representation criterion discussed.

Our paper analyzes parties' electoral financing mechanisms in a more general framework. Our model allows for public funds (which are collected from the entire population by means of taxation and distributed to the parties according to the party-representation proportional rule discussed above) and private contributions from interest groups; we also allow for parties to be both office and policy motivated. The main objectives are to assess how policy decisions (and consequently voters' welfare) are affected by public and private contributions when parties have differing ideologies and to determine the extent to which the type of financing affects parties' representation in congress in the short and long run, as a proxy for unequal party competition.

The electoral competition model focuses on elections for the legislature, using as its main tool the probabilistic voting approach introduced by Lindbeck and Weibull.[20] The hypothesis that campaign spending can influence voters follows Baron, and we borrow the idea of endogenously obtaining lobbyists' private contributions from Grossman and Helpman and from Persson and Tabellini.[21]

Our model shows that in equilibrium, parties tend to announce divergent platforms that reflect the parties' rigid ideology. This leads to policies that are not socially optimal. Moreover, parties' announced policies are biased in favor of lobbyists' interests as a result of the competition for private contributions. If policymakers can enforce a ban on private contributions, then the bias in favor of interest groups disappears. However, the bias stemming from party ideology remains, so a campaign that is completely financed by public funds still will not promote social welfare.

19. Roemer (2006).
20. Lindbeck and Weibull (1987).
21. Baron (1994); Grossman and Helpman (1996); Persson and Tabellini (2000, chapter 3).

In terms of party competition, the fact that policies diverge ensures that interest groups will effectively contribute to electoral campaigns, with a real effect on the parties' probability of success. However, a party's strong ideological rigidity may reduce its received contributions, because strong ideology decreases the bias in favor of interest groups. This effect may be so strong that some interest groups may opt to contribute to a party whose preferred platform is more distant from the group's stance, but that is less rigid in contraposition.[22] Private contributions, in turn, can directly affect a party's chances of success, changing the balance in favor of a party that originally represented only a small part of society. This is the static effect of lobbying on parties' chances of success.

Although the existence of private contributions affects parties' platform announcement decisions, public financing does not have any such effect as it is predetermined and does not change with parties' political positions. Its direct effect in the short run reduces to changing a party's probability of obtaining the majority of seats in the legislature. In the long run, however, the mechanism of public financing based on the parties' relative size in the legislature may provide an extreme advantage to one party, leading to that party's predominance. Such an advantage may arise even when the party is extremely ideologically oriented and therefore may not be very attractive to the majority of the population.

Our results confirm Baron's and Roemer's finding that policy converges to a socially superior policy if there are no private contributions and the parties' ideologies are not very rigid.[23] However, our results related to private contributions and the probability of a party's getting an increasing number of votes completely differ from the conclusions of those two studies. In fact, in our model, lobbyists may even contribute to an opposing party if the party has a very flexible ideology, which affects party competition in the short run.

Under some circumstances, public financing will completely determine a dominant party in the long run, despite the preferences of society or lobbyists. One important caveat is that the effect of public financing depends strongly on its amount. If public financing is too small, it has an insignificant long-run effect, but if it is high enough, it may entirely jeopardize long-term party competition. Our study contributes to the discussion on the optimal regulation of campaign financing by showing that the solution may not be clear-

---

22. This captures the idea of lobbying without imposing the restriction that an interest group can only contribute to one party (contrary to Roemer 2006) and shows the flexibility of our model.

23. Baron (1994); Roemer (2006).

cut and that issues regarding the amount of the public financing may be very important to the resulting political equilibrium. We also highlight the potential negative effects of distributing public funds according to the size of each party in the legislature, which suggests that a more balanced distribution may enhance welfare.

The rest of the paper is organized as follows. The next section presents and solves the model, in which parties are office and policy motivated and electoral campaigns can be financed by interest groups and by the government. We then address long-run party representation in the legislature in an infinitely iterated version of the electoral competition game. A subsequent section briefly discusses the shortcomings and possible extensions of the present study, and the final section presents our main conclusions.

A Model of Electoral Competition

The electoral competition game between parties, lobbyists, and voters is presented in figure 1. The main modeling hypothesis here is that parties announce their policies first, and then lobbyists decide whether to make political contributions based on these announcements. Parties use the private contributions and public funds they receive to influence voters during the electoral campaign. After the electoral campaign, each voter receives stochastic signals that affect his or her preferences for the parties, observes the announced platform of each party, and votes sincerely—that is, for the party that best represents his or her preferences. There is one national electoral district in which each voter has one vote. After elections, each party is assigned a quantity of seats in the legislature that corresponds to the percentage of received votes. Once the new legislature is formed, it decides which policy to implement according to the following rule: the party that has a majority of seats is able to implement its campaign platform.[24] The basic model extends Persson and Tabellini's approach to incorporate three main points: first, we allow for public funding of electoral campaigns in addition to private contributions; second, we allow for partial control of the executive over private contribution; and finally, we allow for the parties to be policy motivated as well as office motivated.[25]

In the figure, only the wider, curved rectangles correspond to real strategic decisions. The top one corresponds to parties' platform announcement;

24. The model assumes that the legislature has an odd number of seats, so one party always has a majority.

25. Persson and Tabellini (2000, chapter 3).

FIGURE 1. The Electoral Competition Game

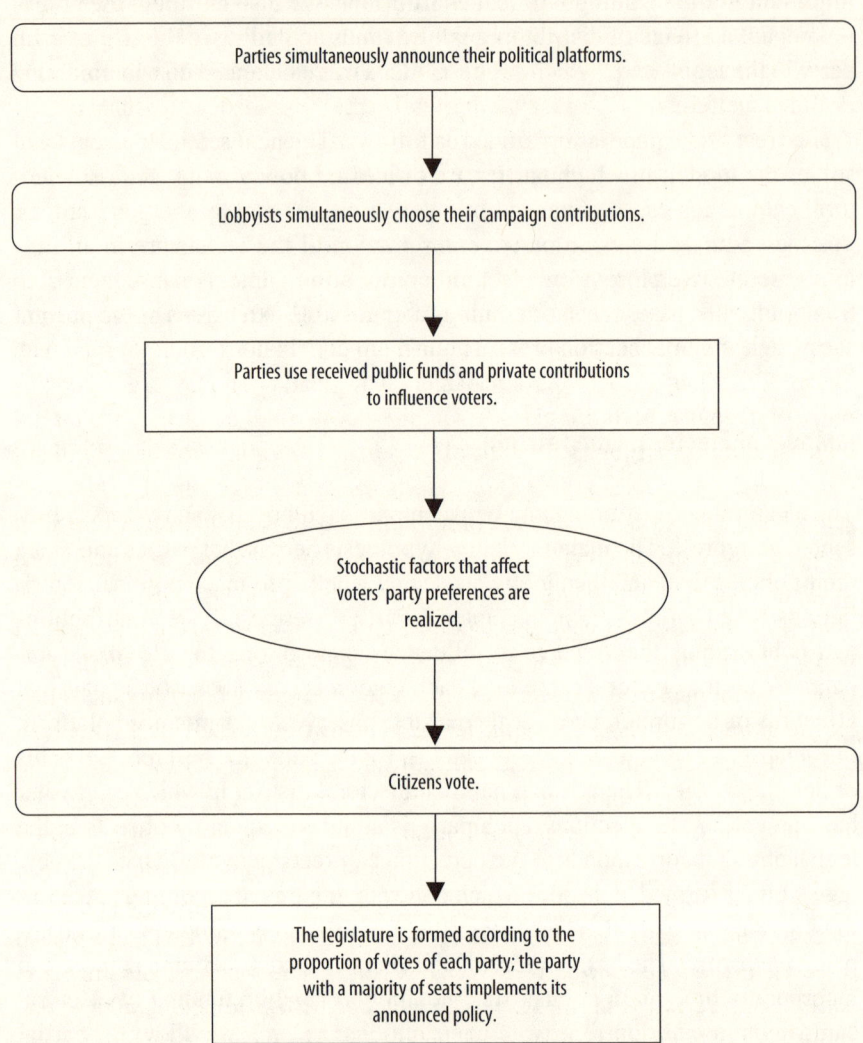

the second one from the top to lobbyists' campaign contribution decisions; and the second one from the bottom to voters' choices. The third (squared) box from the top states the assumption that parties use all available resources in their electoral campaign, so they make no decisions about deviating resources out of the campaign. The ellipse represents the realization of random variables that are out of the players' control, and the last (squared) box states the typical assumption of full commitment made in models of electoral competition (that is, the majority party implements its announced policy).

The remainder of this section details the main elements of the electoral competition model and, simultaneously, solves the game by backward induction.

Voters' Electoral Decision

There is a continuum of unit mass of voters, $\Omega = [0, 1]$. Each voter belongs to one of three social classes based on income: the upper class, R (rich), comprises voters with a high income, y^R; the middle class, M, encompasses voters with an average income, y^M; and the lower class, P (poor), covers voters with a low income, y^P. Thus, $y^R > y^M > y^P$. A social class, J ($J = R, M, P$), has mass α^J, so that $\sum_J \alpha^J = 1$.[26]

There are two parties ($P = A, B$), which compete by announcing the level of production of a per capita public good, g, that will be implemented if the party obtains the majority of seats in the legislature. Public good provision is financed by an income tax given by the rate τ, which is the same for all voters. All tax resources are converted into the public good and public funding for the parties' campaigns. Let c represent the government's per capita cost of public funding of electoral campaigns. The government budget constraint is then $\sum_J \alpha^J \tau y^J = \tau y = g + c$, where $y = \sum_J \alpha^J y^J$ represents the average income of voters.

A voter's utility has two components: a pragmatic component (or sociotropic) and an ideological (or idiosyncratic) component.[27] The pragmatic part of the utility represents the voter's decisions as an economic agent; it depends on the consumption of both a private good and the public good provided by the government. Suppose platform g wins the election. Then, an agent of class J has the following income, net of taxes:

$$c^J = (1 - \tau)y^J = (y - g - c)\frac{y^J}{y},$$

which is normalized to be the agent's private consumption utility. The pragmatic part of the utility of a voter of class J is shown in equation 1. The utility of public good consumption is given by the function H, which is assumed to be strictly increasing and strictly concave.

26. The three-class model is a simple way to characterize differences in wealth among citizens; it is straightforward to extend the model to any finite number of classes.

27. This is the most general way of characterizing an economic agent who also has political concerns. For more on this topic, see Ferejohn (1986) or Bugarin (1999, 2003).

(1)
$$W^J(g) = (y - g - c)\frac{y^J}{y} + H(g).$$

Thus, each class has its own optimal policy for the public good provision. These optimal policies are obtained by maximizing each class's utility function and are given by:

$$g_J^* = (H')^{-1}\left(\frac{y^J}{y}\right),$$

where $J = P, M, R$.

The ideological component of a voter's utility function is represented by two random variables corresponding to the voter's bias toward party B or, equivalently, to party B's popularity at the time elections are held. The first random variable is common to all voters and is associated with the realization of a state of nature that affects the entire population. Examples include a war, an abrupt change in international prices of a commodity that is important to the country, or a countrywide energy crisis. That process is described by a random variable, $\tilde{\delta}$, which the model assumes uniformly distributed on $[-(1/2\psi), (1/2\psi)]$. The parameter $\psi > 0$ measures the level of society's sensitivity to aggregate shocks: the lower the value of ψ, the stronger the effect of the shocks.

The second random variable is particular to each voter i in group J and reflects his or her personal bias toward party B. This bias is modeled as a random variable, σ^{iJ}, which is uniformly distributed on $[-(1/2\phi^J), (1/2 \phi^J)]$. Hence, the greater the parameter ϕ^J, the more homogeneous is class J. For simplicity, and to avoid electoral effects of class heterogeneity, we normalize all the classes' random variable parameters to $\phi = \phi^J$, $J = P, M, R$. Therefore, if party B wins a majority in the legislature with the announced platform g_B, a voter i in the social class J derives utility $W^J(g_B) + \sigma^{iJ} + \tilde{\delta}$.

Positive values for σ^{iJ} and for $\tilde{\delta}$ indicate a favorable bias toward party B, whereas negative values indicate a favorable bias toward party A. The realization of the global random variable can be favorable to party B at the same time that the realization of the individual-specific random variable can favor party A, and vice versa.[28]

---

28. Suppose, for example, that the country faces an economic expansion, so that society approves of the president on the overall conduct of the economy, but the president is involved in a sexual scandal, which can affect voters differently.

Consider now the role of campaign contributions in the model. For simplicity we assume that overall campaign spending will affect the ideological component of a voter's utility function, in a way that is linear to the difference between the total parties' expenditure. Then, the utility of a voter i of class J when party B's (party A's) campaign spending is C_B (C_A) and party B wins the majority of the Legislature seats is

$$(2) \qquad W^J\left(g_B\right) + \sigma^{iJ} + \tilde{\delta} + h\left(C_B - C_A\right).$$

The parameter $h > 0$ represents the effectiveness of campaign spending, that is, how much the difference between party campaign expenditures can affect it's the parties' popularity. If C_B is greater than C_A, then party B gains popularity during the electoral campaign. Otherwise, overall campaign expenditures reduce party B's popularity.

Suppose now that party P announces policy g_P, where $P = A, B$. Then a voter i in group J will prefer party A to party B if $W^J(g_A) > W^J(g_B) + \sigma^{iJ} + \tilde{\delta} + h(C_B - C_A)$. This comparison determines voters' electoral decisions.

A Benchmark for Welfare Comparison

Suppose party P wins the election with policy g_P. Then an agent I of class J derives utility

$$W^J\left(g_P\right) + \theta_P\left(\sigma^{iJ} + \tilde{\delta}\right) + h\left(C_B - C_A\right),$$

where θ_P is the party index function, which is equal to 1 if $P = B$ and zero otherwise. Suppose, moreover, that voters cannot be influenced by the electoral campaign expenditure, that is, $h = 0$. The expected utility of that voter (before the random variables are realized) then reduces to

$$W^J\left(g_P\right) = \left(y - g_P - c\right)\frac{y^J}{y} + H\left(g_P\right).$$

We want to determine what policy maximizes aggregate welfare according to the Bentham social welfare criterion. We should thus maximize

$$W\left(g_P\right) = \sum_J \alpha^J W^J\left(g_P\right),$$

which yields the socially optimal policy, $g_p = g^* = (H')^{-1}(1)$. This is our benchmark for welfare comparison in what follows.

Lobbyists' Contributions Decision

From voters' electoral decision, we can identify for each class J a voter that is indifferent between the two parties, who is called the swing voter of class J. That voter corresponds to the realization of σ^{iJ}, defined as σ^J by:

$$(3) \qquad \sigma^J = W^J\left(g_A\right) - W^J\left(g_B\right) + h\left(C_A - C_B\right) - \tilde{\delta}.$$

Therefore, the number of votes cast for party A is

$$(4) \qquad \pi^A = \sum_J \alpha^J\left(\sigma^J + \frac{1}{2\phi}\right)\phi = \frac{1}{2} + \sum_J \alpha^J \sigma^J.$$

Then, writing $W(g_A) = \sum_J \alpha^J W^J(g_A)$ and $W(g_B) = \sum_J \alpha^J W^J(g_B)$, the probability of party A's getting the majority of seats is $p_A = \text{prob}(\pi^A > 1/2) = \text{prob}[\tilde{\delta} < W(g_A) - W(g_B) + h(C_A - C_B)]$. Equivalently,

$$(5) \qquad p_A = \frac{1}{2} + \psi\left[W\left(g_A\right) - W\left(g_B\right) + h\left(C_A - C_B\right)\right].$$

Symmetrically,

$$(6) \qquad p_B = \frac{1}{2} - \psi\left[W\left(g_A\right) - W\left(g_B\right) + h\left(C_A - C_B\right)\right] = 1 - p_A.$$

We now determine the total amount of campaign resources available to the parties, C_A and C_B. As discussed in the introduction, we follow the proportional public financing distribution rule widely used in Latin America.[29] We thus assume that the total amount of resources directed to party P (where $P = A, B$) is proportional to P's representation in congress during the previous session. Let β_P denote the percentage of the total legislative seats held by party P. Then, $\beta_A + \beta_B = 1$, and the per capita funds received by each party from the government is $\beta_P.c$, where c is the per capita cost to the government of the public funding of electoral campaigns.

As for private financing, the main distinction among classes is that only organized classes who have solved the collective action problem are able to make private contributions.[30] Let the parameter O^J represent whether class J

---

29. Zovatto (2003).
30. See Olson (1971).

is organized (that is, O^J equals 1 if class J is organized and zero otherwise). Thus, if each class J makes the private contribution $O^J C_P^J$ to party $P = A, B$, the total amount of private contributions to a party P is $\sum_J O^J \alpha^J C_P^J$.

To allow for the possibility that the law bans private contributions, we introduce the parameter $\lambda \in (0, 1]$, which measures how efficient the electoral authorities are in exposing illegal contributions.[31] If private contributions are allowed, then $\lambda = 1$; otherwise, the unlawful contributions may be unveiled and confiscated by the electoral authorities with probability $1 - \lambda$. The hypothesis that $\lambda > 0$ implies that it is never possible to completely block illegal contributions. Therefore, the total amount of contributions that party P receives is

$$C_P = \beta_P c + \lambda \sum_J O^J \alpha^J C_P^J, P = A, B.$$

We analyze the interest groups' problem to determine group J's private contributions to party P (C_P^J). An organized class's utility depends on the implemented policy, as well as on the amount of resources spent on political contributions. The present model assumes it takes the following form:

$$(7) \qquad p_A W^J\left(g_A\right) + \left(1 - p_A\right) W^J\left(g_B\right) - \frac{1}{2}\left(C_A^J + C_B^J\right)^2.$$

The first two terms in the above equation reflect the expected economic utility of a member of class J, whereas the last term reflects the utility cost of campaign contributions. The quadratic form of the cost function models the fact that contributions typically involve not only a monetary transfer, but also the personal involvement of organized voters. The ideological components of voters' utilities do not appear in the above equation because the stochastic components, σ^{iJ} and $\tilde{\delta}$, are realized after the contribution decisions are made and have zero expected value.

Therefore, organized class J's maximization problem is as follows, where p_A is given by equation 5.

$$\max_{C_A^J, C_B^J \geq 0} p_A W^J\left(g_A\right) + \left(1 - p_A\right) W^J\left(g_B\right) - \frac{1}{2}\left(C_A^J + C_B^J\right)^2.$$

If the utility an interest group obtains from platforms g_A and g_B is the same, then the group decides not to contribute, so that $C_A^J = C_B^J = 0$. If one platform

---

31. We are indebted to Marco Bonomo for highlighting this issue.

gives more utility than the other, the group contributes only to the party that announces the better platform—that is, C_P^J will be equal to zero for party P if g_P gives less utility to the group, where $P = A, B$. The solution to the interest groups' problem is

$$(8) \qquad C_A^J = \max\left\{0, \lambda \psi h O^J \alpha^J \left[W^J(g_A) - W^J(g_B)\right]\right\};$$

$$C_B^J = \max\left\{0, \lambda \psi h O^J \alpha^J \left[W^J(g_B) - W^J(g_A)\right]\right\}.$$

The above expression elucidates the lobbyists' contribution decisions.

Parties' Platform Announcement Decision

Parties anticipate the contributions they will receive from interest groups by sequential rationality. It follows from equation 8 that

$$(9) \qquad C_A^J - C_B^J = \lambda \psi h \, O^J \, \alpha^J \left[W^J(g_A) - W^J(g_B)\right];$$

$$(10) \qquad C_A - C_B = \lambda^2 \psi h \sum_J O^J (\alpha^J)^2 \left[W^J(g_A) - W^J(g_B)\right] + (\beta_A - \beta_B)c.$$

Plugging equation 10 into equation 5, we obtain party A's probability of receiving a majority of votes.

$$(11) \qquad P_A(g_A, g_B) = \frac{1}{2} + \psi \left\{ \begin{array}{l} W(g_A) - W(g_B) \\ + \psi(\lambda h)^2 \sum_J O^J (\alpha^J)^2 \left[W^J(g_A) - W^J(g_B)\right] \\ + hc(\beta_A - \beta_B) \end{array} \right\}$$

Parties care about winning a majority of votes, but they also care about which policy is implemented. That is, parties have ideological preferences, with party A strictly preferring policy $\bar{g}_A$ and party B, strictly preferring $\bar{g}_B$. The main rationale here is that parties are committed to their founding principles, which establish their preferred political platforms. Thus, announcing a platform that deviates from their optimal one involves a utility loss. This is modeled by introducing a cost of announcing a policy away from the party's optimal one, according to the following functional form:

$$U_A\left(p_A,p_B\right)=p_A\left(g_A,g_B\right)K-\gamma_A\left|\overline{g}_A-g_A\right|;$$
$$U_B\left(p_A,p_B\right)=p_B\left(g_A,g_B\right)K-\gamma_B\left|\overline{g}_B-g_B\right|.$$

The first summand of a party's utility represents its office-seeking motivation, which is the pragmatic or sociotropic part of its utility.[32] The term K represents the return to the party of gaining a majority in the legislature, such that the term is the expected utility of being a majority party. The second summand represents the utility cost that a party bears by announcing a policy other than its established optimal policy, which is the ideological or idiosyncratic part of its utility. This ideological component has two parts. First, the further away the proposed policy is from the party's ideal policy, the costlier for the party. This is the term $\left|\overline{g}_P-g_P\right|$, which represents the pure ideological bias. Second, the coefficient γ_P represents how strongly this deviation affects a party's utility and measures the party's ideological rigidity.

For simplicity, we normalize the return, K, to 1. We further assume that parties' optimal platforms are more extreme than society's, as a result of two reinforcing phenomena.[33] First, there is a self-selection problem, since founding a party is a very demanding activity and only those who have strong and extreme policy positions are willing to bear the corresponding cost. Second, society has evolved over time toward the center of the political spectrum, whereas parties have kept their original, more extreme political positions. We therefore assume that $\overline{g}_A<g_R^*<g_M^*<g_P^*<\overline{g}_B$, where $g_J^*\,(J=R,\,M,\,P)$ represents the optimal policy of the classes.[34]

Since party A takes a leftist position (a small $\overline{g}_A$), we expect that any deviation in the platform increasing p_A will automatically cause g_A to increase. We thus expect that, in equilibrium, $\left|\overline{g}_A-g_A\right|=g_A-\overline{g}_A$. On the other hand, party B will deviate from its optimal policy (a large $\overline{g}_B$) in such a way that g_B will decrease. Thus, in equilibrium, we expect that $\left|\overline{g}_B-g_B\right|=\overline{g}_B-g_B$. We assume this deviation pattern in what follows and confirm it once we solve the political parties' problems. Hence, we can write the parties' utility functions as

(12)
$$U_A=p_A\left(g_A,g_B\right)-\gamma_A\left(g_A-\overline{g}_A\right);$$
$$U_B=p_B\left(g_A,g_B\right)-\gamma_B\left(\overline{g}_B-g_B\right).$$

32. See Ferejohn (1986) for a discussion of the pragmatic or sociotropic part of the utility function vis-à-vis the ideological or idiosyncratic part.
33. We are following Fiorina (1988, 1992, 1996).
34. This assumption is not essential for the model, but it simplifies the solution to the game and supports a more precise analysis of the corresponding equilibria.

FIGURE 2. Groups' and Parties' Optimal Platforms

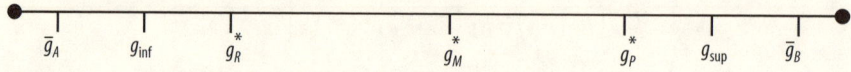

Moreover, we assume that

$$\overline{g}_A < \left(H'\right)^{-1}\left(\frac{y^R}{y} + \frac{\gamma_A}{\psi}\right) < g_R^* = \left(H'\right)^{-1}\left(\frac{y^R}{y}\right)$$

and

$$\overline{g}_B > \left(H'\right)^{-1}\left(\frac{y^P}{y} - \frac{\gamma_B}{\psi}\right) > g_P^* = \left(H'\right)^{-1}\left(\frac{y^P}{y}\right).$$

Let g_{inf} denote $(H')^{-1}[(y^R/y) + (\gamma_A/\psi)]$ and g_{sup} denote $(H')^{-1}[(y^P/y) + (\gamma_B/\psi)]$. The relationship with the preferred policy variable is presented in figure 2.

When all effects of the parties' platform announcement are introduced in the expression of $p_A(g_A, g_B)$ and $p_B(g_A, g_B)$, then sequential rationality reduces the original extensive-form game to a normal-form game between parties A and B, where the utilities are given by equation 12. The resulting dominant-strategy Nash equilibrium is given by

$$(13) \qquad \tilde{g}_A = \left(H'\right)^{-1}\left(\frac{\hat{y}}{y} + \frac{\gamma_A}{\psi\hat{\alpha}}\right) \text{ and } \tilde{g}_B = \left(H'\right)^{-1}\left(\frac{\hat{y}}{y} - \frac{\gamma_B}{\psi\hat{\alpha}}\right),$$

where $\hat{y} = \dfrac{\sum\limits_{J}\alpha^J\left[1 + \psi\left(\lambda h\right)^2 O^J\alpha^J\right]y^J}{\sum\limits_{J}\alpha^J\left[1 + \psi\left(\lambda h\right)^2 O^J\alpha^J\right]}$ and $\hat{\alpha} = \sum\limits_{J}\alpha^J\left[1 + \psi\left(\lambda h\right)^2 O^J\alpha^J\right]$.

Since $y^P \le y^J \le y^R$ for all $J = R, M, P$, with at least one strict inequality, it must be the case that

$$\sum_{J}\alpha^J\left[1 + \psi\left(\lambda h\right)^2 O^J\alpha^J\right]y^P < \sum_{J}\alpha^J\left[1 + \psi\left(\lambda h\right)^2 O^J\alpha^J\right]y^J$$
$$< \sum_{J}\alpha^J\left[1 + \psi\left(\lambda h\right)^2 O^J\alpha^J\right]y^R.$$

FIGURE 3. Parties' Centripetal and Centrifugal Movement[a]

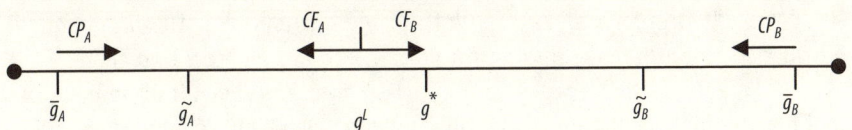

a. CP_P: party P's centripetal movement, where P = A, B; CF_P: party P's centrifugal movement, where P = A, B.

The simplification made in equation 12 is thus justified, that is, $\widetilde{g}_A > \overline{g}_A$ and $\widetilde{g}_B < \overline{g}_B$.

Let us analyze the two expressions in equation 13. First, note that public funds, c, do not enter any of the expressions for the equilibrium announcements. Therefore, public funding of electoral campaigns has no effect on the parties' announced policies. Second, in the absence of both a lobby ($O^J = 0$, $J = P, M, R$) and party ideology ($\gamma_A = \gamma_B = 0$), the two parties converge to the same socially optimal equilibrium announcement: $\widetilde{g}_A = \widetilde{g}_B = g^*$. All deviations from the optimal policy are due either to the existence of a lobby or to ideological rigidity, or to the combined effect of both factors. Third, in the presence of a lobby and the absence of party ideology, the two parties still converge to the same announcements, but now $\widetilde{g}_A = \widetilde{g}_B = g^L = H^{-1}(\hat{y}/y) \neq g^*$. Thus, the very presence of lobbyist groups causes the parties to announce a suboptimal policy. The expression of $\hat{y}$ shows clearly that the deviation occurs toward the preferred policies of the organized groups, although there is no private contribution in equilibrium, since both parties announce the same policy. This is the effect of O^J on $\hat{y}$. This lobby effect can only be circumvented if it is possible to totally ban private contributions (that is, if $\lambda = 0$), which does not seem to be feasible in Latin America or in any other region of the world. Fourth, in the presence of both a lobby and ideological rigidity (that is, positive values of γ_A and γ_B), the two parties will differentiate themselves by announcing opposing policies, with $\widetilde{g}_A < g^L < \widetilde{g}_B$. In this case, there will be no convergence of announced platforms, and there will be private contribution in equilibrium, which will affect the probability of each party's winning a majority of legislative seats.

We can thus decompose parties' decisions into two movements: a centripetal movement (CP) toward platform g^L and a centrifugal movement (CF) away from g^L toward the parties' respective ideological preference, $\overline{g}_A$ and $\overline{g}_B$ (figure 3). The parties' final announcements, $\widetilde{g}_A$ and $\widetilde{g}_B$, are the combination

FIGURE 4. Utility Difference between Poor and Middle-Income Groups

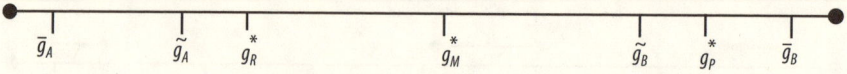

of these two opposing movements. A balance between the desire for interest groups' support and the degree of ideological rigidity will determine the optimal announcement. Note that the higher the ideological rigidity (that is, the higher the value of γ_P), the higher the centrifugal movement, that is, the higher the deviation from the platform g^L toward parties' optimal platforms, $\bar{g}_A$ and $\bar{g}_B$. In other words,

$$\frac{\partial \tilde{g}_A}{\partial \gamma_A} < 0 \text{ and } \frac{\partial \tilde{g}_B}{\partial \gamma_B} > 0.$$

Given the income of each of the three classes, their respective optimal platforms (g_R^*, g_M^*, g_P^*) are such that the higher a class's income, the lower the optimal platform value for this class in the interval $[0, y - c]$. Given that the parties' respective ideologies are extreme and moving toward the center at different rates, we expect that the rich and poor classes will be better represented by parties A and B, respectively. Note that in the present model, a "leftist" policy means low government expenditure, g, and lower taxes, which reflects the preferences of the rich, contrary to the conventional wisdom. If the classes are organized, they will be likely to contribute to the electoral campaign of the party that better represents them. The middle-income group, in contrast, will generically be less likely to finance electoral campaigns, since the announced platforms are both away from their utility. Figure 4 illustrates the situation in which the poor group ends up being more likely to contribute than the middle-income group.

Our model thus points to a polarization in society, according to which the rich and the poor spend the most on electoral campaigns. This polarization occurs because higher contributions are commensurate with the larger utility difference.[35] Elections may be cheaper in countries with predominantly middle-income voters than in countries where the middle class is small; this

---

35. This result would occur even if there were more than two parties. A third ideological party with a more centrist platform would be financed by the middle-income group if the group's risk aversion is high enough to compensate for the cost of electoral financing relative to the group's expected utility under the more extreme platforms announced by the other parties.

FIGURE 5.   Comparison of Parties' Ideological Rigidities

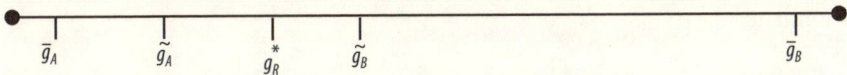

is consistent with Samuels's indication that elections in Brazil are relatively more expensive than in the United States.[36]

The influence of the ideological bias on the level of private contributions is given by the following equation:

$$\frac{\partial\left(C_A^J - C_B^J\right)}{\partial\gamma_A} = \lambda\psi h\sum_J O^J\alpha^J\left(\frac{\hat{y}-y^J}{y}+\frac{\gamma_A}{\psi\hat{\alpha}}\right)\left\{\frac{1}{\psi\hat{\alpha}H''\left[\left(H'\right)^{-1}\left(\frac{\hat{y}}{y}+\frac{\gamma_A}{\psi\hat{\alpha}}\right)\right]}\right\}.$$

If party A's ideological rigidity is sufficiently high, then the right-hand side may become negative. This indicates, for example, that even if the organized rich group prefers party A a priori, its support to this party will decrease with the party's rigidity. This group could even support party B: since party A would have a lower centripetal movement owing to its high ideological rigidity, party B, with relatively lower ideological rigidity, would provide more utility to the rich group. This effect may be heightened if party B has low ideological rigidity, extending its centripetal movement and approaching the platform that would be optimal for the rich group (figure 5).

We now analyze parties' probabilities of winning a majority of votes (equation 11) in equilibrium:

$$(14)\quad P_B = \frac{1}{2} - \psi\left\{\begin{array}{l}\left[W\left(\tilde{g}_A\right)-W\left(\tilde{g}_B\right)\right]\\+\psi\left(\lambda h\right)^2\sum_J O^J\left(\alpha^J\right)^2\left[W^J\left(\tilde{g}_A\right)-W^J\left(\tilde{g}_B\right)\right]+hc\left(\beta_A-\beta_B\right)\end{array}\right\}.$$

The summands inside the brackets in the above expression summarize each of the three factors that affect the probability of victory. The first summand,

$$W\left(\tilde{g}_A\right)-W\left(\tilde{g}_B\right),$$

36. Samuels (2001).

reflects voters' direct welfare concern: the closer the policy to the society's optimal policy, g^*, the higher the party's probability of victory. The second summand,

$$\psi(\lambda h)^2 \sum_J O^J (\alpha^J)^2 \left[W^J(\tilde{g}_A) - W^J(\tilde{g}_B) \right],$$

reflects the battle for lobbyists' contributions. Finally, the third summand,

$$hc(\beta_A - \beta_B),$$

reflects the effect of public funding.

Hence, although the public funding of electoral campaigns does not affect the equilibrium announced policies, it does affect a party's probability of victory by giving additional advantage to a party that had a majority of seats in the previous legislature. The size of the per capita funds, c, is important: if c is reduced, then the effect of public funding may be insignificant, but if c is large, it may offset the other effects and transform a low probability of victory into a high one. We discuss this issue in more detail in the next section, when we consider an iterated version of the game to assess the long-run effects of public financing.

The Iterated Electoral Competition Game

Suppose now that the electoral competition game is repeated an infinite number of times. The main dynamic connection between two successive electoral periods is the number of seats held by a party in one period, which defines the amount of public funding it will receive in the next period. To simplify the analysis, we limit the intertemporal strategic choices of parties by assuming that in each period a party only takes into consideration its utility in that period. This restriction allows us to disregard strategies in which a party would reduce its utility today by strongly deviating from its preferred policy in order to obtain more votes and then, in the future, return to announcing policies closer to its preferred policy, once it has obtained the public funds to run its electoral campaigns.[37] This is a reasonable assumption if politicians have low discount factors, that is, if they highly value the present relative to the future.

37. We thank Ernesto Dal Bó for suggesting the use of the iterated term and Ernesto Dal Bó and Ian Ayres for contributions to this discussion.

Under these assumptions, the iterated game starts at the end of period $t = 0$, where party A holds β_A^0 percent of the seats in the legislature (and, consequently, party B holds $\beta_B^0 = 1 - \beta_A^0$ percent of the seats). Parties make their policy announcements, lobbyists make theirs campaign contributions, parties receive public and private funds and use them to influence voters, and voters cast their ballots based on the platform announcement, the influence of electoral campaigns, and the realization of the stochastic shocks. A new legislature is then formed in period $t = 1$, where the seats occupied by each party are proportional to the quantity of votes received. The majority party implements its announced policy. At the end of period $t = 1$ the game repeats itself, and so on for each period $t > 1$.

The main dynamic component of this iterated game—namely, the evolution of party representation in the legislature—can be analyzed using the following proposition, which relates the probability of winning a majority in the legislature in one period with the expected representation in the legislature next period. The corresponding proof is outlined in the appendix.

Proposition

In a proportional electoral unicameral system, the expected proportion of seats that party A occupies in period $t + 1$, β_A^{t+1}, relates to the probability of winning a majority of votes in period t according to the following equation,

$$(15) \qquad E\left[\beta_A^{t+1}\right] = p_A^t + \left(1 - \frac{\psi}{\phi}\right)\kappa^t,$$

where $\kappa^t = \phi\sum_J \alpha^J \kappa_t^J$ and $\kappa_t^J = W^J\left(g_A^t\right) - W^J\left(g_B^t\right) + h\left(C_A^t - C_B^t\right).$

To simplify the notation, we identify $E[\beta_A^t]$ with β_A^t. Also, since public funds do not affect the announced policy, it must be the case that $\tilde{g}_P = \tilde{\tilde{g}}_P$ (which is the solution to the base game), for $P = A, B$ and for all t. Plugging the announced platforms and expressions 10 and 14 into equation 15 yields[38]

$$(16) \quad \beta_A^t = \frac{1}{2} + \phi\left[\tilde{W} + \psi\left(\lambda h\right)^2 \hat{W}\right]\sum_{i=0}^{t-1}\left(2\phi hc\right)^i + \left(2\phi hc\right)^t\left(\beta_A^0 - \frac{1}{2}\right)$$

---

38. This study postulates that the terms on the right-hand side of expression 16 are small enough to guarantee that $0 \le \beta_A^t, \beta_B^t \le 1$.

and

$$\beta_B^t = 1 - \beta_A^t,$$

where

$$\tilde{W} = \sum_J \alpha^J \left[W^J \left(\tilde{g}_A \right) - W^J \left(\tilde{g}_B \right) \right] \text{ and } \hat{W} = \sum_J O^J \left(\alpha^J \right)^2 \left[W^J \left(\tilde{g}_A \right) - W^J \left(\tilde{g}_B \right) \right].$$

The factors $\tilde{W}$ and $\hat{W}$ compare the weighted average utility of all social classes (welfare criterion) with the weighted average utility of interest groups from the announced platforms $\tilde{g}_A$ and $\tilde{g}_B$, which, in turn, are related to lobbyists' influence. The long-run proportion of parties in the legislature depends fundamentally on the size of the per capita public contributions, as shown below.

Case 1: $c < 1/2\phi h$

The parties' proportions in the legislature can be rewritten as follows:

$$\beta_A^t = \frac{1}{2} + \phi \left[\tilde{W} + \psi \left(\lambda h \right)^2 \hat{W} \right] \left(\frac{1 - (2\phi h \alpha c)^t}{1 - 2\phi h \alpha c} \right) + \left(2\phi h \alpha c \right)^t \left(\beta_A^0 - \frac{1}{2} \right);$$

$$\beta_B^t = 1 - \beta_A^t.$$

In this case, the per capita public contribution is small, so it follows that

$$\lim_{t \to \infty} \left(2\phi h c \right)^t = 0$$

and

$$\lim_{t \to \infty} \frac{1 - \left(2\phi h \, c \right)^t}{1 - 2\phi h c} = \frac{1}{1 - 2\phi h c}.$$

Hence, the parties' expected representations in the long run converge to

$$\lim_{t \to \infty} \beta_A^t = \frac{1}{2} + \frac{\phi}{1 - 2\phi h c} \left[\tilde{W} + \psi \left(\lambda h \right)^2 \hat{W} \right]$$

and

$$\lim_{t \to \infty} \beta_B^t = \frac{1}{2} + \frac{\phi}{1 - 2\phi h c} \left[-\tilde{W} - \psi \left(\lambda h \right)^2 \hat{W} \right].$$

Therefore, public contributions become less determinant of parties' representation in the long run. Since $(1 - 2\phi hc) > 0$, the factors $\widetilde{W}$ and $\hat{W}$ will determine the legislative composition, which shows the combined effect of the direct quest for votes ($\widetilde{W}$) and the competition for private contribution ($\hat{W}$).

If society prefers one party and interest groups prefer the other, their effects are opposite, so we cannot predict, a priori, which party is going to be larger in the long run. One possible outcome is that a party with a strong ideology (but without the support of the majority of social classes) will perpetuate itself in the long run based on the support of lobbyists. In this sense, party ideology may even become an advantage to a rigid party: by receiving financial support from interest groups, an ideologically rigid party guarantees its existence by influencing voters during the electoral campaigns.

In general, we expect the second summand in the above limit to be small enough that both parties are represented in the legislature. In particular, given the stochastic shocks, we would expect a change in party and in implemented policy over time. However, even though public funds have no decisive effect on the long-run party equilibrium, the fact that $(1 - 2\phi hc) < 1$ shows that public funds increase the second summand in the long-run party representation expression. In other words, it reduces party competition in the sense that it amplifies the party that has a positive value for the term in brackets.

Case 2: $c = 1/2\phi h$

In this case, the parties' proportions in the long run become

$$\beta_A^t = t\phi\left[\widetilde{W} + \psi(\lambda h)^2\hat{W}\right] + \beta_A^0$$

and

$$\beta_B^t = t\phi\left[-\widetilde{W} - \psi(\lambda h)^2\hat{W}\right] + \beta_B^0.$$

One party will dominate the other in the long run. The balance between factors $\widetilde{W}$ and $\hat{W}$ will still determine which party will dominate the legislature, that is, the party for which the term in the brackets is positive. In the very specific case in which those effects are opposite and equal, the initial legislative composition will be maintained in the long run as $\lim_{t\to\infty}\beta_A^t = \beta_A^0$ and $\lim_{t\to\infty}\beta_B^t = \beta_B^0$ if $\widetilde{W} = \psi(\lambda h)^2\hat{W}$. However, the main effect of public funding in this particular case is to foster the dominance of one party in the long run.

Case 3: $c > 1/2\phi h$

The parties' proportions in the legislature can be rewritten as

$$\beta_A^t = \frac{1}{2} - \frac{1}{2\phi hc - 1}\left[\phi\tilde{W} - \phi\psi(\lambda h)^2 \hat{W}\right]$$

$$+ \frac{(2\phi hc)^t}{2\phi hc - 1}\left[\phi\tilde{W} + \phi\psi(\lambda h)^2 \hat{W} + \left(\beta_A^0 - \frac{1}{2}\right)(2\phi hc - 1)\right]$$

and

$$\beta_A^t = 1 - \beta_B^t.$$

In this case, public contributions are significant, and the last summand of the above expression increases indefinitely in absolute value. Therefore, one of the two parties will become hegemonic in the long run, as in the previous case. Which party will dominate depends on the sign of the term below, which reflects how attractive the announced policy is to voters ($\tilde{W}$), how attractive it is to lobbyists ($\hat{W}$), how strong the party is at the outset ($\beta_A^0 - 1/2$), and the volume of public funds ($2\phi hc - 1$):

$$\phi\tilde{W} + \phi\psi(\lambda h)^2 \hat{W} + \left(\beta_A^0 - \frac{1}{2}\right)(2\phi hc - 1).$$

A high volume of public contributions may bias the above term so that the third summand dominates the sum of the first two. In this case, an initial, possibly minor advantage of party A in terms of representation in the legislature (that is, β_A^0 higher than, but very close to, 0.5) may give that party hegemony in the long run. Therefore, although public financing has no effect on the announced policy, it may have the unexpected effect of perpetuating a party that obtains a majority as a result of an unlikely realization of the shock variables, such as a war, an unanticipated terrorist attack, or a severe economic crisis.

This reveals the potential for opportunistic changes in the financial campaign legislation to favor a party that obtains a one-time majority in the legislature. Indeed, a party that recently acquired a majority in the legislature may arbitrarily vote for a significant increase in the value of per capita public finance, c, to ensure increasing (expected) representation.[39] Countries must be extremely

---

39. We thank Ian Ayres for emphasizing this issue.

careful when modifying their electoral campaign financing legislation, especially with respect to large increases in public funding.

The potentially negative effect of public finance resides entirely in the fact that different-sized parties receive different amounts of funds. If both parties received the same amount of contributions, then in the present model public funds would have no effect on the probability of obtaining a majority of votes or on the long-run party representation in the legislature. Although none of the eighteen Latin American countries studied by Zovatto use this egalitarian rule, other rules for the distribution of public funds may offer important benefits.[40]

Limitations and Extensions

This study is part of wider research on the different incentives created by public and private campaign financing and the associated consequences for society. The model presented here makes a series of strong assumptions that need to be extended before we can assess its true theoretical and policy contribution. This section explores ideas for addressing these issues in future research.

One of the model's main weaknesses relates to the lobbyists' motivations for contributing to parties. Here lobbyists only contribute to increase the probability of victory for the party that announces a policy that best represents their interests. Although this is clearly one of the lobbyists' motives, the empirical evidence in Latin America suggests that lobbyists also profit from direct benefits granted by the winning party.[41] In that case, it may be profitable for lobbyists to contribute to several parties at once, as a sort of electoral insurance. One option for analyzing such incentives is to include more detailed micropolitical foundations in the lobbyists' utility function, in order to assess their specific individual benefits from supporting a candidate.[42] We could also consider an alternative timing to model a possible negotiation between the lobbyists and the parties before the platform is announced, à la Grossman and Helpman.[43]

The electoral campaign may also play a significant role in revealing information. Many voters may have limited information about important characteristics of the parties, such as the true quality of the politicians or the real

---

40. Zovatto (2003).
41. Transparency International (2004).
42. We thank Ernesto Dal Bó for this insight.
43. Grossman and Helpman (1996, 2001). We thank Francisco Ferreira for this suggestion.

policy to be implemented by the winning party, and the money spent during the electoral campaign may help inform voters.[44] In this case, a certain amount of public financing will always be desirable, although it may be beneficial to limit the amount and distribute it equally among parties.[45] More generally, we would like to analyze the equilibrium effects of alternate mechanisms for distributing public funds.

Moreover, the iterated game is a weak approximation for the dynamic game, as it does not allow the parties to pursue dynamic strategies. If parties are willing to lose some utility by deviating from their optimal policy in one period to gain a majority of votes and then, in the next period, return to their preferred policy, then the centripetal movement could dominate the centrifugal movement. We might then observe a return to converging platform announcements.[46]

An interesting extension relates to the possibility that money spent on campaigns has different effects for different parties. Voters may trust one party more than the other, making them more sensitive to the party's electoral campaign. If so, cheaper campaigns may be as effective for the trusted party as a more expensive campaign, and the electoral equilibrium may be very different from what we modeled in this paper. The optimal distribution of public funds would depend on the equilibrium. We would also like to explore the results of the model using a more general form for including the cost of public contributions in the lobbyists' utility function, as well as the effect of the electoral campaign on voters' utility functions.

Finally, including a postelectoral game could enrich the model significantly, given Transparency International's evidence on direct benefits to lobbyists following elections in Latin American.[47] In that case, the model should incorporate the opportunity for corruption. Voters should consider that possibility in their electoral decision, which, in turn, will generate a concern among voters for the controlling role of the opposition party in the legislature. In such an extended model, the implemented policy would be the result of bargaining in the legislature, and voters may need to choose the composition of the legislature optimally to minimize corruption opportunities, as suggested by Bugarin.[48]

44. See Bennedsen and Feldmann (2002) for a careful discussion on informational lobbying.

45. We thank Eduardo Engel, Rafael Di Tella, and Marco Bonomo for contributions to this discussion.

46. We thank Ian Ayres and Ernesto Dal Bó for comments.

47. Transparency International (2004).

48. Bugarin (1999, 2003).

Conclusion

The present paper studies the interaction between public and private campaign financing and party ideology. We took as our starting point the basic modeling developed by Persson and Tabellini.[49] We expanded their model to incorporate the hypotheses that parties have preferences regarding the political platforms they announce and that electoral campaigns may be financed by both public funds and private contributions.

Our model highlights two opposing movements in terms of equilibrium platforms. A centripetal movement makes parties tend to converge to the lobbyists' preferred platform to secure private financing. At the same time, moving away from a party's established ideological platform is costly, which results in a centrifugal movement when parties have opposing ideologies. This yields an intermediate movement, whereby parties distinguish themselves by choosing different policies, which are typically distinct from the median voter's preferred platform. Public financing affects the likelihood that a party will win a majority in the legislature, but it does not directly affect the equilibrium announced policies.

Since parties diverge in their announced policies, private contributions will be positive in equilibrium. Lobbyist groups will find it optimal to contribute to electoral campaigns, which implies a cost that these groups would not have to face in the absence of ideology. In equilibrium, ideological rigidities determine how much private financing a party will receive from private lobbying groups. In the limit, a lobby could decide to finance a party that has a very different ideological position from its own, but is more flexible in ideological terms.

Based on the divergence of the announced policies, the model suggests that organized poor and rich groups tend to participate more in the electoral process and make larger private contributions than the middle class. This result could explain why political campaigns seem to be relatively more expensive in a country like Brazil (with a relatively reduced middle class) than in the United States (with a more significant middle class), as Samuels argues.[50]

The model highlights two extreme effects of public financing on electoral competition. On the one hand, public financing per se does not affect how

---

49. Persson and Tabellini (2000).
50. Samuels (2003).

political parties decide which platforms they will announce during the electoral campaign. This reflects the fact that public contributions are fixed, while a party's platform announcement is a strategic decision aimed at gaining voters or obtaining private contributions. On the other hand, public funds give strong parties the means to better influence voters, raising their probability of obtaining a majority of votes. In the long run, high levels of public financing may lead to a limiting situation in which one party dominates the legislature, which essentially corresponds to no party competition at all. This implies that the hegemonic party will not change its policy, even though that policy may not maximize social welfare.

This paper's discussions are especially important in present-day Latin America, where several countries are amending their electoral legislation to improve their political institutions. The main policy implication of the study is that governments should be extremely careful in their decisions to allocate large amounts of public funds to electoral campaigns. Furthermore, governments may find it useful to consider new forms of distributing public funds, since an equal-share rule may reduce the large-party advantage highlighted here.

Appendix

This appendix lays out the proof of the proposition stated in the main text regarding the evolution of party representation in the legislature, which relates the probability of winning a majority in the legislature in one period to the expected representation in the legislature next period.

Proposition

Consider a proportional election, in which a party's representation in the legislature is given by the percentage of votes received by that party. Suppose that party P, where $P = A, B,$ proposes policy g_P and collects C_P in private and public funds. Then, the share of legislative seats that party A can be expected to win relates to the probability that the party will win a majority of votes, as follows:

$$E[\beta_A] = p_A + \left(1 - \frac{\psi}{\phi}\right)\kappa,$$

where $\kappa = \sum_J \alpha^J \phi \kappa^J$ and $\kappa^J = W^J(g_A) - W^J(g_B) + h(C_A - C_B).$

Proof

For simplicity of notation, we drop the time index.

PROPORTION OF VOTES. Recall expression 4 defining party A's total number of votes:

$$(A1) \qquad \pi^A = \sum_J \alpha^J \left(\sigma^J + \frac{1}{2\phi} \right) \phi.$$

The swing voter's type is $\sigma^J = W^J(g_A) - W^J(g_B) + h(C_A - C_B) - \tilde{\delta}$. Thus, letting $\kappa^J = W^J(g_A) - W^J(g_B) + h(C_A - C_B)$, we can write

$$\pi^A = \frac{1}{2} + \sum_J \alpha^J \phi \left(\kappa^J - \tilde{\delta} \right).$$

Now let $\kappa = \sum_J \alpha^J \phi \kappa^J$. The above expression can be rewritten as

$$\pi^A = \frac{1}{2} + \kappa - \delta\phi.$$

Since $E[\tilde{\delta}] = 0$, party A's expected percentage of votes is

$$(A2) \qquad E\left[\pi^A \right] = \frac{1}{2} + \kappa - \phi E\left[\tilde{\delta} \right] = \frac{1}{2} + \kappa.$$

EXPECTED REPRESENTATION. Given equation A2 and the proportional electoral system, the expected representation of party A in the legislature is

$$E\left[\beta_A \right] = E\left[\pi^A \right] = \frac{1}{2} + \kappa.$$

PROBABILITY OF GAINING THE MAJORITY IN THE LEGISLATURE. The probability that party A will win the majority in the legislature, $p_A = \text{prob}[\pi^A \geq 1/2]$, can be expressed as follows:

$$p_A = \text{prob}\left(\pi^A \geq \frac{1}{2} \right) = \text{prob}\left(\frac{1}{2} + \kappa - \tilde{\delta}\phi \geq \frac{1}{2} \right) = \text{prob}\left(\tilde{\delta} \leq \frac{\kappa}{\phi} \right).$$

Thus,

$$(A3) \qquad p_A = \frac{1}{2} + \kappa \frac{\psi}{\phi}.$$

From equations A2 and A3, it follows that

$$E\left[\beta_A \right] = p_A + \left(1 - \frac{\psi}{\phi} \right) \kappa.$$

Comment

Ernesto Dal Bó: Portugal and Bugarin build their paper around a standard model of electoral competition and campaign finance, as pioneered by Baron and by Grossman and Helpman.[1] The particulars of the modeling follow Persson and Tabellini's approach.[2] The basic model features two candidates or parties with ideological preferences who want to prevail in a winner-take-all election (although the paper refers repeatedly to a legislature, the model is developed for the case of a winner-take-all election). The authors analyze the cases of candidates receiving private and public funds. Campaign contributions are assumed to improve the candidates' "brand" value. That is, for a given platform pair, an increase in contributions to one party raises voters' inclination to choose that party. The purpose of the paper is to analyze the effects of public financing on platforms and welfare. The authors also explore whether public funds may alter electoral equilibrium in the long run, as defined more precisely below. As developed, the paper is better for achieving the second purpose than the first. Before commenting on that, I briefly lay out the reasons why the model is not well suited to explaining either the welfare implications of public campaign financing or the effects of public funds on platform choices.

In the model, the effect of contributions comes from a black box: the authors provide no microfoundation as to why a party that spends more has a better brand name and receives more votes. The literature analyzes two different possibilities for the connection between money and votes, which I briefly describe here. I then argue that establishing a precise microfoundation of the effects of money on votes is important if one wants to make welfare predictions.[3]

---

1. Baron (1994); Grossman and Helpman (1996).
2. Persson and Tabellini (2000).
3. The next two paragraphs borrow heavily from Prat (2006).

One possibility is that money allows parties to communicate information about their quality.[4] Suppose a lobby is interested in donating money to the candidate who is most likely to win because the winner will be able to return favors to the lobby. Assume also that voters care not just about policy, but also about the quality of candidates. When candidates obtain a contribution, they can pay for an ad that reveals their quality to voters. In this simple world of informative advertising, only high-quality candidates care to advertise, and only high-quality candidates obtain donations in exchange for policy favors. Money allows candidates to transmit valuable information to voters. What is important about money is not where it comes from, but that it is available to sustain communication so that voters can learn about the candidates' features. A second possibility involves a world where advertising per se is uninformative, but the fact that a party was able to raise money does convey information.[5] Why would big campaign spending convey any kind of information? Suppose again that lobbies try to guess who the winning candidate will be in order to decide to whom to donate money. If lobbies observe a better signal about the quality of one candidate versus the other, then lobbies will tend to give more to the candidate they perceive as being higher quality. When voters observe high levels of campaign spending by one candidate, they will think that candidate is more likely to be of high quality, and they will vote accordingly.

In both cases (that is, directly informative versus indirectly informative advertising), being able to spend is correlated with obtaining votes, and private contributions induce policy distortions. Banning private contributions would be desirable if the quality dimension is not very important for voters relative to the policy one. However, the welfare effect of public funds depends crucially on whether advertising is directly informative. In the world of directly informative ads, public funds will allow parties to communicate their quality without selling out to special interests. Thus, by funding campaigns themselves with tax money, voters can obtain valuable information without suffering the policy distortion induced by private contributions. In the world where ads are not directly informative, things are different. Public funds will convey no signal about candidate quality, and the incentives for parties to seek private donations will not be altered. Voters will thus be spending tax money on campaigns to no effect, leading to lower welfare. The conclusion is that because the model lacks a microfoundation for how campaign expenditures

---

4. Ashworth (2006); Coate (2004); Schultz (2007); Wittman (2007).
5. See, for instance, Potters, Sloof, and van Winden (1997) and Prat (2002).

earn votes, it is not well suited to making predictions on the welfare consequences of public campaign financing.[6]

Portugal and Bugarin's model will also have trouble making predictions about how public financing may affect private contributions and platform choices. The reason follows immediately from the model's construction. In the model, parties accept contributions and choose platforms to maximize an objective function in which the cross-partial between private and public funds is zero and the cross-partial between public funds and platform choice is zero. Not surprisingly, the model yields that public finance does not crowd out private funding or affect platforms.

The authors' analysis of an iterated version of their game has important limitations, but it is the freshest part of the paper. It is also the most applicable to Latin America. A natural concern with a system in which parties are financed in proportion to past vote shares is that it may promote entrenchment.[7] When a party receives a majority of the votes, it then obtains a majority of the funds, which reinforces its ability to obtain a majority of the votes. The iterated game captures those effects. The authors look for stable vote share solutions and platform choices. This amounts to a fixed-point solution, and it has some parallels in the model by Ortuño-Ortín and Schultz.[8] The latter, however, impose symmetry assumptions that prevent the analysis of the emergence of hegemonic parties.

The key idea in this section is that when vote shares are sensitive enough to campaign contributions, the initial value of those contributions will dictate the long-run outcome in terms of what party dominates elections. In other words, if a party initially attracts more private contributions, it will obtain more votes in the first election, which entitles it to more public funds and thus allows it to continue to obtain a majority of votes. This means that public funds could introduce a force resembling increasing returns in electoral competition. Although public funds may crowd out private contributions in real life, thereby reducing the exchange of policies for money, they present the danger that increasing returns will create hegemonic tendencies. This problem might be averted by avoiding the precise type of public funding according to

---

6. More cynical views of the role of campaign contributions reinforce the view that microfoundations are necessary to make welfare statements. For example, if campaign money is used simply to buy votes, the particulars of the vote-buying process will be relevant. Dal Bó (2007) studies the inefficiency of vote buying and relates it to specific aspects of the purchase of votes.

7. Dal Bó, Dal Bó, and Snyder (2007) demonstrate the presence of entrenchment effects in democratic politics through the self-perpetuation of political dynasties.

8. Ortuño-Ortín and Schultz (2005).

which money tracks past vote shares. However, such a proportional system may already be in place, since the iterated model may well apply to the problem of illegal public campaign financing.

To illustrate this application, I keep the two-party model and suppose that after the election parties obtain control of government in proportion to their vote shares. That is, if a party gets 60 percent of the vote it will control 60 percent of the government machine, leaving the remainder to the other party.[9] Suppose next that parties extract rents from managing state resources in proportion to the share of government that they control, and they apply those rents to finance the party and its campaign activities. The ensuing situation would be formally similar to one in which some public funds are legally allocated to parties according to their past vote shares, but captures an illegal phenomenon that has been prevalent in some Latin American nations for decades. Party machines extract state-owned resources to fund their activities, and the larger the fraction of government "owned" by a party, the larger the amount of resources that are illegally appropriated. This combination of capture of state resources by victorious political parties and the increasing returns induced by such appropriation may explain the emergence of long-lasting hegemonic parties in Latin American politics, such as Peronism in Argentina and the Institutional Revolutionary Party (PRI) in Mexico.

The preceding comments are speculative for the following reason. The iterated model's ability to capture dynamic play is limited, in that the iteration only mechanically repeats the static game. This approach does not allow for players who are aware of the future and who can condition their play on past events. A more definitive analysis of hegemonic tendencies in electoral competition under state financing (whether legally or through plundering) must await a fully dynamic approach.

---

9. This is for simplicity, given that in presidential systems the winner controls a much higher percentage of state resources than the typical winner vote share.

References

Ashworth, Scott. 2006. "Campaign Finance and Voter Welfare with Entrenched Incumbents." *American Political Science Review* 100(1): 55–68.

Baron, David P. 1994. "Electoral Competition with Informed and Uninformed Voters." *American Political Science Review* 88(1): 33–47.

Bennedsen, Morten, and Sven E. Feldmann. 2002. "Lobbying Legislatures." *Journal of Political Economy* 110(4): 919–46.

Bugarin, Maurício. 1999. "Vote Splitting as Insurance against Uncertainty." *Public Choice* 98(1–2): 153–69.

———. 2003. "Vote Splitting, Reelection, and Electoral Control: Towards a Unified Model." *Social Choice and Welfare* 20(1): 137–54.

Coate, Stephen. 2004. "Political Competition with Campaign Contributions and Informative Advertising." *Journal of the European Economic Association* 2(5): 772–804.

Dal Bó, Ernesto. 2007. "Bribing Voters." *American Journal of Political Science* 51(4): 789–803.

Dal Bó, Ernesto, Pedro Dal Bó, and Jason Snyder. 2007. "Political Dynasties." Working Paper 13122. Cambridge, Mass.: National Bureau of Economic Research.

Ferejohn, John. 1986. "Incumbent Performance and Electoral Control." *Public Choice* 50(2): 5–26.

Fiorina, Morris P. 1988. "The Reagan Years: Turning toward the Right or Groping toward the Middle?" In *The Resurgence of Conservatism in Anglo-American Democracies,* edited by Barry Cooper, Alan Kornberg, and William Mishler. Duke University Press.

———. 1992. "An Era of Divided Government." *Political Science Quarterly* 107(3): 387–410.

———. 1996. *Divided Government,* 2d. ed. Boston: Allyn and Bacon.

Griner, Steven, and Daniel Zovatto. 2005. *Funding of Political Parties and Election Campaigns in the Americas.* San José: Organization of American States and International Institute for Democracy and Electoral Assistance.

Grossman, Gene, and Elhanan Helpman. 1996. "Electoral Competition and Special Interest Politics." *Review of Economic Studies* 63(2): 265–86.

———. 2001. *Special Interest Politics.* MIT Press.

Lindbeck, Assar, and Jorgen W. Weibull. 1987. "Balanced-Budget Redistribution as the Outcome of Political Competition." *Public Choice* 52(3): 273–97.

Olson, Mancur. 1971. *The Logic of Collective Action.* Harvard University Press.

Ortuño-Ortín, Ignacio, and Christian Schultz. 2005. "Public Funding of Political Parties." *Journal of Public Economic Theory* 7(5): 781–91.

Persson, Torsten, and Guido Tabellini. 2000. *Political Economics: Explaining Economic Policy.* MIT Press.

Poiré, Alejandro. 2005. "The Problem of Money in Electoral Politics: A Latin American Perspective." Robert F. Kennedy Professorship Lecture. Harvard University, David Rockefeller Center for Latin American Studies, 17 October 2005.

Potters, Jan, Randolph Sloof, and Franz van Winden. 1997. "Campaign Expenditures, Contributions, and Direct Endorsements: The Strategic Use of Information and Money to Influence Voter Behavior." *European Journal of Political Economy* 13(1): 1–31.

Prat, Andrea. 2002. "Campaign Advertising and Voter Welfare." *Review of Economic Studies* 69(4): 997–1017.

———. 2006. "Rational Voters and Political Advertising." In *The Oxford Handbook of Political Economy,* edited by Barry Weingast and Donald Wittman. Oxford University Press.

Roemer, John. 2006. "Party Competition under Private and Public Financing: A Comparison of Institutions." *Advances in Theoretical Economics* 6(1): 1229.

Samuels, David. 2001. "Money, Elections, and Democracy in Brazil." *Latin American Politics and Society* 43(2): 27–48.

Schultz, Christian. 2007. "Strategic Campaigns and Redistributive Politics." *Economic Journal* 117(522): 936–63.

Transparency International. 2004. *Global Corruption Report 2004.* London: Pluto Press.

UNDP (United Nations Development Program). 2004. *Democracy in Latin America.* Buenos Aires: Agilar, Altea, Taurus, Alfaguara.

Wittman, Donald. 2007. "Candidate Quality, Pressure Group Endorsements, and the Nature of Political Advertising." *European Journal of Political Economy* 23(2): 360–78.

Zovatto, Daniel. 2003. "The Legal and Practical Characteristics of the Funding of Political Parties and Election Campaigns in Latin America." In *Funding of Political Parties and Electoral Campaigns,* edited by Reginald Austin and Maja Tjernström. Stockholm: International Institute for Democracy and Electoral Assistance.

SCOTT E. ATKINSON
MARILYN IBARRA

The Effect of Mexican Workforce Migration on the Mexican *Maquiladora* Labor Market

The Mexican *maquiladora* is a major source of growth in the Mexican economy.[1] Consequently, the *maquiladora* industry influences the country's shifting migration patterns, as *maquiladoras* spread out from their traditional enclave in the north and workers gravitate to *maquiladora* centers in search of better employment opportunities. This paper measures two forces that act as determinants of the wages and employment of skilled and unskilled workers in Mexican *maquiladoras:* Mexican interstate labor migration and international return labor migration.[2] We examine the impacts of these two forces for a low-value-added sector of the Mexican *maquiladora* industry, which should be particularly sensitive to wage changes. We then speculate on the ability of Mexican workers to withstand competition from lower-wage Chinese workers.

New migration patterns developed in Mexico in the 1990s. Urban-to-urban migration supplanted the earlier phenomenon of rural-to-urban migration, a process the National Population Council (CONAPO) termed the new geography of migration. In addition, industrialized centers developed in the central and southern states as the *maquiladoras* shifted from their historic northern geographic locations. For example, from 1990 to 2000, *maquiladora*

Atkinson is with the University of Georgia; Ibarra is with the U.S. Bureau of Economic Analysis.

We thank Juliano Assunção, Carmen Pagés-Serra, and Eric Verhoogen for their comments on a previous draft. Comments by Ned Howenstine, Ralph Kozlow, and Obie Whichard from the Bureau of Economic Analysis are also gratefully acknowledged.

1. *Maquiladoras,* or in-bond manufacturing assembly plants, are part of free enterprise zones established in the 1960s. The special tax status of the industry requires U.S. firms in Mexico to report to the Mexican government on output, expenses, and inputs. These zones allow duty-free importation of raw materials and payment of export duties only on the value added in production.

2. We do not attempt to measure the nonpecuniary effects of migration, such as disruption of family life, stress on children living without one or both parents, and the loss of community support for migrants.

textile employment grew by 145 percent in the border regions, compared with 918 percent in the nonborder regions. Consequently, the border region's share of textile employment fell from 49 percent in 1990 to 17 percent in 2000.[3]

The majority of *maquiladora* employees are interstate migrants. Fernández-Kelly finds that 70 percent of the *maquiladora* workers in her sample are so classified.[4] In a similar study, Young and Fort report on interviews of 1,246 women in the labor force in Ciudad Juarez, Mexico.[5] Of these, 46 percent were employed in the *maquiladoras,* 26 percent in commerce, 20 percent in services, and 8 percent in a variety of other industrial sectors. The authors conclude that the *maquiladora* workers were more likely to have migrated to Ciudad Juarez than were the women working in other industries (72 percent versus 43 percent). Of the *maquiladora* workers, 82 percent were interstate migrants, almost double the 45 percent share of non-*maquiladora* workers.

A study of migration patterns and their impact on the wages and employment of *maquiladora* workers is timely, given that numerous U.S. firms have left Mexico in the last few years and relocated to China. This exit is commonly attributed to relatively higher wages in Mexico vis-à-vis China.[6] However, interstate migration in pursuit of employment in manufacturing assembly plants can either reduce or increase the market wage for unskilled and skilled workers, depending on a number of factors. Immigration should shift labor supply. If immigration occurs without an increase in the turnover rate, the labor supply will shift right as a result of the increase of workers in a given skill category. This causes the equilibrium wage to fall. Immigration could shift the labor supply to the left, however, if immigrants exhibit high turnover rates. Two patterns of employment that have been traced to internal migration in Mexico may increase turnover and hence employers' costs. First, *maquiladoras* absorb workers in transit to the United States. Second, they employ young, inexperienced females and males from rural areas. Therefore, the assembly plant's labor pool is largely composed of individuals with a high tendency to switch jobs, migrate to the United States, or, in the case of women, exit the labor market for childbearing. Picou and Peluchon estimate that the annual turnover rate in the *maquiladoras* routinely exceeds 100 percent.[7] Sargent argues that high turnover not only imposes significant personnel costs, but also inhibits the

3. See U.S. General Accounting Office (2003).
4. Fernández-Kelly (1983).
5. Young and Fort (1994).
6. However, in a pooled regression using the 1990 and 2000 Mexican census, we find that log wages in the *maquiladora* industry decreased over the decade in real 2000 pesos.
7. Picou and Peluchon (1995).

installation of sophisticated manufacturing facilities that demand substantial worker training.[8] Higher turnover rates will shift the labor supply curve to the left, and the equilibrium wage will rise.

Borjas, Freeman, and Katz, as well as Card, address the issue of how an influx of immigrants can lead to an outflow of natives.[9] In theory, if the native labor supply curve is upward sloping or perfectly inelastic, then an influx of immigrants would decrease the supply of native workers. In Mexico, native workers, particularly unskilled workers, may respond to inflows of immigrants by seeking employment in the informal sector. In addition, many native workers may migrate permanently to the United States, depleting their numbers in Mexico.

Immigration could shift labor demand to the right, which would increase the equilibrium wage. This shift could reflect an increase in productivity from more skilled migrants or an increase in demand for goods produced by the migrants. Migrants may be more skilled than natives or may have innate abilities not captured by educational attainment or work experience, if workers prone to migrate are among the most able, motivated, or productive workers in the population. Mexican workers who do not emigrate to the United States, but instead migrate internally, may be positively selected. In this case, an influx of migrants into another Mexican state could increase wages if firms seek out migrant workers, on average, more than native workers. This would change the mix of workers employed in an industry, such that the industry would largely be composed of more productive migrants.[10]

While our focus is on the impact of Mexican migration on the Mexican *maquiladora* industry, the literature on the impact of Mexican immigration on the wages of U.S. workers guides our analysis. Considerable disagreement exists regarding the impact of Mexican migration on the wages of native workers in the U.S. labor market. In a natural experiment involving the *Marielitos,* Card estimates the impact of immigration on the Miami labor market.[11] He finds that a 7 percent increase in the workforce raised the wages of black and other workers (except Cubans), presumably as the result of a demand shift offsetting a supply shift. Card later argues that while migration shifts the supply curve for the migrants' labor type outward, migration of new workers into a region also shifts the demand curve for many goods and services and their labor type

8. Sargent (1997).

9. Borjas, Freeman, and Katz (1991); Card (1990).

10. This prediction is consistent with the evidence found by Fernández-Kelly (1983) and Young and Fort (1994).

11. Card (1990). *Marielito* is a term applied to the Cuban refugees who fled to the United States from the Cuban port of Mariel in 1980.

outward.[12] In addition, native workers are less likely to be affected if the skill set of immigrants differs from that of natives. A widely cited review article by Friedberg and Hunt concludes that the effect of immigration on the labor market outcomes of natives is small.[13] In contrast, Borjas concludes that immigration causes a substantial reduction in the wages of native-born unskilled workers: a 10 percent increase in the supply of immigrant workers reduces wages of skilled native workers by 3–4 percent and by as much as 8 percent for all workers.[14]

A more recent strand of literature studies the impact of Mexican emigration on wages in Mexico. The first to examine this subject, Mishra gauges this impact using the 1970–2000 Mexican and U.S. censuses.[15] She concludes that emigration from Mexico to the United States had a statistically significant and positive effect on Mexican wages and increased wage inequality in Mexico.

Hanson considers the regional impact of emigration on wages in Mexico for high- and low-migration states.[16] He finds that the distribution of male earnings in high-migration states shifted to the right relative to that in low-migration states. In the 1990s, average hourly earnings in high-migration states rose relative to that in low-migration states by 6–9 percent. However, because he assumes Mexican labor is immobile across Mexican regions, region-specific labor supply shocks would not affect regional earning differentials in his model.

Mollick and Wvalle-Vázquez examine the impact of variations in U.S. real output and of real Chinese wages on the demand for Mexican *maquiladora* workers.[17] They find that growth in U.S. real output has a relatively strong impact on *maquiladora* employment, but that the effect on employment of higher real wages in Mexico relative to China is small and statistically insignificant. However, they do not distinguish skilled from unskilled workers, and they use aggregated *maquiladora* data.

In this paper, we replace data aggregated across production sectors with disaggregated data for the textile *maquiladora* sector. Panel data at the state level are available for this sector from 1998 to 2001, allowing us to estimate labor demand functions for skilled and unskilled workers using fixed effects. Since our data are at the state (rather than plant) level, to obtain enough observations our analysis is necessarily limited to the low-value-added textile *maquiladora*

---

12. See Roger Lowenstein, "Immigration Equation," *New York Times,* July 9, 2006.
13. Friedberg and Hunt (1995).
14. Borjas (2003).
15. Mishra (2007).
16. Hanson (2005).
17. Mollick and Wvalle-Vázquez (2006).

division that is prevalent throughout Mexico. We assume that *maquiladora* firms are short-run cost minimizers subject to exogenously determined output constraints (driven almost exclusively by U.S. demand), exogenously determined prices for skilled and unskilled labor, and a set of demand curve shifters (namely, quantities of materials inputs and time). We then compute state-level own-price and cross-price elasticities of demand for both types of workers. High own-price and cross-price elasticities would bode well for the Mexican *maquiladora* industry in terms of remaining competitive with Chinese producers. Using the 2000 Mexican census, we estimate the impact of changes in interstate migration and international return migration rates on wages. Finally, we combine these migration rates with our estimated labor demand elasticities to determine the ultimate impact of migration on each type of wages and employment in this *maquiladora* sector.

The remainder of this paper is organized as follows. In the next section, we present a cost minimization model of the *maquiladora,* from which we obtain input demand functions for skilled and unskilled workers and derive the own-price and cross-price elasticities of demand. We also describe our methodology for estimating the impact of migration on wages. The subsequent section describes the firm-level production data and the demographic data that are used jointly to determine the impact of changes in immigration on wages and employment. We then present our empirical results, while our conclusions follow in the final section.

The Model

The objectives of our econometric models are threefold. First, we wish to estimate demand functions for skilled and unskilled labor in the textile *maquiladora* sector, computing the impact of changes in wages on employment by skill type. Second, we wish to estimate wage equations for interstate migrants and returning international migrants for skilled and unskilled workers and to estimate wage changes for each type of worker that have resulted from actual migration levels. Third, we wish to apply these wage changes to our estimated demand functions for each labor type to determine the effect of migration-induced wage changes on employment in this *maquiladora* sector.

Cost Minimization by the Firm

We assume that the *maquiladora* meets exogenously determined production goals subject to exogenously determined input prices. We find that *maquiladoras* account for only a small proportion of production in each state, so *maquiladoras* are reasonably assumed to be price takers in the labor market. Defining variable costs as $C_f = \Sigma_n p_{nf} x_{nf}$, we obtain the restricted cost function, C_f, for *maquiladora* firms aggregated to the level of state f as

$$(1) \qquad C_f\left(y_f, \frac{\mathbf{p}_f}{b_f}; \mathbf{z}\right) = \min_{b_f \mathbf{x}_f}\left[\left[\left(\frac{\mathbf{p}_f}{b_f}\right)(b_f \mathbf{x}_f)\right] \middle| f\left(\mathbf{x}_f; \mathbf{z}_f\right) = y_f\right],$$

where $\mathbf{p}_f = (p_{1f}, \ldots, p_{Nf})$ is a vector of N ($n = 1, \ldots, N$) input prices, $\mathbf{x}_f = (x_{1f}, \ldots, x_{Nf})$ is a vector of N input quantities, y_f is output, $\mathbf{z}_f$ is a vector of quasi-fixed inputs (such as materials inputs) that can shift the cost function, and b_f is a state-specific parameter (since we are using aggregate *maquiladora* production data at the state level).

The first-order conditions corresponding to equation 1 are given by

$$(2) \qquad y_f = f\left(\mathbf{x}_f; \mathbf{z}_f\right)$$

and

$$(3) \qquad p_{nf} = \frac{\phi \partial f\left(\mathbf{x}_f; \mathbf{z}_f\right)}{\partial x_{nf}}, \quad n = 1, \ldots, N,$$

where ϕ is the Lagrange multiplier. Applying Shephard's Lemma to equation 1, we obtain the input demand functions for factor n:

$$(4) \qquad \frac{\partial C_f}{\partial p_{nf}} = x_{nf}\left(p_{1f}, \ldots, p_{Nf}, y_f; \mathbf{z}_f\right), \forall n.$$

The Translog Cost Function and Labor Demand Equations

Assuming the availability of panel data (T time series observations on F states), we define factor cost shares as $s_{nft} = \partial \ln C_{ft} / \partial \ln p_{nft}$, where $t = 1, \ldots, T$ and $f = 1, \ldots, F$. A fixed effects approach leads to stochastic cost and share equations with the general form

$$(5) \qquad C_{ft} = \frac{1}{b_f} C\left(p_{1ft}, \ldots, p_{Nft}, y_{ft}; \mathbf{z}_{ft}\right) \exp\left(v_{ft}\right)$$

and

(6)
$$\frac{\partial \ln C_{ft}}{\partial \ln p_{nft}} = s\left(p_{1ft}, \ldots, p_{Nft}, y_{ft}; \mathbf{z}_{ft}\right) + \omega_{nft}, \forall n,$$

where v_{ft} and ω_{nft} are two-sided random error terms. In equation 5, we interpret b_f as a state-specific dummy variable that controls for unobserved time-invariant heterogeneity (such as distance to the border). By specifying an appropriate functional form for the cost function, we derive an estimable expression for variable cost and for cost shares given in equations 5 and 6. We employ the translog functional form, which provides a convenient second-order approximation to an arbitrary, continuously twice-differentiable restricted cost function. The translog approximation to the cost function in equation 1 is

(7) $\ln C_{ft} = \gamma_0 - \ln b_f + \gamma_y \ln y_{ft} + \frac{1}{2}\gamma_{yy}\left(\ln y_{ft}\right)^2 + \sum_n \gamma_n \ln p_{nft}$

$+ \frac{1}{2}\sum_n\sum_f \gamma_{nl} \ln p_{nft} \ln p_{lft} + \sum_r \gamma_r \ln z_{rft} + \frac{1}{2}\sum_r\sum_n \gamma_{rn} \ln z_{rft} \ln z_{sft}$

$+ \sum_r \gamma_{ry} \ln z_{rft} \ln y_{ft} + \sum_n y_{ny} \ln y_{ft} \ln p_{nft} + \sum_r\sum_n \gamma_{rs} \ln z_{rt} \ln p_{nft}$

$+ \gamma_t t + \gamma_{tt} t^2 + v_{ft},$

where $\gamma_{nl} = \gamma_{ln}$, for all n and l, $n \neq l$, and $t = 1, \ldots, T$. The share equations corresponding to equation 7 are

(8) $s_{nft} = \frac{\partial \ln C_{ft}}{\partial \ln p_{nft}} = \gamma_n + \sum_l \gamma_{nl} \ln p_{lft} + \sum_r \gamma_{rn} \ln z_{rft} + \gamma_{ny} \ln y_{ft} + \omega_{nft}, \forall n.$

While we could have adopted an error-components approach by moving $-\ln b_f$ to the error term, the fixed effects specification avoids the strong assumptions required by this random-effects approach. These include distributional assumptions for both components of the error term, as well as the unlikely assumption that both components of the error are uncorrelated with the explanatory variables in equation 7. With the fixed effects approach, by contrast, we require no distributional assumptions and assume only that the v_{ft} and ω_{nft} terms are uncorrelated with the regressors.

Given these assumptions, and with output held constant, C_{ft} is linearly homogeneous in prices. This implies the following restrictions on the cost function parameters:

$$(9) \qquad\qquad \sum_n \gamma_n = 1;$$

$$(10) \qquad\qquad \sum_n \gamma_{ny} = 0;$$

$$(11) \qquad\qquad \sum_n \gamma_{nz} = 0, \forall z;$$

$$(12) \qquad\qquad \sum_n \gamma_{nl} = \sum_n \sum_l \gamma_{nl} = 0.$$

Since the cost shares sum to one, we estimate $N - 1$ share equations (to avoid linear dependency). We estimate our cost system using nonlinear least squares, so the results are invariant to the share equation dropped.

After estimation, we obtain own-price and cross-price elasticities of demand, holding output and the prices of other inputs constant, as

$$(13) \qquad\qquad \eta_{nn} = \frac{\left(\gamma_{nn} + s_n^2 - s_n \right)}{s_n}, \forall n,$$

and

$$(14) \qquad\qquad \eta_{ln} = \frac{\left(\gamma_{ln} + s_l s_n \right)}{s_l}, \forall l, n; l \neq n.$$

For these elasticities, the first subscript represents a quantity and the second a price.

The Impact of Migration on Wages and Employment

In this section we develop our methodology for estimating the impact of migration on wages. Table 1 illustrates some of the differences in the characteristics of natives and immigrants. Immigrants, on average, are more educated, earn higher incomes, and are more likely to be married than natives. This is

T A B L E 1. Average Characteristics of Natives and Immigrants, by Skill Type[a]

Variable	Natives			Interstate immigrants			Returning international immigrants		
	All	Unskilled	Skilled	All	Unskilled	Skilled	All	Unskilled	Skilled
Experience	16.4008	16.2240	16.9593	14.3017	14.5562	13.7637	17.0238	17.3576	8.567
Indigenous	0.0475	0.0576	0.0157	0.0376	0.0483	0.0151	0.0201	0.0194	0.0223
Log income	7.6026	7.3858	8.2873	7.8178	7.5009	8.4878	7.8736	7.580	8.7731
Male	0.8397	0.8552	0.7908	0.8294	0.8317	0.8246	0.9229	0.9343	0.8880
Married	0.5692	0.5215	0.7196	0.6068	0.5428	0.7420	0.6733	0.6204	0.8358
Schooling	7.5266	6.4102	11.0527	8.6052	6.7576	12.5108	7.9596	6.6520	11.9701
Skilled	0.2405	...	...	0.3123	...	...	0.2549	...	...

Source: 2000 Mexican census.

... = Not applicable.

a. See table 2 for a definition of the variables.

consistent with Chiquiar and Hanson, who conclude that there is positive selection of migrants.[18]

We first estimate a log wage equation using data from the 2000 Mexican census for all workers in the manufacturing sector. Although we have no way of knowing whether they are employed in *maquiladoras*, we assume that workers in each sector are part of one relatively homogeneous labor market. For an individual m in state j, with skill category i (equal to u for unskilled and s for skilled), each equation has the following form:

$$(15) \qquad w_{mji} = \beta_0 + d_j + \beta_1 \text{PINM}_{ji} + \beta_2 \text{PRINT}_{ji} + \beta_3 \mathbf{X}_m + e_{mji},$$

where w_{mji} is the log of the hourly wage, PINM_{ji} is the ratio of interstate migrants to the sum of all immigrants and all native workers (that is, the total stock of workers) for the individual worker's skill type in his or her state of residence, PRINT_{ji} is the ratio of returning international migrants to the sum of all immigrants plus all native workers for the individual worker's skill type in his or her state of residence, d_j is a dummy indicating state of residence, and $\mathbf{X}_m$ is a vector comprising sociodemographic variables (see table 2 for variables and definitions). Finally, e_{mji} is a random error term. We define PINM_{ji} and PRINT_{ji} as measures to reflect the aggregate supply conditions for the individual's labor skill type.

Since immigrants may be drawn to states where the relative demand for labor is increasing, we treat PINM_{ji} and PRINT_{ji} as endogenous and compute a two-stage least squares estimator using two instruments based on networking effects, which should be exogenous but highly correlated with the endogenous variables. For skill type i, the instrument for PINM_{ji} is based on

$$(16) \qquad z_{kji}^I = \left(\frac{c_{kji,1990}}{c_{ki,1990}} \right) \left(\frac{c_{ki,1995-2000}}{c_{ji,2000}} \right),$$

where $c_{kji,1990}$ is the number of people who were born in state k and living in state j in 1990, $c_{ki,1990}$ is the number of people who were born in state k and were migrants living in another Mexican state in 1990, $c_{ki,1995-2000}$ is the number of migrants from state k living in another Mexican state from 1995 to 2000, and $c_{ji,2000}$ is the total number of workers in state j in 2000. The first term in parentheses measures the 1990 historical probability of an interstate migrant from state k living in state j, while the second term in parentheses measures

---

18. Chiquiar and Hanson (2005).

TABLE 2.   Definition of Variables

Variable	Definition
Experience	Work experience (worker's age minus fifteen years)
Experience squared	Work experience squared
Indigenous	Dummy equal to 1 if indigenous and 0 otherwise
$INM_{ij,t}$	Number of interstate immigrant workers
$PINM_{ij}$	Total interstate immigrant workers in skill class i of worker m divided by total workforce for skill type i of worker m in state j
Log income	Log of income in pesos
Male	Dummy equal to 1 if male and 0 otherwise
Married	Dummy equal to 1 if married and 0 otherwise
Native	Dummy equal to 1 if native and 0 otherwise
$RINT_{ij,t}$	Number of returning international migrant workers
$PRINT_{ij}$	Total returning international migrant workers in skill class i of worker m divided by total workforce for skill type i of worker m in state j
Schooling	Number of years of schooling
Skilled	Dummy equal to 1 if skilled and 0 otherwise
Urban	Dummy equal to 1 if worker lives in urban area and 0 otherwise

the change from 1995 to 2000 in the total migration from state k to any state relative to the work force in state j. The product of these two terms yields an exogenous measure of the expected amount of migration from state k to state j from 1995 to 2000 relative to the workforce in state j.

The instrument for $PRINT_{ji}$ is based on

$$(17) \qquad z_{kji}^R = \left(\frac{c_{kji,1990}}{c_{ki,1990}} \right) \left(\frac{r_{ki,1995-2000}}{c_{ji,2000}} \right),$$

where $r_{ki,1995-2000}$ is the number of returning international migrants born in state k migrating from the United States to any state in Mexico from 1995 to 2000. The product of the two terms in parentheses yields an exogenous measure of the expected amount of international return migration from state k to the United States and back to state j from 1995 to 2000 relative to the workforce in state j.

The final step in computing our networking-effects instruments is to sum z_{ki}^I and z_{ki}^R over all K states except for the receiving state j to obtain

$$(18) \qquad z_{ji}^I = \sum_{\substack{k=1 \\ k \neq j}}^{K} z_{ki}^I, \forall j,$$

and

(19)
$$z_{ji}^R = \sum_{\substack{k=1 \\ k \neq j}}^{K} z_{ki}^R, \forall j.$$

Card uses a similar instrument.[19]

Given these instruments, our next step is to estimate the log wage equation 15 using two-stage least squares. We then compute the wage elasticities, $\tau_{\text{INM},sj}$ and $\tau_{\text{RINT},uj}$, for skilled and unskilled workers, respectively, for each state and each immigrant class. We then use the Mexican census data for 1990 and 2000 to compute the percentage change in the supply of interstate migrants by skill category as $\Delta_{\text{INM},sj}$ and $\Delta_{\text{INM},uj}$:

(20)
$$\Delta_{\text{INM},sj} = \frac{\text{INM}_{sj,2000} - \text{INM}_{sj,1990}}{0.5\left(N_{sj,1990} + N_{sj,2000}\right) + \text{INM}_{sj,1990}}, \forall j,$$

and

(21)
$$\Delta_{\text{INM},uj} = \frac{\text{INM}_{uj,2000} - \text{INM}_{uj,1990}}{0.5\left(N_{uj,1990} + N_{uj,2000}\right) + \text{INM}_{uj,1990}}, \forall j,$$

where $N_{ij,t}$ is the native workforce with skill level i in state j, at time t, and $\text{INM}_{ij,t}$ is the actual level of interstate immigrant workers with skill level i in state j, at time t. Similarly, we use the percentage change from 1990 to 2000 in the supply of returning international migrants by skill category,

(22)
$$\Delta_{\text{RINT},sj} = \frac{\text{RINT}_{sj,2000} - \text{RINT}_{sj,1990}}{0.5\left(N_{sj,1990} + N_{sj,2000}\right) + \text{RINT}_{sj,1990}}, \forall j,$$

and

(23)
$$\Delta_{\text{RINT},uj} = \frac{\text{RINT}_{uj,2000} - \text{RINT}_{uj,1990}}{0.5\left(N_{uj,1990} + N_{uj,2000}\right) + \text{RINT}_{uj,1990}}, \forall j,$$

19. Card (2001). We wish to thank a referee for suggesting these instruments.

where $RINT_{ij}$ is the actual level of international return migration with skill level i in state j, at time t. Since the native workforce in many states has changed dramatically over time, we follow Borjas in averaging the 1990 and 2000 levels and treating the preexisting immigrant population as part of the native stock in the denominator.[20]

For each state, we next carry out the following sequential calculations. First, we multiply each $\Delta_{INM,ij}$ and $\Delta_{RINT,ij}$ by the computed wage elasticity (τ) for the corresponding skill and immigrant type to yield the implied percentage change in wages for each skill level and migratory type. We then multiply each percentage change in wages by the corresponding elasticity of demand for each skill type (η), obtained from equations 13 and 14, to produce estimates of changes in the share of *maquiladora* employment resulting from changes in labor supply within each migrant category. The percentage change in wages stemming from the observed change in interstate migration is

$$(24) \qquad \Delta \log w_{INM,sj} = \tau_{INM,sj} \Delta_{INM,sj}, \forall j,$$

and

$$(25) \qquad \Delta \log w_{INM,uj} = \tau_{INM,uj} \Delta_{INM,uj}, \forall j.$$

The percentage change in wages stemming from the observed percentage change in international return immigration is

$$(26) \qquad \Delta \log w_{RINT,sj} = \tau_{RINT,sj} \Delta_{RINT,sj}, \forall j,$$

and

$$(27) \qquad \Delta \log w_{RINT,uj} = \tau_{RINT,uj} \Delta_{RINT,uj}, \forall j.$$

Letting the variables L_s and L_u denote the quantity of skilled and unskilled labor, respectively, for interstate migration, the percentage change in employment is

$$(28) \qquad \Delta \log L_{INM,sj} = \eta_{ss,j} \Delta \log w_{INM,sj} + \eta_{su,j} \Delta \log w_{INM,uj}, \forall j,$$

and

$$(29) \qquad \Delta \log L_{INM,uj} = \eta_{uu,j} \Delta \log w_{INM,uj} + \eta_{us,j} \Delta \log w_{INM,sj}, \forall j.$$

20. Borjas (2003).

For international return migration, the percentage change in employment is

$$(30) \qquad \Delta \log L_{\text{RINT},sj} = \eta_{ss,j} \Delta \log w_{\text{RINT},sj} + \eta_{su,j} \Delta \log w_{\text{RINT},uj}, \forall j,$$

and

$$(31) \qquad \Delta \log L_{\text{RINT},uj} = \eta_{uu,j} \Delta \log w_{\text{RINT},uj} + \eta_{us,j} \Delta \log w_{\text{RINT},sj}, \forall j.$$

The Data

The *maquiladora* production data are drawn from the *maquiladora* yearbook published by the National Institute of Statistics, Geography, and Information (INEGI).[21] The yearbook identifies six major *maquiladora* sectors: food, beverage, and tobacco; textiles, clothing, and leather; wood and wood products; chemicals and by-products of petroleum, rubber, and plastics; social and personal services; and metal products, machinery, and equipment. Our empirical analysis uses aggregated state-level data on the textiles, clothing, and leather sector (which we refer to simply as textiles). This sector includes operations in twenty Mexican states.[22] The yearbook provides data on production, value added, materials, and the quantity and earnings of skilled and unskilled workers. Production is defined as the sum of value added and material costs. Material costs are defined as the value of both domestic and imported primary materials, packaging, and other costs incurred in the processing stage.[23] Data on production, value added, materials expenses, and earnings were adjusted to the base year 2001 by the national consumer price index provided by the Bank of Mexico.[24]

Figure 1 shows average value added in all sectors for each of the twenty Mexican states in our sample. Perhaps surprisingly, the states with relatively high value added in textile production are Chiapas and Colima. Chiapas' population has relatively low levels of human capital and relatively high levels

21. INEGI (2005).

22. The twenty states with textile production are Aguascalientes (Ags), Baja California Norte (BCN), Baja California Sur (BCS), Chiapas (Chs), Colima (Col), Durango (Dur), Federal District (DF), Guanajuato (Gto), Hidalgo (Hgo), Jalisco (Jal), México (Mex), Nuevo León (NL), Puebla (Pue), Querétaro (Qtr), San Luis Potosí (SLP), Sonora (Son), Tamaulipas (Tamp), Tlaxcala (Tla), Yucatán (Yuc), and Zacatecas (Zac).

23. According to INEGI (2005), 3.0 percent of material costs were generated in Mexico in May 2004 and 3.4 percent a year later.

24. The national consumer price index is available online at the Bank of Mexico website (www.banxico.org.mx). Since we were not provided with data on capital, we must assume separability with respect to this input.

FIGURE 1. Average Value Added in the *Maquiladora* Industry, 1998–2001[a]
Constant 2001 dollars

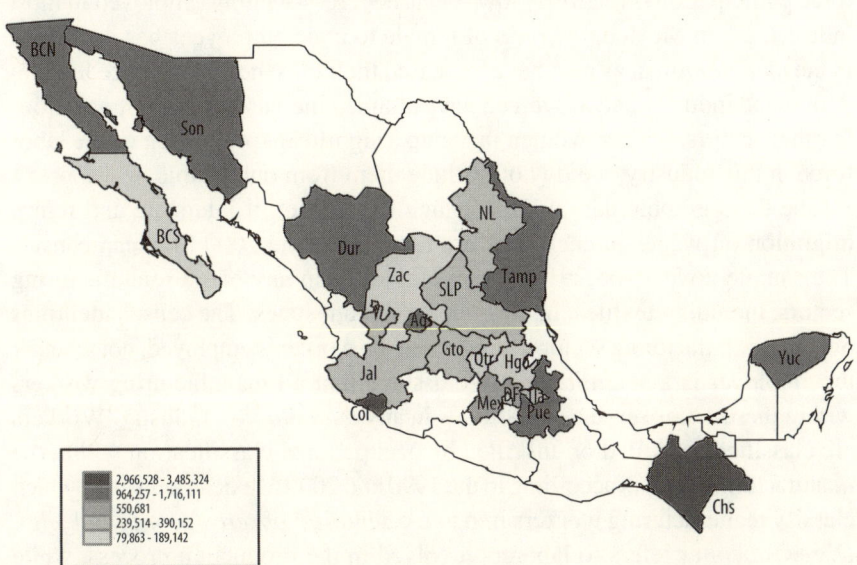

	2,966,528 - 3,485,324
	964,257 - 1,716,111
	550,681
	239,514 - 390,152
	79,863 - 189,142

a. States in white are not included in our sample. The abbreviations are as follows: Aguascalientes (Ags), Baja California Norte (BCN), Baja California Sur (BCS), Chiapas (Chs), Colima (Col), Durango (Dur), Federal District (DF), Guanajuato (Gto), Hidalgo (Hgo), Jalisco (Jal), México (Mex), Nuevo León (NL), Puebla (Pue), Querétaro (Qtr), San Luis Potosi (SLP), Sonora (Son), Tamaulipas (Tamp), Tlaxcala (Tla), Yucatán (Yuc), and Zacatecas (Zac).

of indigenous people. Colima is a relatively small state in central Mexico with a significant amount of production in the textile industry. Both states have low migration rates. Given the growing presence of the *maquiladora* industry in these poorer states, we would expect to see increased rural-to-urban and urban-to-urban intrastate and interstate migration over time.

Labor employed in the *maquiladora* industry is sorted into two types of workers: skilled workers, defined empirically as workers involved in the administrative process, and unskilled workers, defined as workers directly involved in the production process.[25] An ideal classification of labor would be by skill type, education, experience, and occupation; however, the data available to us are disaggregated only into wages paid for quantities of unskilled and skilled labor employed. In all states for which data are available, a large proportion of wage payments goes to skilled workers, even though the textile industry predominantly employs unskilled workers.

25. INEGI (2005) terms the two categories *obreros* and *personal administrativo*.

Studies carried out for the United States commonly exclude women from the sample in an attempt to reduce measurement error, given that female labor force participation is relatively low for earlier cross-sections employed in most industries.[26] In Mexico, the ratio of female to male employees has decreased in the *maquiladoras,* as men have increased their presence in this once female-dominated industry and as women have attained increased labor opportunities in other sectors.[27] Since women make up a significant proportion of the labor force in this industry, we do not exclude them from our sample.

The demographic data used to gauge the impact of interstate and return migration on wages in each state are taken from the 2000 Mexican census. The sample covers 105,291 workers employed in any of six manufacturing sectors, including textiles, in the twenty relevant states. The census identifies only the manufacturing sector within which the worker is employed, not whether the employer is a *maquiladora.* We assume that all manufacturing workers within these states serve as substitutes in any *maquiladora* industry. Workers are classified as skilled or unskilled by occupational classification within the manufacturing sectors according to the 1990 and 2000 Mexican censuses, which classify manufacturing workers into two categories: *obreros/peones* and *jefes.* *Obreros/peones* refers to laborers involved in the production process, while *jefes* refers to workers involved in administration. The classification of workers is the same as that in INEGI's yearbook, although the categories are given somewhat different names in the two publications. Hence, it is accurate to make inferences from the Mexican census and use them in conjunction with labor demand estimates obtained using our *maquiladora* data.

An issue that arises in analyzing the impact of immigration is determining which workers are substitutes—that is, which workers compete in the same labor market. For the United States, immigrants and natives can be viewed as imperfect substitutes in certain occupations, given that immigrants, on average, have less human capital and do not speak English as well as natives. Friedberg and Hunt examine labor market changes associated with the exodus of 600,000 Russian Jews to Israel; they find that immigrants compete more with one another than with natives.[28] In Mexico, we have two possibilities. One is to treat interstate migrants, returning international immigrants, and natives as perfect substitutes in the *maquiladora* labor market, since they speak the

26. Borjas (2003).

27. See MacLachlan and Aguilar (1998) for background information on changes in the structure of the labor force of this industry.

28. Friedberg and Hunt (1995).

same language and have roughly the same skill set. In this case, all workers can be viewed and treated as a single factor of production. The second possibility is to treat immigrants differently from natives, since immigrants may have different motivations and proficiencies than natives. Also, returning international migrants may have accumulated human capital in the United States that is highly rewarded in the manufacturing industry in Mexico. We think that the second scenario is probably more consistent with how immigration affects Mexico's labor market. We thus assume that natives and immigrants are imperfect substitutes, and we treat them as unique categories. Based on these assumptions, we treat workers employed in the other five divisions of the manufacturing industry as perfect substitutes for workers in the textile sector, in order to capture as many substitutes as possible for these workers.[29]

The sample is restricted to individuals aged sixteen to sixty-four who participated in the labor force. The inclusion of individuals as young as sixteen is not unreasonable for a developing country such as Mexico, especially since the *maquiladora* industry attracts young workers with relatively little work experience. Monthly earnings are drawn from the subsample of persons who were employed in the year of the survey, were not students, and reported positive monthly earnings. A person is defined to be an interstate migrant if he or she resided in a different Mexican state in 1995 than in 2000. Figure 2 shows the average interstate migration for the twenty Mexican states in our sample. If the person resided abroad in 1995, returned to Mexico, and was interviewed in the 2000 Mexican census, then that person is regarded as a returning international migrant. If a person resided in the same state in 2000 as in 1995, that person is regarded as a native worker.

Based on the 2000 Mexican census, table 3 presents the percentage of interstate and returning international migrants relative to the total population for skilled and unskilled workers for the twenty Mexican states with textile *maquiladora* production. The percentage of migrants relative to the total workforce is greater for interstate migrants than for returning international migrants by approximately an order of magnitude. The average percentage for skilled interstate migrants is typically larger than that for unskilled interstate migrants. Some of the highest percentages for skilled interstate migrants are found in Baja California Norte, Baja California Sur, and Zacatecas. Few differences in mobility exist, however, between skilled and unskilled returning

---

29. The difficulty of capturing the true pool of workers in the manufacturing labor market is exacerbated by unreliable unemployment measures in Mexico. The sample only includes employed workers, so it does not capture the potential number of workers in a given occupation.

FIGURE 2. Average Interstate Immigration in Mexico, 1998–2001[a]

Number of migrants

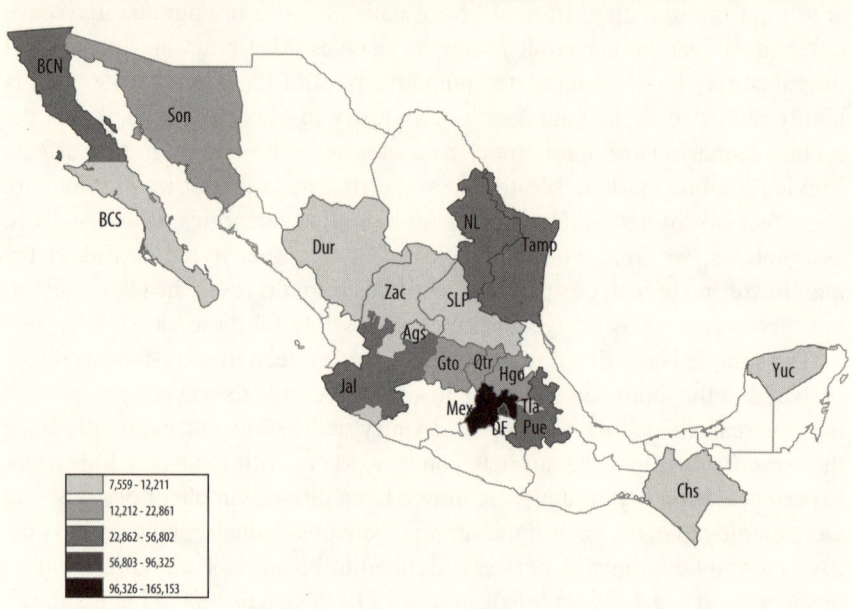

	7,559 - 12,211
	12,212 - 22,861
	22,862 - 56,802
	56,803 - 96,325
	96,326 - 165,153

a. States in white are not included in our sample. See figure 1 for a list of abbreviations.

international workers. In comparison, the United States is also characterized by high labor mobility, with about three percent of the population moving across state lines in any given year and almost 10 percent of the population changing states over a five-year period.[30] Movements in labor among some Mexican states are clearly greater than this.

Empirical Results

We estimate the translog cost and share equations for skilled labor in equations 7 and 8, with respective R^2 values of 0.99 and 0.25 for the textile sector. Own-price and cross-price elasticities of demand for skilled and unskilled workers are computed for the textile sector using equations 13 and 14. They are reported in table 4, where η_{ss} represents the own-price elasticity of demand for skilled labor with respect to skilled wages and η_{uu} represents the own-price

30. Borjas (1996).

TABLE 3. **Percent Interstate Migration and International Return Migration Relative to Total Population, by State**[a]

State	Percent skilled workers		Percent unskilled workers	
	INM	RINT	INM	RINT
Aguascalientes	5.6572	0.6656	3.1983	1.4215
Baja California Norte	14.1364	1.4091	18.7765	1.5142
Baja California Sur	19.1257	0.0000	18.5455	0.3636
Chiapas	9.7938	2.0619	7.4180	0.9986
Colima	7.2607	0.0000	1.6403	0.1789
Durango	6.4961	0.7874	2.8670	1.3761
Federal District	4.6318	0.2342	6.4410	0.1245
Guanajuato	10.8922	0.3476	5.8011	0.6215
Hidalgo	4.9143	0.6095	3.1470	1.4563
Jalisco	8.8141	0.2648	6.5397	0.0853
México	6.6315	0.9797	2.5263	1.0307
Nuevo León	5.7133	0.7350	6.1596	0.3911
Puebla	7.0558	0.5131	4.1677	0.6364
Querétaro	10.3139	0.2242	4.3222	0.5894
San Luis Potosí	5.9361	0.4566	2.2357	0.9384
Sonora	6.7455	0.6954	4.5483	0.6901
Tamaulipas	10.3995	0.7638	8.4194	0.3226
Tlaxcala	8.5515	0.3490	5.2230	0.1205
Yucatán	4.1966	0.5995	1.6156	0.1393
Zacatecas	12.2857	0.5714	3.0315	2.0599
Average	7.5500	0.5727	5.0126	0.5944

a. RINT and INM refer to returning international migrants and interstate migrants, respectively.

elasticity of labor demand for unskilled workers with respect to unskilled wages. Both estimates indicate that labor demand curves for skilled and unskilled workers are downward sloping.[31] The own-price elasticities indicate that the demand for skilled labor, with an average own-price elasticity ranging from about −0.34 to −0.49, is more wage elastic than that for unskilled labor, with an own-price elasticity ranging from about −0.04 to −0.10.[32] Firms thus exhibit a greater relative responsiveness to changes in the wages of skilled workers than to changes in the wages of unskilled workers. Fajnzylber and Maloney obtain similar findings for Chile, Mexico, and Colombia.[33] They estimate elasticities ranging from −0.20 to −0.80; our estimates typically fall within this range. The estimates of η_{su} and η_{us}, which are the cross-price elasticities of demand, indicate that skilled workers are at higher risk of replacement

31. This is consistent with Borjas (2003).
32. Borjas (1996) finds short-run elasticities in the range of −0.4 to −0.5 for the United States.
33. Fajnzylber and Maloney (2001).

TABLE 4. Textile Sector: Estimated Price Elasticities of Factor Demand, by State[a]

State	η_{ss}	η_{uu}	η_{su}	η_{us}
Aguascalientes	−0.3619	−0.0471	0.3619	0.0471
Baja California Norte	−0.4291	−0.0636	0.4291	0.0636
Baja California Sur	−0.4388	−0.0695	0.4388	0.0695
Chiapas	−0.4701	−0.0831	0.4701	0.0831
Colima	−0.4534	−0.0738	0.4534	0.0738
Durango	−0.3351	−0.0399	0.3351	0.0399
Federal District	−0.4653	−0.0812	0.4653	0.0812
Guanajuato	−0.4151	−0.0590	0.4151	0.0590
Hidalgo	−0.4678	−0.0814	0.4678	0.0814
Jalisco	−0.4768	−0.0884	0.4768	0.0884
México	−0.4211	−0.0604	0.4211	0.0604
Nuevo León	−0.4940	−0.1004	0.4940	0.1004
Puebla	−0.3939	−0.0525	0.3939	0.0525
Querétaro	−0.4802	−0.0897	0.4802	0.0897
San Luis Potosí	−0.4945	−0.1017	0.4945	0.1017
Sonora	−0.4550	−0.0753	0.4550	0.0753
Tamaulipas	−0.4600	−0.0776	0.4600	0.0776
Tlaxcala	−0.4439	−0.0698	0.4439	0.0698
Yucatán	−0.4049	−0.0554	0.4049	0.0554
Zacatecas	−0.4905	−0.0975	0.4905	0.0975

a. Price elasticities, where the first subscript refers to quantity and the second to price; s and u refer to skilled and unskilled, respectively.

by unskilled workers than conversely. Firms may be able to reduce costs by training unskilled workers to replace skilled workers. They may also be able to easily substitute away from skilled workers into more capital-intensive processes requiring fewer skilled workers in production.

In the second step, we estimate equation 15 using two-stage least squares to determine the impact of interstate migration and international return migration on the wages of skilled and unskilled workers in any of the states with *maquiladoras* in the textile sector. To assess the strength of our instruments, we regress each endogenous variable on the full set of instruments (that is, the networking-effects instruments plus the other exogenous variables in the model). We obtain F statistics equal to 33,795 and 30,261 for the regressions of INM and RINT, respectively, on the full set of instruments. The corresponding R^2 values are 0.90 and 0.89. The F statistics are clearly in excess of the rule-of-thumb value of ten, which allows us to conclude with confidence that the instruments employed are sufficiently strongly correlated with the endogenous variables.

Table 5 reports the results for ordinary least squares (OLS) and two-stage least squares (2SLS). The 2SLS results indicate the impact of using the networking-effects instruments, where we allow for heteroskedasticity of

TABLE 5.   Textile Sector: Estimated Log Wage, 2000 Mexican Census[a]

| | OLS | | 2SLS | |
Variable	Estimated coefficient	Estimated standard error	Estimated coefficient	Estimated standard error
Constant	6.1349*	0.0136	6.1457*	0.0151
INM	1.1900*	0.1830	−3.9031*	1.2640
RINT	0.0688*	0.0110	0.5337*	0.1189
Urban	0.0966*	0.0042	0.1148*	0.0061
Schooling	0.0573*	0.0007	0.0584*	0.0007
Male	0.2224*	0.0046	0.2139*	0.0052
Indigenous	−0.0617*	0.0097	−0.0608*	0.0099
Experience	0.0236*	0.0005	0.0236*	0.0006
Experience squared	−0.0003*	0.0000	−0.0004*	0.0000
Married	0.0880*	0.0042	0.0915*	0.0043
Skilled	0.5510*	0.0058	0.6530*	0.0258
Aguascalientes	0.2715*	0.0191	−0.1427	0.1086
Baja California Norte	0.4887*	0.0353	0.5370*	0.0567
Baja California Sur	0.6359*	0.0497	1.4102*	0.1966
Colima	0.2549*	0.0264	0.0355	0.0703
Durango	0.2043*	0.0211	−0.2318*	0.1144
Federal District	0.2523*	0.0132	0.4138*	0.0425
Guanajuato	0.2993*	0.0159	−0.0475	0.0908
Hidalgo	0.0811*	0.0166	0.1128*	0.0228
Jalisco	0.3431*	0.0176	−0.1075	0.1172
México	0.2340*	0.0135	0.4840*	0.0634
Nuevo León	0.4299*	0.0144	0.4254*	0.0190
Puebla	0.1542*	0.0138	0.0628*	0.0302
Querétaro	0.3401*	0.0174	0.3723*	0.0222
San Luis Potosí	0.0735*	0.0164	−0.2213*	0.0774
Sonora	0.3510*	0.0157	0.2387*	0.0361
Tamaulipas	0.3023*	0.0193	0.4782*	0.0487
Tlaxcala	0.1223*	0.0151	0.3053*	0.0475
Yucatán	0.0708*	0.0135	0.0306	0.0170
Zacatecas	0.1599*	0.0256	−0.5439*	0.1846

* Statistically significant at the 5 percent level using a two-tailed test.
a. See table 2 for a definition of the variables.

unknown form by employing the Newey-West covariance matrix estimator.[34] The estimated R^2 value of the log wage regression is 0.49 for the OLS regression and 0.43 for the 2SLS regression using the textile sector data.[35]

The positive estimated coefficient on $PRINT_{ji}$ is consistent with Card and with Friedberg and Hunt, who suggest that the migration-induced demand shift

34. See Newey and West (1987).
35. Since RINT is very small, we rescale it by multiplying by 100 to avoid roundoff error. This has no impact on any of the other results that we report.

can outweigh the supply shift.[36] However, the negative coefficient on PINM$_{ji}$ is consistent with Borjas.[37] The use of instruments changes the sign of this variable from that obtained using OLS, whose findings suggest that migration causes an increase in supply that outweighs any rightward shift in demand. The estimated coefficients of the rest of our explanatory variables are consistent with our maintained hypotheses. For example, the human resource literature finds evidence of male wage premiums. We find gender-based and racial-based wage premiums in the textile sector. Women earn approximately 21 percent less than men, on average, while indigenous textile workers earn about 6 percent less than nonindigenous workers. We also find a wage premium for an additional year of education (approximately 6 percent) and for marriage (about 9 percent). Another result consistent with the literature is that the effect on wages of an additional year of experience increases at a decreasing rate. Furthermore, the partial effect of the dummy variable for skilled workers indicates a skilled-worker wage premium of 65 percent for workers employed in the textile sector.

We also compute the average elasticities of wages with respect to each type of migration. We find that the average elasticity of wages with respect to interstate migration is –0.22, while the average elasticity with respect to international return migration is 0.31. The coefficients on all but five state dummy variables were statistically significant at the 5 percent level with a two-tailed test, indicating that individuals living in a state other than Chiapas (the omitted dummy category) receive higher wages than workers in Chiapas.[38] The dummy for Zacatecas is significant at the 10 percent level using a two-tailed test.

Table 6 provides the actual percent change in migration from 1990 to 2000 by skill type and source of migration, computed from the Mexican census for these two years. Skilled workers have registered substantial interstate immigration into the states of Baja California Norte, Baja California Sur, Hidalgo, Tamaulipas, and Zacatecas, while Baja California Sur and Hidalgo have been the most important destinations for unskilled workers. Considerable interstate emigration of unskilled workers has occurred from Baja California Norte. International return migration has been relatively small in comparison.

As described earlier, we use these estimates of migratory percentage changes, by immigration and skill type, in conjunction with the estimated log wage equation elasticities with respect to immigration type to estimate the impact of

---

36. Card (1990); Friedberg and Hunt (1995).
37. Borjas (2003).
38. Chiapas is one of the poorest states in Mexico.

TABLE 6. Percent Change in Immigration from 1990 to 2000[a]

State	RINT-U	RINT-S	INM-U	INM-S
Aguascalientes	1.26	0.63	−1.79	−3.40
Baja California Norte	0.79	1.69	−7.55	7.51
Baja California Sur	0.25	0.80	8.72	15.81
Chiapas	−0.06	0.00	1.13	1.38
Colima	0.76	2.84	2.14	1.90
Durango	1.03	1.07	−0.45	−0.59
Federal District	0.06	0.02	−0.45	0.41
Guanajuato	0.75	1.09	0.52	1.03
Hidalgo	0.95	0.47	6.18	6.92
Jalisco	1.34	0.59	0.01	0.67
México	0.03	0.21	−2.11	−3.29
Nuevo León	0.33	0.40	0.12	2.72
Puebla	0.92	0.42	4.14	2.52
Querétaro	0.71	0.14	0.54	−0.37
San Luis Potosí	1.00	−0.15	0.09	−0.85
Sonora	0.65	0.52	0.72	0.40
Tamaulipas	0.32	1.50	2.03	7.82
Tlaxcala	0.12	0.54	5.66	2.92
Yucatán	0.21	0.78	0.97	0.74
Zacatecas	2.26	0.00	2.61	9.60
Weighted average	0.62	0.98	0.83	1.86

a. RINT and INM refer to returning international migrants and interstate migrants, respectively, while U and S refer to unskilled and skilled workers, respectively.

immigration on wages. We then average these estimates by skill type. Table 7 shows the estimated percentage changes in wages caused by immigration for the textile sector. The weighted average effect of migration on wages is typically small and positive for international return migration. However, most states experienced a reduction in wages as a result of interstate migration. The most notable reductions occurred in Baja California Sur, where the wages of skilled and unskilled workers fell approximately 12 percent and 6 percent, respectively, and in Baja California Norte, where skilled workers saw a 4 percent decline. Wages declined from 3.0 to 4.6 percent in Hidalgo, Tamaulipas, and Zacatecas. These results for skilled interstate migrants are reasonably close to those of Borjas, who estimates for the United States that a 10 percent increase in the labor supply of immigrants reduced the wages of skilled native workers by 3 to 4 percent and by as much as 8 percent for all native workers.[39]

Table 8 shows the extent to which these estimated percentage changes in wages translate into estimated percentage changes in employment in the

39. Borjas (2003).

TABLE 7. Textile Sector: Estimated Percent Change in Wage as a Result of Immigration[a]

State	RINT–U	RINT–S	INM–U	INM–S
Aguascalientes	0.96*	0.22*	0.22*	0.75*
Baja California Norte	0.64*	1.27*	5.54*	−4.14*
Baja California Sur	0.05*	0.00*	−6.31*	−11.80*
Chiapas	−0.01*	0.00*	−0.07*	−0.39*
Colima	0.40*	3.12*	−0.62*	−0.73*
Durango	0.76*	0.45*	0.05*	0.15*
Federal District	0.00*	0.00*	0.11*	−0.07*
Guanajuato	0.42*	0.57*	−0.05*	−0.27*
Hidalgo	0.31*	0.09*	−1.40*	−2.94*
Jalisco	1.04*	0.19*	0.00*	−0.13*
México	0.00*	0.03*	0.54*	1.13*
Nuevo León	0.07*	0.16*	−0.03*	−0.61*
Puebla	0.31*	0.11*	−0.67*	−0.69*
Querétaro	0.22*	0.02*	−0.09*	0.15*
San Luis Potosí	0.50*	−0.04*	−0.01*	0.20*
Sonora	0.24*	0.19*	−0.13*	−0.11*
Tamaulipas	0.06*	0.61*	−0.67*	−3.18*
Tlaxcala	0.01*	0.10*	−1.15*	−0.97*
Yucatán	0.02*	0.25*	−0.06*	−0.12*
Zacatecas	2.49*	0.00*	−0.31*	−4.60*
Weighted average	0.36	0.72	0.03	−0.82

* Statistically significant at the 5 percent level using a two-tailed t test.
a. RINT and INM refer to returning international migrants and interstate migrants, respectively, while U and S refer to unskilled and skilled workers, respectively.

maquiladora textile sector. The weighted average effects of migration on employment are very small for all but skilled interstate migrants. The largest positive effect is about 4 percent in Baja California Norte, with an approximate 2 percent increase in Baja California Sur and Zacatecas. In Tamaulipas, the increase is approximately 1 percent.

Finally, we use the delta method to compute the significance of the entries in tables 7 and 8, since they are functions of previously estimated parameters as well as data.[40] All the entries in table 7 are significant at the 5 percent level using a two-tailed t test. The estimated standard errors are equal to those provided in table 5. To compute the significance of the entries in table 8, we must take the estimated percent changes in wages from table 7 as given (that is, not random variables), since we have not estimated their covariances together with those of the labor demand equation parameters. Although the results in table 8

40. See the TSP Reference Manual, version 5.0, for details on the delta method calculations.

TABLE 8. Textile Sector: Estimated Percent Change in Employment as a Result of Immigration[a]

State	RINT–U	RINT–S	INM–U	INM–S
Aguascalientes	−0.0290*	0.2524	0.0209	−0.1818*
	(0.0049)	(0.1808)	(0.0164)	(0.0424)
Baja California Norte	0.0444	−0.2827*	−0.6763*	4.3090*
	(0.0287)	(0.0914)	(0.0934)	(0.7947)
Baja California Sur	−0.0035*	0.0217*	−0.4046	2.4885*
	(0.0001)	(0.0068)	(0.2672)	(0.8792)
Chiapas	0.0004*	−0.0027*	−0.0236*	0.1446*
	(0.0001)	(0.0009)	(0.0090)	(0.0102)
Colima	0.2208*	−1.2713*	−0.0086	0.0493
	(0.0714)	(0.0533)	(0.0167)	(0.0817)
Durango	−0.0125	0.1077	0.0041	−0.0349*
	(0.0098)	(0.1412)	(0.0034)	(0.0095)
Federal District	−0.0001	0.0007	−0.0125*	0.0816*
	(0.0002)	(0.0007)	(0.0017)	(0.0166)
Guanajuato	0.0094	−0.0657	−0.0130*	0.0908*
	(0.0128)	(0.0646)	(0.0060)	(0.0080)
Hidalgo	−0.0128*	0.0930	−0.0870	0.6309*
	(0.0020)	(0.0505)	(0.0653)	(0.2251)
Jalisco	−0.0698*	0.3998*	−0.0104*	0.0596*
	(0.0045)	(0.1369)	(0.0030)	(0.0003)
México	0.0022*	−0.0131*	0.0467	−0.2755*
	(0.0008)	(0.0003)	(0.0259)	(0.0724)
Nuevo León	0.0089*	−0.0436*	−0.0582*	0.2855*
	(0.0038)	(0.0080)	(0.0143)	(0.0034)
Puebla	−0.0111*	0.0805	−0.0012	0.0083
	(0.0026)	(0.0499)	(0.0155)	(0.1079)
Querétaro	−0.0221*	0.1035*	0.0257*	−0.1203*
	(0.0005)	(0.0248)	(0.0036)	(0.0102)
San Luis Potosí	−0.0464*	0.2557*	0.0177*	−0.0978*
	(0.0010)	(0.0634)	(0.0046)	(0.0011)
Sonora	−0.0034	0.0208	0.0016	−0.0098
	(0.0045)	(0.0334)	(0.0025)	(0.0178)
Tamaulipas	0.0440*	−0.2578*	−0.1989*	1.1651*
	(0.0140)	(0.0075)	(0.0725)	(0.0891)
Tlaxcala	0.0056*	−0.0392*	0.0110	−0.0764
	(0.0023)	(0.0013)	(0.0218)	(0.1788)
Yucatán	0.0119*	−0.0916*	−0.0031	0.0237*
	(0.0056)	(0.0027)	(0.0028)	(0.0104)
Zacatecas	−0.2268*	1.2016*	−0.3915*	2.0743*
	(0.0001)	(0.3051)	(0.1066)	(0.0379)
Weighted average	0.03	−0.17	−0.06	0.39

* Statistically significant at the 5 percent level using a two-tailed *t* test.
a. RINT and INM refer to returning international migrants and interstate migrants, respectively, while *U* and *S* refer to unskilled and skilled workers, respectively. Estimated standard errors are in parentheses.

are less precise than our other findings, the vast majority of the estimates are significant.

Conclusion

Although a number of researchers examine the impact of immigration on wages and employment in the United States, few studies for Mexico focus on the effects of interstate migration and international return migration. This paper sets out to fill this gap. By modeling firm productivity and employment in conjunction with an analysis of the impact of migration on wages, we avoid the shortcomings of the U.S. studies by Borjas, Card, and Mishra, all of whom use census-level data without linking wage changes to the type of employer.[41]

Two basic conclusions emerge from this study. First, our estimates of worker demand functions indicate substantial sensitivity to changes in price. While the demand functions of skilled and unskilled *maquiladora* workers slope downward, skilled workers face a higher own-price elasticity of demand and a higher cross-price elasticity of demand than do unskilled workers. Second, inflows of skilled interstate migrants into the textile manufacturing labor market from 1998 to 2001 generated substantial reductions in wages for Baja California Sur and to a lesser extent for Zacatecas, Baja California Norte, Tamaulipas, and Hidalgo. Wages were also reduced in most Mexican states by the influx of interstate unskilled migrants, but to a much lower degree. Consequently, modest increases in the employment of skilled interstate migrant labor are found in Baja California Norte and, to a lesser extent, Baja California Sur, Zacatecas, and Tamaulipas. The large amounts of interstate migration in Mexico have thus produced modest wage reductions, potentially helping to stem any further flight of *maquiladora* production to China.

---

41. Borjas (2003); Card (1990); Mishra (2007).

Comments

Juliano Assunção: The Mexican *maquiladora* industry constitutes an interesting economic environment in which to study the impact of migration on the labor market. Because most of the *maquiladora* employees are interstate migrants, migration flows can arguably be directly associated with the shift in the labor supply curve. Moreover, the relocation of U.S. firms to China has changed the configuration of the *maquiladora* industry. The impact of migration on the labor market, however, is still a matter for debate in the migration literature. Atkinson and Ibarra contribute to this literature by investigating the effects of internal interstate migration and international return migration on the wages and employment of skilled and unskilled workers in the textile *maquiladora* industry.

The results are derived in two steps. First, the authors use the 2000 Mexican census to estimate the effect of interstate migration and international return migration on wages. From this analysis, the authors compute the effect of migration on the wages of skilled and unskilled workers from 1990 to 2000. The two main right-hand-side variables regarding migration are considered endogenous and are thus instrumented with the corresponding network effect measures. The authors' concern about the endogeneity of migration is appropriate and consistent with the literature on the determinants of migration. Indeed, table 1 shows that natives and immigrants are different. Solving this problem is a much harder issue, however. The use of networking effects as a source of exogenous variation is interesting and finds support in the literature, but it also has its limitations. The hypothesis here is that wages are affected by networking effects only through the migration channel. In particular, Atkinson and Ibarra assume that the existence of immigrant groups does not affect the balance of power between firms and workers, which could, in principle, increase or decrease wages. Unfortunately, the analysis is restricted to this set of instruments, so the robustness of the results under different assumptions cannot be checked.

A really surprising result, reported in table 5, is that the effects of interstate migration and international return migration point in opposite directions. While the negative coefficient for interstate immigration suggests an increase in the labor supply, the only way to explain the positive and quantitatively high coefficient for return migration is through an increase in the average turnover rate or a change on the demand side. This result is even more puzzling given the extremely low percentage of returning international immigrants in the population: this type of immigrant accounts for less than 1 percent of the population in thirteen out of twenty states (see table 3).

The second step is based on the state-level panel data for 1998–2001 and studies the effect of wages on the employment of skilled and unskilled workers in the *maquiladora* industry. The authors derive structural cost and share equations from which they compute the own-price and cross-price elasticities of demand for skilled and unskilled workers. Results indicate that the demand for skilled labor is more elastic (to wage) than the demand for unskilled workers, as found in similar studies for other countries in the region.

The impact of total (interstate and international) immigration on employment is obtained by combining the two steps described above. This combination, in turn, involves matching the two data sets, which is not directly feasible. The census identifies laborers working in the manufacturing sector, without specifying whether their employer is a *maquiladora*. A similar problem arises with the immigration measures, which come from the same source. As a consequence, the results comprise the effect of international return and interstate migration on the wages of skilled and unskilled workers in the manufacturing sector; and the effect of wage changes on employment in the *maquiladora* sector. In other words, the estimated effects of migration on wages apply to the whole manufacturing sector, such that only the estimated effects of wages on employment are clearly specific to the *maquiladora* industry. The underlying hypothesis behind the authors' interpretation is that wage responses do not differ substantially in the manufacturing and *maquiladora* industries. Without this assumption, it is not possible to combine the two steps.

In summary, the authors have documented a number of relevant effects, and explored some new and interesting aspects of Mexican migration flows and the *maquiladora* industry. The issues described above are important for contextualizing the analysis within the limits imposed by the empirical environment.

Eric Verhoogen: This is a welcome contribution on a topic—internal migration—that is both important and underresearched. I begin my comments with a few words about the motivation of the paper and then turn to my main comment about the three-stage methodology used to estimate the effects of migration.

Part of the reason that internal migration is underresearched, despite its importance in terms of sheer numbers, is that it is often unclear what the stakes are. To put it another way, what is the policy issue that research on internal migration informs? International migration raises an obvious issue: how large a fence, literal or figurative, to put at the border. Governments are not typically in the business of putting up barriers to internal migration, so there is no natural policy "hook." Nevertheless, governments do many things that affect the costs and benefits of internal migration—from offering training for new migrants in occupations facing high demand, to implementing reforms to make social security benefits more portable, or even to providing disparate levels and quality of public services in rural areas versus urban areas or small towns versus cities. It is appropriate, then, to ask whether internal migration is a good thing and thus whether governments should actively try to facilitate or impede it. The set of winners from internal migration seems pretty clear: by revealed preference, one can infer that the migrants themselves are better off migrating. Internal migration has also played an important role in facilitating the growth of the *maquiladora* sector in Mexico, as Atkinson and Ibarra discuss. But are there losers? If so, how severe are their losses? Economic logic suggests that workers already present in a particular region are likely to lose, but convincing evidence of such negative effects has been elusive in the United States as well as other countries. Answering this question is a crucial step in addressing the larger policy issue of whether internal mobility is a desirable thing to promote. I take it that this is part of the motivation of the current paper; this point could have been brought out more explicitly.

My main comment about the empirical exercise in the paper is that it seems to be unnecessarily complicated and indirect. The authors implement a three-step procedure. First, they use a translog cost-function approach to estimate the elasticity of labor demand with respect to wages. Second, they use an instrumental variables procedure to estimate the effect of internal migration on wages. Third, they plug the estimated effect of migration on wages back into their estimated labor demand function to estimate the effect of internal migration on employment. In my view, the strongest part of this procedure is the second step. The instruments—namely, interactions of the number of emigrants or returning international migrants from a particular state in a particular period with the pre-existing distribution of emigrants from that state in receiving states—are plausibly uncorrelated with labor demand shocks in receiving states and yet correlated with migration flows. (A small but important point: the authors should report the first-stage regression of actual migration flows on the instruments.) The issue is whether, once one has found such instruments, the first and third steps are necessary. If the instruments are valid, then it should be possible to estimate the effect of internal migration on employment (*maquiladora* or otherwise) in receiving states by a straight-forward two-stage least squares procedure in which receiving-state employment is regressed on migration inflows instrumented by the network-effect instruments described above. This simpler procedure would seem to be more robust and less susceptible to endogeneity concerns than the procedure the authors implement, which is open to several objections. For instance, if, as the authors argue, the weak effect of international return migration on wages stems from its tendency to boost labor demand, shouldn't the migration itself be taken into account in the labor demand estimation? Another issue is precision: although the authors do not report standard errors on their final estimates of the effect of migration on employment in receiving states, I suspect that the estimates are quite a bit less precise than would be obtained from the simpler two-stage least squares procedure. This issue leads me to think the jury is still out on the magnitude of the true effect of internal migration on *maquiladora* wages and employment. Nonetheless, this paper is a useful step in investigating the important broader question of who wins and who loses from internal migration.

References

Borjas, George J. 1996. "Labor Mobility." In *Labor Economics,* pp. 280–315. New York: McGraw-Hill.

———. 2003. "The Labor Demand Curve Is Downward Sloping: Reexamining the Impact of Immigration on the Labor Market." *Quarterly Journal of Economics* 118(4): 1335–374.

Borjas, George J., Richard B. Freeman, and Lawrence F. Katz. 1991. "Searching for the Effect of Immigration on the Labor Market." *American Economic Review* 86(2): 246–51.

Card, David. 1990. "The Impact of the Mariel Boatlift on the Miami Labor Market." *Industrial and Labor Relations Review* 43(2): 245–57.

———. 2001. "Immigrant Inflows, Native Outflows, and the Local Labor Market Impacts of Higher Immigration." *Journal of Labor Economics* 19(1): 22–64.

Chiquiar, Daniel, and Gordon H. Hanson. 2005. "International Migration, Self-Selection, and the Distribution of Wages: Evidence from Mexico and the United States." *Journal of Political Economy* 113(2): 239–81.

Fajnzylber, Pablo, and William F. Maloney. 2001. "How Comparable Are Labor Demand Elasticities across Countries?" Policy Research Working Paper 2658. Washington: World Bank.

Fernández-Kelly, María Patricia. 1983. *For We Are Sold, I and My People: Women and Industry in Mexico's Frontier.* Albany: State University of New York Press.

Friedberg, Rachel M., and Jennifer Hunt. 1995. "The Impact of Immigrants on Host Country Wages, Employment, and Growth." *Journal of Economic Perspectives* 9(2): 23–44.

Hanson, Gordon H. 2005. "Emigration, Labor Supply, and Earnings in Mexico." Working Paper 11412. Cambridge, Mass.: National Bureau of Economic Research.

[INEGI] Instituto Nacional de Estadísticas, Geográficas e Informática. 2005. *Industria Maquiladora de Exportación.* Mexico City.

MacLachlan, Ian, and Adrian G. Aguilar. 1998. "*Maquiladora* Myths: Locational and Structural Change in Mexico's Export Manufacturing Industry." *Professional Geographer* 50(3): 315–31.

Mishra, Prachi. 2007. "Emigration and Wages in Source Countries: Evidence from Mexico." *Journal of Development Economics* 82(1): 180–99.

Mollick, Andre V., and Karina Wvalle-Vázquez. 2006. "Chinese Competition and Its Effects on Mexican *Maquiladoras.*" *Journal of Comparative Economics* 34(1): 130–45.

Newey, Whitney K., and Kenneth D. West. 1987. "A Simple, Positive, Semi-Definite, Heteroskedasticity and Autocorrelation Consistent Covariance Matrix." *Econometrica* 55(3): 703–08.

Picou, Armand, and Emanuel Peluchon. 1995. "The Texas-Mexico Maquila Industry: Expectations for the Future." *Journal of Borderland Studies* 10(2): 75–86.

Sargent, John. 1997. "*Maquiladora*s and Skill Development." *Journal of Borderland Studies* 12(1–2): 17–39.

U.S. General Accounting Office. 2003. *International Trade: Mexico's Maquiladora Decline Affects U.S.-Mexico Border Communities and Trade; Recovery Depends in Part on Mexico's Actions.* Report to Congressional Requesters 03-891. Washington.

Young, Gay, and Lucía Fort. 1994. "Household Responses to Economic Change: Migration and *Maquiladora* Work in Ciudad Juárez, Mexico." *Social Science Quarterly* 75(3): 656–70.